THE BRITISH SCHOOL AT ROME
One Hundred Years

The British School at Rome
One Hundred Years

by
Andrew Wallace-Hadrill

with contributions by
Jacopo Benci, Sarah Court,
Gill Clark, Alistair Crawford,
Caroline Egerton, Stephen Farthing,
Andrew Hopkins, Sarah Hyslop,
Anthony Majanlahti, Helen Patterson,
Cristiana Perrella, Geoffrey Rickman,
Valerie Scott, Jane Thompson,
Jo Wallace-Hadrill, Katherine Wallis

Published by The British School at Rome
at The British Academy
10 Carlton House Terrace
London SW1Y 5AH

THE BRITISH SCHOOL AT ROME
Via Gramsci, 61
00197 Rome

Registered Charity No. 314176

ISBN 0-904152-35-9

Design by Silvia Stucky
Printed by Studio Lodoli Sud, Rome, Italy

Front cover
Arnold Mason RA (1885-1963)
Winifred Knights and the British School at Rome 1922.

CONTENTS

PREFACE

An architect, returning from his two-year scholarship in Rome in the early 1930s, summed up his impressions in a lecture to the Royal Institute of British Architects. William (later Lord) Holford evoked the visual images fired on his mind by the bright Mediterranean light, and then affectionately recalled the chiaroscuro sequence of the approach to his home for those years, the British School:

> 'Those of us who had the good fortune to be given an opportunity not only to visit Rome but to live and work there will be able to recall the more domestic details as well – the hazardous crossing of the via Flaminia and the plunge into the cool, green tunnels of the Borghese Gardens, the blinding glare of the steps and terraces as one descended to the Valle Giulia, the hideous details of the Gallery of Modern Art, the steady pull up the hill to the portico of the British School, and then the quiet cortile, with ilex and cypress and orange trees and the startled deer in Skeaping's fountain.'

Those familiar with the School will recognise how little has changed. Those who know the building only from outside may be surprised at the lack of comment on the conspicuous neo-classical façade designed by Edwin Lutyens. Is not the bold statement of British Imperial confidence the important thing? Insiders know that it is the contrast that matters: first the bright steps, then the cool green of the garden, the oasis which has been home to an exceptional mixture of architects, artists, archaeologists and students of all things Roman and Italian. Of that community, William Holford also had sharp recollections:

> 'Nor, in fairness, may I give an objective account of the relations between the architects of the School and their fellow members – the painters, the sculptors, the industrious engravers, the librarians, and the inscrutable company of archaeologists. These relationships have been co-operative, argumentative and critical, but they have always been stimulating. That they were also collaborative in a high degree cannot be doubted. For did not Eros himself mingle with the Muses in frequent visits to the studios?'

Holford collaborated to the full. In his time in Rome, he collaborated with an archaeologist, the Director Ian Richmond, in a study of the town plan of Verona (he was to become a major authority on town-planning himself), and married the Painting Scholar, Marjorie Brooks. The marriage he embodies between architecture, archaeology and painting could scarcely have been consummated elsewhere.

This is a book written from the inside, a Director's view of a century of his institution's history. It is partial in every sense. It represents a take on the School's story from a particular viewpoint and at a specific moment. Some features of the School's life are so recurrent that it is hard not to write into the past the debates of the present. It does not tell the whole story: some parts of it have already been written far better, by Peter Wiseman in his *Short History of the British School at Rome* (BSR 1990), which remains the best account of the original foundation, by Hugh Petter in his *Lutyens in Italy: the Building of the British School at Rome* (BSR 1992), which tells the full story of the Lutyens building, and by Richard Hodges in his recent *Visions of Rome: Thomas Ashby Archaeologist* (BSR 2000), which gives a far fuller picture of this critical figure. It draws on a great deal of material from the School's archives which has not been published before; but anyone who has had the pleasure of working with this rich source will know that the following account does no more than skim. There is so much more that could be said, for instance about the scholars of the twenties and thirties, which has been difficult to access before the present reorganisation of the Archive.

There are many to thank for the common effort that lies behind the volume. First, Alistair Crawford and Stephen Farthing, for their contributions on the artists which a Roman historian could not have tackled with conviction. Second, my colleagues, both for their own contributions to the last chapter, and for their patience in putting up with a Director lost for weeks on end in the Archive. Third, Valerie Scott and her colleagues in the Library, particularly Alessandra Giovenco, not only made me aware of the potential of our archival collections, but helped enormously in identifying suitable images. One of the basic aims of the volume is to give an idea of the wealth of these collections: we are still only at the threshold of cataloguing, studying and publishing them.

Next, my warmest thanks go to two superb research assistants, Sarah Hyslop and Sarah Court, supported by my long-suffering P.A., Katherine Wallis, who spent months assembling information about our scholars in a database, identifying and selecting photographs, and assembling material for the press. Our idea was that we should celebrate the School's centenary by recovering some of the knowledge of our past that has been not so much lost as buried under piles of paper. It is a tribute to their labours that we have managed to recover as much as we have. The book has been saved from a thicket of errors by the sharp eyes of Alistair Crawford, Caroline Egerton, Geoffrey and Anna Rickman, and Peter Wiseman; I have myself to blame for the rest. Silvia Stucky has gone far beyond the usual role of a designer in helping the volume gradually come to light.

Finally our heartfelt thanks go to the sponsors, Richard and Janet Cooper, who through their Charitable Trust enabled the School to celebrate its Centenary in style with a Private View at the Royal Academy of Arts in March 2000 of the *Genius of Rome* exhibition. The money so raised has enabled the publication of this volume. They are the most recent in a century's tradition of donors without whose support the School could never have achieved what it has. We hope that future generations too will warm to the cause.

AWH

August 2001

THE BRITISH IN ROME
to 1900

THE BRITISH IN ROME
(to 1900)

THE BALANCED RHYTHMS of Sir Edwin Lutyens' neo-classical façade for the British School at Rome embody a long dialogue between cultures. The façade is a conscious, and elaborately studied, quotation from that of Sir Christopher Wren's St Paul's Cathedral. It therefore offers to Rome a powerful symbol of British identity. But, as Lutyens knew, Wren's inspiration lay in an Italian architectural tradition codified by Palladio, a renaissance rediscovery or reinvention of the architecture of ancient Rome. Not, then, a symbol of British difference, but of British awareness of the depth of its engagement with Italy and Rome, stretching in complex continuity from the present to the renaissance to antiquity.

To understand the dialogue with Italian culture the School represents, it is helpful to see it in a longer context. If a hundred years have passed of this specific British establishment in Rome, Britain's engagement with Rome and Italy has far deeper roots. Against the background of more than a millennium of visitors from the British Isles, the development of the British School makes fuller sense.

The history of English residential communities in Rome goes back to the eighth century.[2] Caedwalla, king of the West Saxons, came to the city as a pilgrim, followed in AD 725 by Ine, also king of the West Saxons, who gave up his throne and 'set out for Rome, to exchange a temporal for an eternal kingdom. On his arrival he built a house with the consent of Pope Gregory and gave it the name of Schola Anglorum.'

Thus began the first phase of continuous English inhabitation in Rome. This first community of the English, the *Schola Saxonum*, which occupied the site of the present Ospedale di Santo Spirito in Sassia, had a life that stretched over almost five hundred years, and played host to King Alfred in 854 and the Scottish king Macbeth in 1050. Scholars and monks, pilgrims and emissaries alike forged Britain's links with Rome in the early Middle Ages; only with the European turmoil of the twelfth and thirteenth centuries did visits from the British isles decline, and in 1201 Innocent III founded his great poor hospital of Santo Spirito *in Sassia* on the site of the moribund *Schola Saxonum*. The English left behind another

(above and previous)
Joseph Woods (1776-1864), view of the Palatine from the Colosseum, around 1817; BSR Library.[1]

10

Il Viaggatore Moderno (Venice 1780),
by Francesco Locatelli, frontispiece;
BSR Library, from the collection
of Thomas Ashby.

*Via Appia Illustrata ab Urbe Capua
ad Romam* (Rome 1794),
by Carlo Labruzzi (1748-1817),
frontispiece with dedication
to Sir Richard Colt Hoare;
BSR Library, from the collection
of Thomas Ashby.

memento of their presence: the *burgus Anglorum* left its name in the 'Borgo'.

In 1300 Boniface VIII instituted the Jubilee, which offered remission of sins to pilgrims who visited the seven great basilicas of Rome, made confession and acts of contrition, and repented, within the space of the year. An estimated two million pilgrims visited in the first Jubilee year. The English were among the many who were badly treated by the rapacious Roman innkeepers. The English Hospice came into existence in response, as did other national hospices, like those of the Germans, the Portuguese, the Spaniards, and the Swedes. These groups formed national guilds, or confraternities, which gave their communities a structure and leadership.

The foundation of the English Hospice itself in its location on what is today known as the via di Monserrato involved the purchase by the previously existing confraternity of the English on 27 January 1362 of the house belonging to John

Shepherd, *paternostrarius* or bead-seller, for forty gold florins. The hospice prospered through careful investment in property in the redeveloping area of central Rome close to the riverbank of the Tiber bend. By the end of the fifteenth century it had been commandeered by the English crown and functioned, indeed, as an informal residence for royal orators.

The break with Rome in the mid 1530s caused a devastating trauma to the English presence in the city, the second in a decade, as the Sack of Rome in 1527 had already destroyed many of the hospice's precious rental properties and ransacked the glittering decorations of the hospice church of St Thomas. Paul III re-established the hospice confraternity, which had dwindled to only one decrepit brother, in 1538, staffing it with the household of the English Cardinal Reginald Pole. The medieval association continued to function, however vestigially, until 1579, when Gregory XIII founded the English College, a Catholic seminary, in the former hospice buildings.

The Reformation intensified the division between English visitors to Rome who had religious motives and those who were interested in the secular study of the ancient world. Much of the seventeenth century was torn with religious wars, and the environment in Rome was far from tolerant; despite this, visitors from England persisted. In the guest-book of the English College appear names like William Harvey, Royal Physician, and John Milton. In his diary for 29 December 1644, John Evelyn reported that 'we were invited to the English Jesuits to dinner, being their great feast of Saint Thomas of Canterbury.' These visitors, whose curiosity was more social, literary, and historical than religious, were the precursors to the Grand Tourists of the eighteenth century.

Already in the seventeenth century, a new vision of Rome as a cultural, not just a religious centre, was emerging. A critical moment for the institutions that were to spring up later was the foundation in 1666 of the Académie de France by Colbert, minister of Louis

XIV, under the inspiration of Poussin and Lebrun, and with the advice and collaboration of Bernini. Not only did it promote artistic interest through the Prix de Rome, but it served as a centre for collecting and copying ancient sculpture for the French court, and promoted the study of art history. Art and archaeology were allied from the start in the cultural rediscovery of Rome.

By the eighteenth century, the city had become the magnet for the strange mixture of aristocrats, artists and antiquarians that was to be the Grand Tour. For the English, it offered a non-religious approach to Rome, particularly when it was still compromised by the presence of the exiled Stuart court between 1717 and 1788. The 'tour' was conceived as educational in purpose – the young aristocrat was accompanied by his tutor or 'bear-leader', who was only too often seen as an obstruction to the preferred education in win-

Detail from the *Plan of Rome* (1593) by Antonio Tempesta, with the English College visible bottom left.

ing and women. The tension is made visible in Sir Joshua Reynolds' well-known portrait group of the Society of Dilettanti (a society founded in 1732 to promote scholarships for travel to Italy by artists) in which various members brandish glasses of wine, books of antiquities, and a lady's garter. The political atmosphere became easier after the Peace of Paris in 1763: the Young Pretender was no longer recognised by the Papacy, and British Royalty started to visit Rome, notably Edward Augustus, Duke of York, and Prince Augustus Frederick, and to acquire, like their continental counterparts, antiquities.[3]

The flow of visitors was stimulated by the discovery of Herculaneum (1738) and Pompeii (1748), creating a mandatory Rome-Naples tour. A vital role was played by Sir William Hamilton as British Ambassador to the Kingdom of the Two Sicilies in Naples from 1764-1803: his high society connections and study of antiquities helped to define a new British interest in archaeology, and his collection formed a basis for the British Museum vase collection. Many other English *milordi* like Sir Richard Colt Hoare, the builder of Stourhead, were serious students of art and antiquities; a volume like Carlo Labruzzi's *Via Appia Illustrata* (1794), the outcome of Hoare's journey with Labruzzi from Rome to Benevento, both blazes the trail and provides material evidence for the later, more scientific studies of Thomas Ashby.[4] At the same time, there was a boom of British archaeology in Rome. British artist/entrepreneurs like Gavin Hamilton, Thomas Jenkins and Robert Fagan were notably successful in being granted papal excavation licences, resulting in collections of marbles such as that of Charles Townley (1760s to 90s), which formed the basis of the British Museum sculpture collection. There was a vigorous interest of artists in Rome: the visit of Joshua Reynolds in 1752 led to the creation of an 'English group' for visiting Grand Tour artists. Through Reynolds, the Royal Academy soon after its foundation created a Gold Medal Travelling Scholarship to promote visits to Italy (in 1771). Architects took no less active an interest: over 40 British architects are on record as in residence in Rome in the second half of the

Porta San Paolo and Pyramid of Sestius (1783-4) by Nicolas-Didier Boguet; BSR Library.

eighteenth century, and their concern to measure and analyse classical architecture fed directly into the foundation of the Institute of British Architects in 1834.[5]

If the heyday of the aristocratic Grand Tour was past by the end of the eighteenth century, interest in Rome continued to grow and gradually institutionalise itself. An era of professionalism challenged that of the dilettanti. Reynolds' artistic group was formalised as the 'British Academy of Arts in Rome' in 1823: Sir Thomas Lawrence as President of the Royal Academy secured its support and the patronage and donation of £200 by George IV. The British Academy established itself in via Margutta, an area still today occupied by artists' studios. Numerous architects followed the example of Inigo Jones and, later, Sir John Soane, and made detailed studies of ancient and renaissance architecture through measured drawings: those of Joseph Woods, who travelled through Italy around 1817, are no more than a sample of the material that was to prove valuable later to the School's collection. By the mid nineteenth century, photography had also emerged as a medium of prime importance for recording ancient buildings and landscapes: British photographers represented in the BSR collection, such as James Graham and Robert MacPherson, were pioneers of such photography in Italy.

English archaeological interest, too, became more scholarly and less entrepreneurial. The most notable figure was Sir William Gell: active in Italy between 1814 and 1836, he is best known for his *Pompeiana*, reporting with J.P. Gandy the latest work in Pompeii, from 1817 to 1819, then from 1819 to 1832. Printed in many editions, his volumes helped to inspire Edward Bulwer Lytton's *Last days of Pompeii* of 1834, in its turn the inspiration for numerous plays and later films. But his studies of the topography of Rome and its vicinity, conducted in collaboration with the Irish artist, Edward Dodswell, and the Italian archaeologist, Antonio Nibby, laid the foundation of generations of British study of the ancient Roman landscape. His *Topography of Rome and its Vicinity* (1834) is based on a series of notebooks, which Thomas Ashby was later to acquire: through them, the link to the School's later topographical research is clear.

Archaeological study acquired a character as an international activity with the foundation in 1828-29 of the Istituto di Corrispondenza Archeologica by the Prussian Minister, Karl Bunsen, housed in Palazzo Caffarelli on the Capitoline. The institute was international in its conception (Thomas Arnold was a member), though it was dependent on Prussian funding and largely under Prussian control. By 1870, the international mood was very different: the Risorgimento transformed Rome from the city of the Popes to a national capital, and the secular strand of cultural interest in Rome that had long competed with the religious pull of pilgrimage now acquired full political sanction. In 1871, the international institute was converted on the orders of Wilhelm I to the Royal Prussian Institute of Archaeology. This was a critical moment for the formation of international scholarly activity in Rome. The Institute, from 1874 renamed the German Archaeological Institute, is the archetype of a model that was to spread swiftly. A parallel German

Robert Macpherson (1814-72), view of the Cloaca Maxima and Forum Boarium.

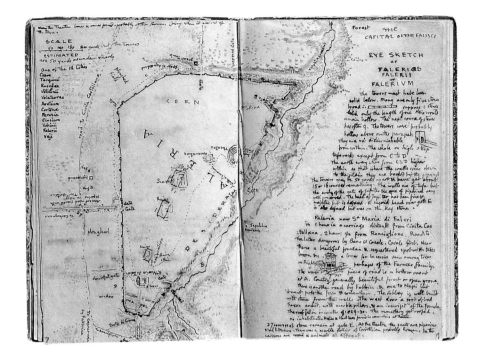

Falerii, eye sketch, c.1828, from the notebooks of Sir William Gell; BSR Library, Thomas Ashby collection. Gell's central interest was in mapping the classical landscape. The walled republican town of Falerii was later to be of interest to Ashby, Ward-Perkins, and in the current Tiber valley project to Millett and Keay.

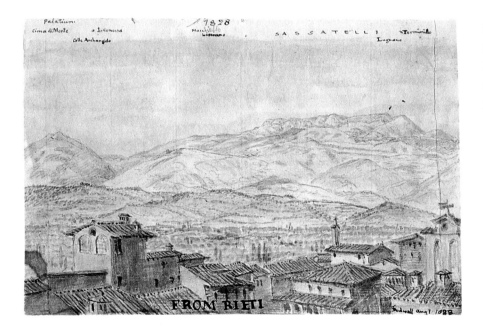

View from Rieti, Edward Dodswell, 1828, from the notebooks of Sir William Gell. Dodswell frequently accompanied Gell and inserted watercolour views of the landscape in his notebooks.

Institute was set up in Athens in 1874, where there had been an Ecole Française since 1846. In conscious rivalry, France now set up an Ecole in Rome (1873). The British and Americans had a new model to follow.

Longstanding British archaeological interest in Rome had already by 1865 crystallised in the formation of the British (later 'and American') Archaeological Society of Rome; inspired especially by John Henry Parker. Parker was a figure of major importance: well aware of the world of commerce through the family bookshop in Oxford, his archaeological interests took him to the Keepership of the Ashmolean Museum. His eight-volume publication on *The Archaeology of Rome* (1873-77) made avowed use of British archaeological method absent in previous scholarship. It also benefited from his collection of over 3300 photographs (often commissioned from professional photographers), which were sold commercially, and form the fullest surviving visual record of mid-nineteenth century Rome. His archaeological society served to put British students in contact with the latest discoveries of Roman archaeology, and those in the rapidly expanding Roma Capitale were nothing short of dramatic. Members of the society included Rodolfo Lanciani, the most important single figure in the systematisation of the archaeological knowledge of Rome, and a strong Anglophile. Another member of the society was a retired Quaker brewer, Thomas Ashby, a keen bibliophile collecting books and prints on Rome. Their common bonds were formed in Parker's society.

As the newly founded French and German Institutes or Schools established themselves in Rome and Athens, a seachange was taking place in British universities, remodelling themselves under the influence of the new and professional German approaches to *Wissenschaft*. Classicists with a broader vision wanted to get beyond the cosy old tutorial system with its emphasis on prose and verse composition in Latin and Greek, and to plug into the new models of learning. It was the hellenists, led by Richard Jebb of

Porta S. Lorenzo (1864-66), view of interior with arch of gate destroyed in 1869, by Carlo Baldassare Simelli (attrib.); albumen print from the collection of J.H. Parker.

Cambridge, who showed the way: his public appeal for funding, supported by the Prince of Wales (later Edward VII) in 1883 raised enough to launch the British School at Athens, in operation from 1886. The same movement that created foreign schools created learned societies and learned journals: the Society for the Promotion of Hellenic Studies with its annual publication, the Journal of Hellenic Studies, had been founded in 1880, in clear imitation of continental rivals. Romanists were to follow hellenists with a significant time lag: the Roman Society and its Journal of Roman Studies were only launched in 1910.

The creation of a British School at Rome comes out of this ferment. On the one hand, a history going back to Saxon England of visitors to the Eternal City, with a more recent surge, thanks to the Grand Tour, of interest in Rome as a centre of art and archaeology. On the other hand, a transformation on the continent of the world of learning towards systematisation of knowledge, driven by the rise of nation states, finding in Risorgimento Rome its perfect location. British artists and British archaeologists had been a notable presence in Rome since the mid eighteenth century, and the way to institution formation had been pointed by the British Academy of the Arts and the British Archaeological Society. But the British state was less inclined than its continental rivals to contribute public finance to culture, so that British initiative was to follow with a slight time lag, and on the basis of private not public funding.

THE EARLY YEARS
1900-1910

THE EARLY YEARS
(1900-1910)

THE LEAD IN LAUNCHING the new institution was taken by the Camden Professor of Ancient History at Oxford, Henry Pelham. One of the champions of what was then called 'the new scholarship', he recalled his first visit to Rome in 1870 'when Pio Nono was still King and Pope'. He had visited the excavations on the Palatine conducted by Cav. Rosa for Napoleon III, and reflected,

> 'at that time we English people hardly did justice to what Napoleon was doing in the way of science...Rosa made the visit to the Palatine hill very interesting even at that day. Oh, the enormous interest which had occurred since then! We had before us an intensely interesting field of operations in classical Rome, to say nothing of medieval Rome, and it was of the utmost importance that we should have young and trained experts on the spot. The Germans had been foremost in the field, and it was of the utmost importance that England should not be altogether unrepresented.'[1]

Pelham's enthusiasm to give his country a share in the new wave of French and German scholarship was shared by his pupil (and later successor) Francis Haverfield, tutor in ancient history at Christ Church, Oxford. Haverfield happened to have a pupil ideally qualified to fulfil the role of a 'young and trained expert on the spot' in Thomas Ashby. The family had moved to Rome in 1890, and Thomas Ashby senior was able to devote time to Parker's Archaeological Society, and much of the wealth derived from the family brewery in Staines to assembling an extraordinary collection of rare books, manuscripts, prints and watercolours that was to be the core of his son's library.[2] His son already had an unusual knowledge of Rome when he went up to Christ Church in 1893; he must have played his part in urging his tutor, Haverfield, and Pelham to visit Rome in 1898, to meet Lanciani, and talk to the Ambassador and English residents about setting up a permanent British base. Their visit was recorded by the diary of one of the circle in Rome, St Clair Baddeley.[3]

(above and previous)
The Columbarium
of Pomponius Hylas
by F.G. Newton.

Group photographed
by Thomas Ashby, 28 March 1901,
including Rodolfo Lanciani *(left)*,
Henry Pelham *(third from right)*
and Gordon Rushforth *(right)*.

On his return, Pelham proposed to the Managing Committee of the British School at Athens, founded 13 years previously, the setting up of a sister school in Rome; forming a committee that included George Macmillan of the publishing house, a keen supporter of Classics, Percy Gardner, the Professor of Classical Archaeology at Oxford, and J.S. Reid, Professor of Ancient History at Cambridge, they drew up a scheme of 'Objects of the School', and launched a public appeal. The central interest of this group was clearly in classical archaeology: they envisaged a School of Archaeology following in Rome where the School in Athens had led, and this just at the moment when Arthur Evans was preparing to launch his excavations in Knossos (he purchased the site in 1894, and started digging in 1900). But from the first, they appreciated that Rome offered quite different opportunities from Athens, and their vision was explicitly phrased as a broad one stretching beyond classical antiquity. So their appeal brochure, after emphasising a need for a base for classical archaeologists, drew attention to the impossibility of excavating in Italy under Italian law, and the emphasis rather on topographic studies, work in museums, and the growing importance of prehistory:

'It is obvious, too, that in some respects the work of a School at Rome would be more many-sided than is possible in Athens. It would be less predominantly classical and archaeological, and its students would be found in the galleries, libraries, and churches, as well as in the museums, or among the monuments of the Palatine or the Forum. A School at Rome would also be a natural centre from which work could be directed and organized at Naples, Florence, Venice, and elsewhere in Italy.

It is therefore not only to those who are interested in classical history or archaeology that the proposed School should be of service, but equally to students of Christian Antiquities, of Mediaeval History, of Palaeography, and of Italian Art.'

This broad vision, as Pelham and his colleagues realised, was not only inherent in the nature of Rome in all its millennial layers, but would strengthen the institution in every sense, in providing a broader base of support among donors, and in enriching the experience of its varied students. Even before launching the appeal, the committee had a successful meeting with Sir Edward Poynter, President of the Royal Academy, Sir Henry Maxwell Lyte of the Public Record Office, and Sir E.M. Thompson of the British Museum, all of whom promised collaboration; letters were also sent to the Royal Institute of British Architects offering to enrol their students.

The initial appeal was for a capital of £3000 and an annual income of £1000. The appeal was circulated privately in the early months of 1900, amid anxieties about the impact of the war in South Africa. They may have been a little disappointed they had only collected £879 in donations, and £321 in annual subscriptions, and bitter words were spoken about the willingness of people to give much larger sums to other, they felt less worthy, charitable causes, and to the relative ease of raising such sums in America. But the truth was that they had done well, and had found a winning formula: it merely took time to set the ball rolling. The four hundred subscribers and donors attracted by the end of 1901 seem an impressive achievement from the perspective of a century later; the subscription income rose to over £500 the next year, remained at that level for the rest of the decade, and reached a peak of £728 by 1914, by which time over 500 institutions or individuals were contributing.

GORDON McNEIL RUSHFORTH (1900-1903)

Such sums, in days when £200 could be offered as salary to a Director, were enough to make a start, and so it was that Gordon McNeil Rushforth, Tutor in Classics at Oriel College, Oxford was chosen in March 1900 to go out to Rome as a one-man band to launch the School. Rushforth, like Pelham, was an admirer of the great Theodor Mommsen, who, among his numerous other achievements, blazed a trail in Roman history by collecting Latin inscriptions for the first time systematically in a Corpus; Rushforth in 1893 published a selection of a hundred historical Latin inscriptions, a handy compilation for student use. But, apart from being a Roman historian in the Pelham mould, he was a man of broad culture with a particular interest in Italian art, and had just in 1900 published a monograph on the fifteenth-century Venetian painter Carlo Crivelli. His range embodied something of the nascent School's ambitions.

The School had now to establish itself an identity: place, people and programme. Rushforth left for Rome only in November 1900, when sufficient financial support had accumulated. By January 1901 he had identified a home for the School in the Palazzo Odescalchi on Piazza SS Apostoli, close to Piazza Venezia: it was ceremonially opened by the British Ambassador, Lord Currie, on 11 April 1901. Its nine rooms, on

GORDON McNEIL RUSHFORTH (1862-1938). He graduated from St John's, Oxford in 1885, was appointed College Lecturer at Oriel in 1893, and Classical Tutor in 1897. He published *Latin Historical Inscriptions illustrating the History of the Early Empire* (Oxford 1893), especially acknowledging the help of Professor Pelham. After returning from Rome in 1903, he retired to Malvern; he translated three volumes on architectural history by G.T. Rivoira, and published a series of papers on the stained glass of Great Malvern Priory, culminating in *Medieval Christian Imagery* (Oxford 1936).[4]

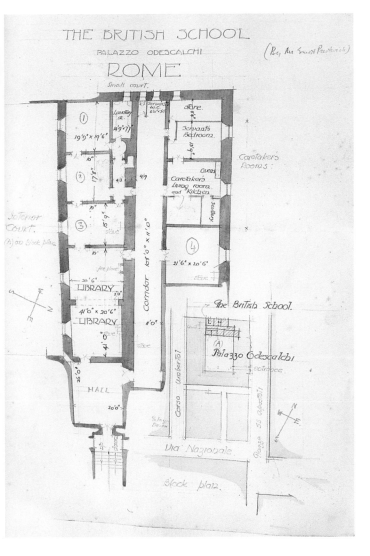

PALAZZO ODESCALCHI

(above) Interior of library photographed by Ashby.

(above left) The courtyard of Palazzo Odescalchi photographed by Ashby.

(left) Plan of the BSR apartment.

An old property of the Colonna family, the Palazzo Odescalchi was rebuilt by Carlo Maderna; passed to Cardinal Flavio Chigi in 1661, who commissioned Bernini to complete it in 1665; it then passed to Don Livio Odescalchi, nephew of Pope Innocent XI.

Ashby wrote: 'The photographs give an idea of the quiet dignity of the building, in the summer sunlight of early July. The deep cool shadows formed a delicious contrast to the glare without, and one realised that Renaissance Rome (and I imagine Classical Rome as well) was built for and by people who lived in the summer and existed in the winter, such stress did they lay on coolness in the hot months, without sufficiently providing for warmth in the cold season. So it was at the best season that we left the first residence of the School, when the mellow colour of the travertine showed at its best against the brilliant blue of the summer sky. Most of the students had gone before, some seeking refuge from the heat, more called by military duties which were soon to absorb the rest, as the claims upon us became more and more imperious. But the Palazzo Odescalchi never seemed more beautiful, more reposeful, more stately, than at the moment when the School left it; and though our new home in the Valle Giulia promises to be far cooler and fresher, with its lovely views and surroundings... it was impossible not to feel a real and deep regret at leaving the historic building with which, in however indirect a way, we had been connected for some fourteen years.'[5]

Giacomo Boni's excavations of the via Sacra
photographed by Thomas Ashby (1899-1900).

the second floor of the north wing, were sufficient for a library, a Director's flat, service rooms, and accommodation for a caretaker. There was no accommodation for students, who were expected to find their own lodgings, and use the School as a base. The apartment was regarded with considerable affection by those who used it over the next fourteen years.

The first priority was to establish a library. The collection got off to a head start with donations of books from the major publishing houses, led by Macmillans, which thanks to George Macmillan, who served loyally on the Managing Committee, was a generous contributor of funds. One particularly significant donation was a large collection from the library of James Peddie Steele, a retired physician living in Florence, introduced to Rushforth by Pelham; the obituary of Steele in the *Papers* after his death in 1917 underlines not only his generosity, but his important role in introducing English visitors to distinguished Italian scholars like Comparetti.[6] Through Steele and others, the Library had already acquired a thousand volumes by the end of its first year.

As well as books, the School needed people. There was no endowment or government grant at the outset, and no prospect of offering scholarships. But what was offered was a base, and the rules defined carefully who was eligible to be admitted as a 'student'. The requirements that 'no person shall be admitted who does not intend to reside at least three months in Italy' and that they were 'expected to pursue some definite course of study or research' made clear that the School was not a base for casual visitors or holidaymakers; it was a privilege to be a student, and the Managing Committee had to give its permission for each individual to be admitted. The categories specified of eligible students already embody some of the vital characteristics of the later institution. They could be,

(i) Holders of travelling fellowships, studentships, or scholarships, at any University of the United Kingdom or of the British Colonies.

(ii) Travelling Students sent out by the Royal Academy, the Royal Institute of British Architects, or other similar bodies.

The School was envisaged from the first as serving artists and architects as well as scholars. The RIBA was one of the biggest subscribers from 1902 onwards, and the early students included many from the RIBA and the Royal Academy. It is noteworthy too that students from the 'British Colonies' were envisaged from the outset. Canterbury

College, Christ Church, New Zealand and McGill University, Montreal were among the earliest institutions to subscribe, and already in 1901 the Committee received a letter from the architect Herbert Baker in Cape Town suggesting an application to the Colonial Government of South Africa for funding.

By the end of its first year, the School had already admitted four students. The first was Thomas Ashby. His family had been behind the plot from the first, and his father, mother and he appear in the first list of subscribers. He was presumably self-funded, though he had previously held a Craven Fellowship from the University of Oxford, and so became the first in a long series of Craven Fellows to be enrolled as students. The second student was Cuthbert Blakiston, the Craven Fellow of that year, working on the architecture of the fourth century AD; the following year, after touring Roman antiquities in Dalmatia, Germany and Austria, he was forced by ill-health to return home, the first of a long list of students and staff who found Rome bad for their health, and he settled down to teach at Eton. The third was Bernard Webb, Gold Medallist and Travelling Student in Architecture of the Royal Academy. Webb was studying Renaissance buildings in Italy, and came to focus on Baldassare Peruzzi. The fourth student, Peter McIntyre from St Andrews, extended the range of the School's interests into palaeography, a discipline for which the Vatican was an obvious centre; his work on the manuscripts of Plato formed a contribution to the new Oxford text of Plato edited by John Burnet of St Andrews.

The School had a home, a library and students; but what were to be its projects? As the Appeal had anticipated, there was no chance of a significant excavation in Italy to paral-

Detail of the 'palimpsest' fresco from Santa Maria Antiqua.

View of the Campagna around S. Gregorio; from Thomas Ashby collection (the figure in the carriage appears to be Ashby himself)

Ashby recorded the countryside around Rome aware that it was changing swiftly. He wrote: 'The rapid spread of cultivation in the country around Rome leads to the continual discovery of roads, buildings, inscriptions, works of art, coins, &c.; but the object with which the work is done usually excludes any attempt at scientific exploration, and in many cases, discovery and destruction are simultaneous...By thus describing them one is able to estimate the relative density of population, to observe which parts of the Campagna were inhabited by the wealthy owners of large villas, and which by agriculturalists; and the record is the more important inasmuch as the continual destruction just alluded to will, in all probability, soon preclude the possibility of compiling it.'[7]

lel the work now in full swing at Knossos. But it was a moment when Giacomo Boni's excavation of the Forum Romanum was at its most exciting. The British interest in new excavations in Rome had been kindled and kept alive by the series of 'Notes from Rome' sent by Rodolfo Lanciani, which by the turn of the century were as frequent as once a month.[8] By February 1901 Lanciani was reporting the rediscovery of the church of S Maria Antiqua, buried beneath the later S Maria Liberatrice: its eighth century AD frescoes were recognised as of great interest and importance. Rushforth found in these frescoes a suitable project; and though he could not publish photographs of them ahead of the official publication, his careful description and analysis was a significant contribution to art history. His lengthy paper formed half of the first volume of the *Papers of the British School at Rome*, published with astonishing promptness (thanks also to Macmillans) in 1902.

As Pelham remarked in the introduction to this first volume, it was an illustration of 'the variety and richness of the field which Rome and Italy offer to the student, and suggest the work which a properly equipped British School should be able to offer for the advancement of learning'. Balancing Rushforth's contribution to early medieval art history was the first of Thomas Ashby's essays on the Classical Topography of the Roman Campagna (others followed in 1906, 1907 and 1910). Pelham thought that in comparison the Director's paper on Santa Maria Antiqua 'will no doubt be found the most interesting by the majority of readers'. There is something austere about Ashby's endlessly thorough traversing of the Roman countryside and his careful descriptions of all Roman remains; Arthur Smith in his obituary even dared to call his topographical work 'sometimes pedestrian in more senses than one'.[9] But it was pioneering work of fundamental importance, recording primary material often for the first time; and it succeeded in carving out an area of specifically British expertise that is one of his greatest legacies to the institution. He recognised as his major forerunner Sir William Gell, whose *Topography of Rome and its Vicinity* of 1834 pioneered the subject.

Ashby's account is underpinned by a real vision of the significance of landscape archaeology. He was witnessing in his own day the gradual reclamation of the landscape, the draining of salt marshes, the elimination of malaria, and the extension of agriculture, such that 'it is not impossible that a hundred years of prosperity may make the Campagna once again a huge garden, as it was in the days of the Empire'.[10] His theme was this constantly changing usage of the landscape, as populations rose and fell, and agricultural systems changed, and the system of communication represented by the roads was created; a hundred years on, his predictions of the transformation of the Campagna are more than exceeded, and his theme has lost none of its relevance. His first paper on the subject, over 150 pages long, is an astonishing achievement for any scholar, let alone one so young.

Ashby's work evidently exceeded the level expected of a mere 'student', and he must have hoped from the start to make the School his life. In October 1902 the Committee decided to promote him to 'lecturer' if finance could be found. Meanwhile, Rushforth resigned on grounds of ill-health, and Ashby was asked to stand in as Acting Director until the new Director could arrive. By March 1903, Ashby's father offered to donate £250 to pay for his son as Assistant Director for the next two years from September. Ashby effectively ran the School for most of 1903.

Henry Stuart Jones (1903-1905)

The new Director, Henry Stuart Jones, was another Oxford ancient historian, a Fellow of Trinity College. He was to succeed Francis Haverfield in due course as Camden Professor of Ancient History. He had a strong interest in sculpture, and proposed to the Committee a major project for the School, of preparing a catalogue of the sculptures held in the three museums of the Comune: the Capitoline, the Conservatori, and the Antiquarium on the Caelian. An explicit motive for the project was that the Germans were in course of

SIR HENRY STUART JONES (1867-1939). His wide-ranging activities and publications were marked by a talent for the organization of collaborative work. A graduate of Balliol (1890), he was inspired by Percy Gardner's lectures on Greek art, and went out to the British School at Athens, where he met Eugénie Sellers (Mrs Strong); in 1891 he studied in Italy, but suffered from malaria. Elected Tutor at Trinity in 1894, he published a handbook of *Select Passages from Ancient Writers Illustrative of the History of Greek Sculpture* (1895), companion to the handbook on *The Elder Pliny's Chapters on the History of Art* by Eugénie Sellers and Katherine Jex-Blake (1896). He also edited the Oxford Classical Text of Thucydides (1898-1900). He launched his collaborative *Catalogue of the Ancient Sculpture preserved in the Municipal Collections of Rome* as Director, but continued as editor after his resignation in 1905, publishing the first volume, *The Sculptures of the Museo Capitolino* in 1912, and the second, *The Sculpture of the Palazzo dei Conservatori* in 1926. He served on the Managing Committee (later the Faculty of Archaeology) 1905-29. He was in charge of the revision of the Greek Lexicon of Liddell and Scott from 1911, held the Camden Chair 1919-27, was Principal of the University College of Wales, Aberystwyth 1927-34, and knighted in 1933.[11]

publishing the sculptures of the Vatican – again a German model was followed.

This project was to last for several years, and to engage the labours of a series of scholars. The first of these was Alan Wace, Craven student from Cambridge, admitted as a student in 1903; promoted to Librarian in 1905, he refused the Assistant Directorship in 1906, and went on to fame as excavator of Mycenae, Director of the British School at Athens, and professor of Archaeology at Cambridge. Overlapping with Wace was A.H.S. Yeames, first as a student from 1903, then recruited as Assistant Director 1907-9, who went on to a career in the British Museum. Meanwhile, Augustus Daniel served as Assistant Director in 1906-7; his career took him on to the Directorship of the National Gallery, and as Sir Augustus he long served on the School's committees. The project fulfilled the purpose of giving the School a sustained collaborative activity over a number of years, long after Stuart Jones' departure, stimulating the study of Roman sculpture in Britain, and forwarding the careers of promising young scholars.

THOMAS ASHBY (1906-1925)

Stuart Jones found that his health was not up to the Roman climate, and indicated his intention to leave in May 1904, trying to arrange things so that Wace would take over in his place. The Committee offered the Directorship to A.H. Smith, the Honorary Secretary, but the British Museum refused him secondment; he was to have his chance later. They next approached Percy Gardner, Professor of Archaeology at Oxford and one of the moving spirits of the School's creation; he too declined. Next the name of Roger Fry was raised, and indeed he was interviewed for the job. It is very striking and significant that so long before the invention of Arts scholarships, they were considering someone from the Arts world, and one whose views were the opposite of conventional. In the event Fry went to be Curator of European Painting at the Metropolitan Museum.[12] In June 1905, with Stuart Jones about to depart, there was still no decision, and the recommendation to appoint Ashby, which appears never to have occurred spontaneously to the Committee, was received from Mrs Strong. Strong and Ashby were interwoven from the start in the story of his Directorship. In September, the Committee decided to make Ashby Acting Director for 1905-6, and to retain Wace with the title of Librarian. Only in May 1906, after interviewing unsuccessfully the Rev. Gerald Davies, did the Committee finally decide to offer the Directorship for 3 years to Ashby. With such hesitation and reluctance was the School's greatest Director chosen.

Thomas Ashby
by George Clausen RA (1925).

With Ashby's Directorship there is an upwards surge in activity which is the product of the passion with which he believed in the School, and his vision of its potential. But he was aided by the fact that the School was at last given government support, at the rate of £500 per year, so transforming its finances, and realising the initial ambition of an income of £1000 per annum. The grant came in response to a petition made to the Prime Minister, Balfour, in 1905: its signatories, approaching a thousand, were a formidable show of institutional solidarity, including 11 bishops and archbishops, 21 Right Honourables, the Presidents of the British Academy, the Royal Academy, the RIBA, the Royal Society, the Society of Antiquaries, and the Society of Dilettanti, the Director of the British Museum, the Principals and Vice-Chancellors of 17 universities and university colleges, and hundreds of individuals from universities and public schools. From the first payment, on 1 April 1906, the government grant was a vital element, though never the whole, of the School's source of income.

It was a manifestation of public confidence that the institution had found its feet. Ashby seized his advantages: the School boomed in every way. The numbers of students admitted rose from the 3-5 per year of the first quinquennium to over 10 a year for Ashby's first two years (see Appendix). By 1908, they could report 'some 20 young scholars working at various subjects ranging from Greek vases to glass-work of the Renaissance and the survivals of pagan customs in Sardinia'. Those students included J.D. Beazley, working on his catalogue of Attic Red Figure Vases (he was to be a frequent visitor), and W.M. Calder, on his way to excavate with Sir William Ramsay in Asia Minor. It is clear from the enthusiastic accounts of their work in the Annual Reports that Ashby wished to extend the range of the School's activity in every way. It is likely too that the School made a major intellectual impact: the 'Morellian' method of identifying artists from their rendering of minor features that is claimed to be Beazley's contribution to the study of Greek art was explicitly advocated by Eugénie Strong, from whom he would have learnt in Rome.[13]

It is from now on that a regular stream of artists and architects from the Royal Academy and the RIBA and other colleges of art was admitted – compared to 2 between 1901 and 1905, there were 37 between 1906

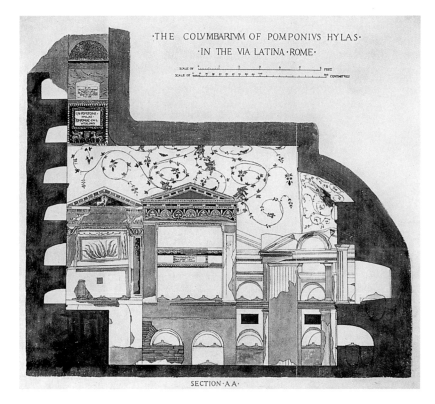

The Columbarium of Pomponius Hylas by F.G. Newton.[14]

and 1910. Ashby not only encouraged them in general, but involved them actively in archaeological projects. Thus the architect F.G. Newton, admitted in 1907, returned regularly to work with him in the Campagna, Sardinia, Malta and elsewhere, and so set a model for collaboration between architect and archaeologist that is one of the persistent features of the School's history. His beautiful watercolour copies of the Columbarium of Pomponius Hylas added to the range of the *Papers*. Reciprocally, Ashby, who was elected an ARIBA, contributed regularly to architectural journals like the *Builder*.

Another aspect of Ashby's 'outreach' was the welcome offered to teachers. The Annual Report for 1907-8 commends Eton College for sending out A.C. Sheepshanks to study the topography of Rome: 'such visits to classical sites give to the teaching of the classics in England additional reality and life'. The same notes are heard in the Report for 1911-12 when Arnold Toynbee spent seven weeks touring Lazio and Umbria, partly with Ashby: 'there is no doubt that such firsthand knowledge on the part of the teacher makes classical and historical teaching gain greatly in reality and interest'. Ashby could not guess that the inspiration which fed directly into Toynbee's lecture course in 1913 would half a century later ripen to the magnificent volumes of *Hannibal's Legacy*.[15]

The desire to broaden the School's base is also visible in the extension of the category of 'Associates' (those who did not qualify as students under the 3 months residence rule) and the creation of a new category of 'Honorary Associates', giving an association with the School to more senior figures, especially those resident in Rome, who could not be counted among students. Before Ashby there had been one; in 1906 alone he had 14 Honorary Associates admitted, including his old friends St Clair Baddeley, Father Mackey, keen photographer and companion of several of his projects, and Mrs Arthur Strong, his future Assistant Director, and an old admirer. Among these, note should be taken of S.J.A. Churchill, the British Consul in Palermo, and evidently another friend of the Ashbys. Churchill had a special interest in the history of Italian goldsmiths; he published an article on the goldsmiths of Rome in the *Papers*,[16] and on his death in 1924, his widow donated his specialist library on medieval goldsmiths to the School; the Goldsmiths' Company contributed generously both to

THE CHURCHILL ROOM. The walnut shelving of the Churchill Room was designed by Marshall Sisson (Jarvis Student, 1924) and financed by a grant of £500 from the Goldsmiths' Company in 1926; its upper layer was designed in 1996 by Robert Adam (Special Scholar in Architecture 1973), and financed by a further donation of £5000 also from the Goldsmiths' Company in 1997.

HENRY PELHAM.

Henry F. Pelham (1846-1907), Fellow of Exeter College, Oxford 1870-89, Camden Professor of Ancient History 1889-1907, President of Trinity College, Oxford.

His role was warmly appreciated by the Managing Committee: 'The Committee of the B.S.R. desire to express the deep regret with which they have learnt the death of their Chairman, the late Professor Henry Pelham, President of Trinity College, Oxford, and their sense of the grave loss which the School has sustained. The foundation of the School was due to the initiative of Prof. Pelham; his zeal and influence were largely instrumental in securing the necessary funds; his wise and kindly guidance led the School successfully through its early years, to its present position.'[17]

their original walnut shelving in 1926, and to its extension in 1996.

The continued dream of Ashby was to find money for studentships. One opportunity was created by the untimely death of Henry Pelham in 1907. By a twist of fate, Ashby lost Pelham within months of the death of his own father. What Ashby owed to his father in terms of shared enthusiasms is evident in the photographs in which he features, and in the moving restraint of his thanks in his Roman Campagna volume. What Ashby's father was to him, Pelham was to the School, and the Committee recorded its indebtedness appropriately. An appeal was launched for contributions to a Pelham Studentship to be awarded by Oxford: the first Pelham Student, T.E. Peet, was appointed in 1909. The Craven Committee of Oxford still occasionally recalls the link by sending out a Pelham student.

THOMAS ASHBY senior. The bearded figure with the umbrella has been taken to be Ashby's father, though this is not certain and may be an uncle. Ashby wrote in the preface to *The Roman Campagna in Classical Times* (1927): 'To the latter [Lanciani] and to my father (the best of companions while he lived) I owe my first introduction to the delights of the exploration of the Campagna.'

Borore (Nuoro) 'Giants' Tomb' of Imbertighe (1898-99)

by Father Peter Paul Mackey (1851-1935)

For the archaeologist, the glory of the Ashby years lies in his projects. His work on the Roman Campagna was big enough to absorb the efforts of several scholars for many years; yet rather than wishing it on the institution, he maintained it as a personal research project, and set about building up more ambitious schemes. Already in the summer of 1906, he visited Sardinia in the company of Duncan Mackenzie, the field director for Arthur Evans' excavations of Knossos; they saw the possibility of drawing links between early Aegean civilization and the western Mediterranean, and of extending from Crete to Sardinia the technique of craniological study. There were frequent follow-up visits: good relationships were established with the local archaeologists, Taramelli and Nissardi, and even the London secretary, John Baker-Penoyre, joined in an exploration in the spring of 1907. Another significant companion was Ashby's friend Father Mackey: his earlier photographs of the Nuraghi in 1898 and 1899, along with those of Ashby himself, now represent a valuable historical record. Mackenzie made a second more thorough exploration in 1908 with the architect F.G. Newton (albeit 'hampered by a severe chill'), and the results were published in a major contribution to the Papers of 1910.[18]

But, ever energetic, Ashby could not contain his interest only to prehistoric Sardinia. By the end of 1907, Ashby was dreaming of a far larger project, comparing the prehistoric remains of Sardinia to those of Corsica, the Balearic islands, Malta and Gozo. So the idea of a Western Mediterranean project grew, and an appeal was made for funding. One key player was Eric Peet (in his later career famous as an Egyptologist), admitted as a student in 1907; his article on the early Iron Age in south Italy in the fourth volume of the *Papers* was the School's first contribution to prehistory,[19] and his book on the *Stone and Bronze Ages in Italy* followed soon after. After playing with the idea of Sardinia, Peet was more drawn to Malta; there in 1908 Ashby had a successful visit, establishing his friendship with Theodor Zammit, and launched a series of successful seasons of digs on Malta and Gozo.[20] This British Colony offered what other countries in the western Mediterranean did not, a ready licence to dig. The Maltese connection was to last long, through Ward-Perkins, Tony Luttrell and the excavations on Gozo of Simon Stoddart and Caroline Malone.

Behind the Malta project lurked a never fully realised vision: that just as Evans could reveal a Minoan civilization in the eastern Mediterranean, new worlds could be studied

(left) Thomas Ashby with Joseph ('Pip') Whittaker
at his house on Motya, c.1911; from Ashby collection.

(below left) Excavations at the North Gate
necropolis, Motya, c.1911; from Ashby collection.

(below) Excavations of prehistoric temples at Mnajdra
on Malta; sent by T.E. Peet to Ashby.

in the west. Ashby was continuously in pursuit of openings. He was drawn to Sicily to the Punic settlement on the tiny island of Motya by Joseph Whittaker, of the family of great Marsala producers, and recorded Whittaker's excavations there with great attention in May 1911. He was also exploring Tripoli in this period. Between 1909 and 1911 there was active discussion of an excavation at 'Lebda', i.e. Lepcis Magna in Libya, then under Turkish rule, strongly pushed by one of Ashby's Oxford tutors, Sir John Myres. The project foundered on the hesitations of the Turkish authorities; by a twist of fate, it was to become the centre of a major School project half a century later under Ward-Perkins.

Ashby's was a School that looked outwards, in disciplinary range, in chronological scope, and in geographical spread. There were initiatives that did not take off, but rightly assessed the institution's potential. Among these was active negotiation with the Public Record Office to link up the small team they employed at the Vatican to create a basis for historical study at the School. For two years running, in 1909-1911, John Rigg of the PRO was officially nominated as Adviser in Historical Studies, though to their disappointment, historians failed to arrive as students. The desire to involve historians had been there from the start: in 1902, the *Times* reported Dr Charles Waldstein as observing at a subscribers' meeting 'that the continuity of history from ancient times and throughout the Middle Ages was better realised in Rome than on any other spot; and the Renaissance really centred in Rome'. If this vision was not fully realised until the early 1930s, it was not for want of trying.

Amid all these new developments, the established project of the cataloguing of Capitoline sculptures continued unabated. When Yeames resigned as Assistant Director in 1909, and Eugénie (Mrs Arthur) Strong offered her services, it was the dream choice: an established expert on Roman sculpture, a friend of the School from its conception, and one who already knew Rome intimately. Ashby and Strong were the most powerful academic team the School has yet fielded: between them they spanned the two central areas of research in Roman archaeology: Ashby representing the various possibilities of fieldwork, from landscape survey to excavation, Strong maintaining the great German tradition of art history. What is more, Ashby provided the link between the two by his work in a field in which he must count as a pioneer, and which is only a century later beginning to come of age: the history of excavation and antiquarianism. His interest in rare books and drawings was driven by a perception of the richness of information preserved in early travellers, collectors and artists: from the drawings attributed to Andreas Coner from the Soane collection to the Paper Library of Cassiano dal Pozzo at Windsor (a project still ongoing today), he drew attention to sources of lasting significance for the understanding of antiquity and revealed the importance of what is now called 'excavation in the archives'.

The institution had made astonishing strides forward in its first decade; if it grew subsequently, it was because those who launched it had a broad vision, grasped its rich potential, and pursued it with imagination and passion. True, the Committee in London continued to dither, notably about the renewals of Ashby's tenure, but it did not have the benefit of historical hindsight to measure his achievement.

THOMAS ASHBY, by Gilbert Ledward (RS Sculpture 1913). Ledward, the first Sculpture Scholar, sketched Ashby during his brief visit to Rome in 1914 before the outbreak of war. They met again on the front in Northern Italy. Ledward wrote to Shaw (29 May 1917): 'Dr Ashby came over to see me the other day and had tea with us in our cleft in the mountains. He seems very fit, and it was quite interesting to talk a bit again about old times in Rome. I took him up to the top of the hill from where you get a magnificent view of enemy country'.

THE NEW BUILDING
1911-1925

THE NEW BUILDING
(1911-1925)

(above and previous)

Façade of School c. 1916.

THE NUMEROUS ARCHITECTS and artists who visited the School in its first decade made clear a larger potential. By the end of the decade, a number of initiatives were brewing. In March 1908, the Architectural Association was enquiring about the possibility of setting up a scheme of studentships. In June 1910, a letter was received from Herbert Baker proposing a scholarship for South African architects. He seems to have funded it personally. The first Herbert Baker student, Gordon Leith, arrived in 1911, and worked with Boni on a reconstruction of the palace of Domitian. He also collaborated with the other new scholar of 1911, funded by the Gilchrist Trustees, J.S. Beaumont. Together they made drawings of the Vigna di Papa Giulio, next to the Villa Giulia: as if in anticipation of the future location of the School, they were drawn to the Valle Giulia. There was to be a distinguished series of Herbert Baker Students down to the declaration of sanctions against South Africa in 1961, and a distinguished series of Gilchrist Students down to 1934.

THE·FLAVIAN·PALACE ROME

Reconstruction of Domitian's palace by Gordon Leith.

George E. Gordon Leith was the first holder of the Herbert Baker Studentship for South African architects (1911-13). On his death in 1965 he left to the School 'all drawings, photographs, diagrams and related documents dealing with the Flavian Palace, Rome. I was privileged to attend the excavations during the years 1910-1913 which were carried out under the supervision of Commendatore Giacomo Boni which may well be the only records available of relics then discovered.'

Entrance hall with carpet given by Herbert Baker, c.1924.

Herbert Baker, the great architect of colonial South Africa, was an enthusiastic supporter of the School from the start. He wrote in 1901 suggesting a studentship for South African architects paid by the Colonial Government, and found the money himself from 1910. He also made smaller contributions, including, in 1926, a gift of £100 to pay for a carpet for the Entrance Hall (Exec Ctee 21.1.26). (This carpet is now in the Director's flat).

The RIBA too was thinking seriously of founding a School or Institute of its own in Rome; in early 1909 negotiations were opened with the School. John W. Simpson, elected RIBA representative to the Committee, explained their need of establishing a residential hostel. In November 1910, the RIBA were still pursuing their scheme: John Simpson made a visit to Rome, investigating the British School, the British Academy of Arts, the French and American Academies. In a printed memorandum to the RIBA he recommended the establishment of a single institution that would unite archaeological, architectural and artistic interests, which was very much the idea of the Ambassador, Sir Rennell Rodd; but given the high costs (he estimated a capital outlay of £100,000), suggested that as a temporary measure the RIBA should rent the apartment immediately adjacent to that of the School in Palazzo Odescalchi for five years and establish two architectural scholarships, with Ashby as Director of both institutions. Simpson was fully alive to Ashby's virtues:

> 'The present Director is Dr. T. Ashby, a distinguished archaeologist, who has lived nineteen years in Rome, and has a thorough knowledge of the City and its inhabitants, and is in full sympathy with the R.I.B.A. intentions. The library is well furnished as regards classic, archaeological and topographical works, many of which are of extreme interest to architects.'[1]

The ambitions of the RIBA in fact coincided with Ashby's ambitions for developing the scope of the School. What was lacking was the large funding required to realise the vision. At this stage, a much larger player entered the game, the Royal Commissioners of the Exhibition of 1851. The London exhibition of 1851 that created Crystal Palace had made a large profit, which the Commissioners were supposed to apply to 'increasing the means

of industrial education and extending the influence of science and art upon productive industry'. Its newly appointed Chairman, Lord Esher, set his sights on establishing Art Scholarships on the model of the Prix de Rome. By November 1910, his able young Secretary, Evelyn Shaw, was reporting back on consultations with a number of prominent members of the Arts establishment, including Sir Aston Webb, Sir Thomas Brock, and George Frampton; among those most enthusiastic about the proposals was Edwin Austin Abbey, R.A., who thought that Decorative Painting would particularly benefit, and underlined the importance of establishing a Home in Rome. Shaw simultaneously made contact with the Committee of the School, and complicated negotiations ensued in which the 1851 Commission, the RIBA and the School all seemed to want to call the tune.

The solution was engineered by Sir Rennell Rodd, HBM Ambassador in Rome. He had been elected to the School's Committee in 1901, on the recommendation of Lord Currie, under whom he served in the Embassy in Rome; promoted Ambassador to Italy 1908-19, his loyalty to the School was unflagging over the next forty years, including a decade's service as its Chairman (1930-39). Rodd strongly disapproved of the idea of setting up separate archaeological and architectural schools in Rome; by a closely parallel movement, the Americans, who had separate Schools of Architecture (founded in 1894 by Charles McKim) and Classical Studies (founded 1895), united them as the American Academy in 1912, and their magnificent new building by McKim, Mead and White was opened in 1914.

As Ambassador, Rodd was centrally involved in the British contribution to the international exhibition in Rome of 1911. He recruited both Ashby and Strong to the organising committee in Rome: they were directly responsible for the organisation of the successful exhibition of drawings of Rome and the Campagna by British artists at Castel Sant' Angelo, a theme clearly close to Ashby's heart. It was for the 1911 exhibition that Sir Edwin Lutyens was commissioned to design a British Pavilion in the Valle Giulia, where all the

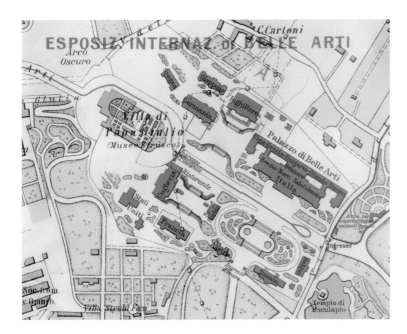

THE VALLE GIULIA SITE

(left) 1911 official plan of Esposizione Internazionale di Belle Arti; from BSR Archive.

(below) Aerial view of Rome in the 1920s, northwards. The School and the Galleria d'Arte Moderna are visible isolated in an area only sparsely built up.

The choice of the Valle Giulia as a site proved controversial. The case against was put by Sir Arthur Evans: 'Having studied the local conditions on the spot I can only repeat

once more – and my conclusions are confirmed by the opinion of old residents in Rome- that the position chosen for the new School itself must be absolutely fatal to its successful working. It is proposed to set down our students out of all convenient reach of the great Museums and Libraries and at the opposite pole from the other foreign schools. It has been urged that access from Rome will be easy through the Villa Borghese. As a matter of fact the Borghese is always closed at sundown, and frequently all day on the occasion of fêtes and shows. The routes, very bad in wet weather, vary in length from three-quarters of a mile by the via Po, to about half a mile by the Porta del Popolo. On the west side the tram which took visitors to the Valle Giulia during the Exhibition will be discontinued, and the nearest will be by the via Flaminia about a mile off, with another half mile, amidst slums, stables, factories and gas-works, to the Porta del Popolo...'

Rodd's vision stretched very much further than that of Evans: 'Anyone who could have seen the site this autumn in all its beauty would inevitably have rejoiced in our prospects...Things have changed in Rome today, rents are so high, and ground is so scarce, that it is quite hopeless to expect to obtain a site for the School and a hostel in the centre of the old city...The new site is within easy reach of the Vatican, a couple of hundred yards from the Villa Papa Giulio, and very near the Borghese Gallery. It will be practically included in the Villa Umberto (Borghese Gardens), the most beautiful and characteristic Roman part. It is on high ground, where the air is good and sanitary conditions will be satisfactory. I can only say that our prospects are envied by everyone here. The city will spread beyond us in the future, but we shall remain in a garden and park-like area, which will be as essentially Roman as anything can be in a city which, throughout its history, has always been changing.'

RENNELL RODD, portrait by 'Spy' (*Vanity Fair*, 7 January 1897).

James Rennell Rodd (1858-1941) was a man of wide culture; he won the Newdigate Prize in Oxford in 1880, and belonged to the circle of Oscar Wilde, with whom he collaborated in a production of Aeschylus' *Agamemnon* in Greek in the summer of 1880. That year they went together on a walking tour of the Loire. Rodd's first volume of poems, published in 1881 as *Songs in the South*, was reissued by Wilde in the States in 1883 as *Apple Leaf and Rose Leaf* with a dedication to Wilde as 'Heart's Brother', in consequence of which Rodd renounced his friendship. He served as Counsellor in the British Embassy in Rome from 1902-4, and was Ambassador 1908-19. He served on the Managing Committee of the School 1901-3 and 1908-12, then joining the new Executive Committee in 1912, to be its Chairman 1930-39 in succession to Lord Esher. He was created 1st Baron Rennell of Rodd in 1933. He is remembered as a founding figure by the Keats-Shelley Memorial House, the British Institute in Florence and the Non-Catholic Cemetery in Rome. He published three volumes of memoirs, *Social and Diplomatic Memoirs* (1922-1926) in addition to his poetry and prose.

Rennell Rodd, *Social and Diplomatic Memories*, 1909-1919 ch. VI:

'Of more permanent interest to record is the important sequel to our participation in the Exhibition. My good friend Nathan the Syndic who, as the pupil of Mazzini, was often accused of an anti-clerical and republican bias, but was really one of the most public-spirited and kindliest of men, expressed to me the hope that our pavilion might be allowed to remain as a permanent head-quarters for Exhibitions of art, in which case the area on which it stood would be conceded to us by the Municipality, if not in fee-simple at any rate on a perpetual lease at a peppercorn rent. The same offer would be made to the other nations which had been represented. I accordingly suggested to him a scheme which appeared to me more practical and comprehensive, and which did not exclude his idea of occasional exhibitions... I therefore suggested to the Syndic that the area in question should be offered to the British School, which was rather cramped in its actual domicile, and should become its permanent seat. Nathan readily assented, and obtained the cordial agreement of the Municipality. The land was then handed over to three trustees – Prince Arthur of Connaught, Lord Esher, and myself.'

foreign pavilions clustered. His adaptation of the upper order of Wren's façade of St Paul's met instant acclaim. Rennell Rodd entered negotiations with the strongly anglophile Mayor of Rome, Ernesto Nathan, and cut a deal whereby the Comune of Rome would grant the plot of the pavilion in perpetuity to the British Nation on condition that it was used only as a British School. With this plot of land, Rodd held the trump card: he overcame the qualms of the existing School about turning into a hostel for architects and artists, outflanked the RIBA's plot to set up a hostel independent of the School under their direct control, and bounced Lord Esher into making a snap decision that the 1851 Commission would fund the costs of acquiring and converting the pavilion, rather than see it pass into the control of any other body.

By April 1911 the parties involved had agreed to collaborate in creating a united institution. Evelyn Shaw had by July drafted a new constitution which satisfied the Committee. The 1851 Commissioners would finance the conversion of the pavilion, and a new scheme of scholarships for painters, sculptors and architects, one of each to be appointed each year with a three-year tenure, providing nine scholars at any one time. A new Faculty of Arts would take responsibility for selecting these scholars (in the event, there were separate Faculties for each discipline, Painting, Sculpture and Architecture). The old Committee would become the Faculty of Archaeology, and would take responsibility for the Library, the research programmes and the continuation of current activities. Management would pass to a new Council of 30, drawn from architects, painters, sculptors, archaeologists, and representatives of the main institutions involved; real control would be vested in a small Executive Committee. A petition was submitted to the King for a Royal Charter of Incorporation, approved by Privy Council in April 1912 and receiving the royal signature on 22 June. The new Council had its inaugural meeting two days later, and Ashby was confirmed as Director of the newly incorporated institution, and Shaw as its Honorary General Secretary.

The merger was complete, and control passed to the 1851 Commission, in the persons of Lord Esher, who doubled as Chairman of the Commission and of the Executive Committee, and Shaw, who doubled as Honorary Secretary of both bodies. Since the new Executive Committee met only once a year (unlike its predecessor which met if necessary monthly), power devolved to the Honorary Secretary. Shaw was a consummate bureaucrat: determined to maintain control of the running of the School in every matter however minute, he bombarded Rome with his correspondence, at the rate sometimes of dozens of letters a month, for the next 35 years until his retirement and knighthood in 1947. No matter was too trivial to elude his purview: Ashby could not buy a tennis ball unauthorised without receiving a rebuke. His correspondence, all surviving neatly filed in the School's archive, is a monument to micromanagement. It came close to smothering the institution.

The first challenge was to get the new building made. The initial assumption was that the exhibition pavilion would only need minor changes to adapt it ('Sir Rennell has ascertained from Mr Lutyens that the building is practically permanent, and that only the stucco front would, in time, require renewal').[2] The initial estimate of £2,500 proved wildly over-optimistic: in the event, the entire façade, in all its Palladian elaboration, had to be reconstructed, at the high cost of £15,000, the entire capital sum granted by the Commissioners. Costs soon rose towards £40,000, and it became necessary to absorb an anonymous benefaction of £10,000, intended to provide a working capital, to cover costs. Timely help also came from the offer of not less than £6,000 from the widow of Edwin Austin Abbey, the muralist who had so enthusiastically backed the 1851 Commission project.

So the story of the building is one of ever-changing plans, attempting to stay within costs.[3] The earliest plan for the School envisaged re-use of the exhibition room structures behind. The design that now seems so natural and obvious, of a four-sided structure around a central courtyard, was ironically the result of spending cuts. The original pavilion had no central courtyard. The first design substituted a small courtyard with Doric pillars for one of the exhibition rooms. The revised design had a central service block, again leaving only a small courtyard in front and behind. But for lack of funds, only three sides of the building designed by Lutyens were constructed, and it was not until 1938 that a fourth side gave the School its now definitive shape.

Sir Edwin Lutyens. O.M., K.C.I.E., P.R.A.
29ᵗʰ March 1869 – 1ˢᵗ January 1944.
From the original painting by Meredith Frampton R.A in the hall of
the Art Workers' Guild of which Sir Edwin was Master in 1933

Lutyens was originally excited by the prospect of designing what would be his first large institutional project. He wrote to Lady Emily that the Syndic of Rome was 'so pleased with our Pavilion they are to *give* the site – a valuable one and Rodd wants me to get the RIBA to buy the building and to fit it up as the British School at Rome', although he also immediately added, 'There will be a good deal of criticism about my building and its adaptability.'

The difficulties were not only due to the escalation of costs so typical of a project on this scale. A basic problem was that the architect was from January 1913 distracted by a more important job, the Viceroy's Palace at New Delhi. This was compounded by his insistence on attempting to build in Rome as if in England, with an English contractor, and frequently English materials. The firm of Humphreys got the contract by 'donating' the pavilion buildings, which eventually proved impossible to recycle. Rennell Rodd blamed them for the failure to complete the project:

'The whole trouble has been doing everything from London and through English contractors. I always urged getting estimates here, but my modest arguments were swamped by Lutyens at once and after all the building has been built by local people... It seems to me we have spent the maximum of money for a comparatively small result.'

To make things worse, materials were shipped out from England, and the outbreak of war made problems acute.

'We hear that the SS. Bittern has been torpedoed and is a total loss. Our goods which were being carried by this vessel for the Rome contract were chiefly 4 in eared cast iron pipe bends, junctions, and inspection pieces. We have already enquired if the iron-founders can supply replacements immediately and will let you know as soon as we have a definite reply.'

Lutyens for his part blamed the conflicting wishes of different committees in England and the staff in Rome. He writing to Lady Emily from Boulogne, on the train to Rome:

'War with three committees, one in Rome two in England make the British School so difficult and everyone seems X with me! as though I could help it, and ascribe everything to my being in India. Then the Roman Municipality and their absurd drainage rules, Mrs Strong, Rodd and all I suppose I have given them £1500 worth of fees at least.'

The succession of designs made by Lutyens for the building shows the impact of these factors.

THE LUTYENS BUILDING

by Andrew J. Hopkins

THE BRITISH PAVILION OF 1911

(left) The 1911 Pavilion, façade.
(below left) The 1911 Pavilion, ground plan.
(below right) The 1911 Pavilion, interior gallery.

Edwin Lutyens commented on the pavilion façade: 'The condition to copy, i.e. to adapt the upper order of the west front of St Paul's was given by the Board of Trade. They thought it all very like, but it wasn't a bit which is where the fun came in for me. The whole order had to be altered, and I think it takes more architectural technique to do this, and make every other part fit in, with the design of an undoubted master like Wren. The cornice, columns, etc.; a great labour but it was very interesting. To the lay mind a copy is good enough but to an architect, except some tradesman, it means a very good deal of thought, insight, knowledge.')[4]

The correspondent of *The Graphic* commented on the pavilion: 'The result is a spacious palace of a dozen splendid galleries, constructed in rolled steel and concrete, as if the building was not merely designed for a temporary building but intended as a national safe deposit for permanent use.'[5]

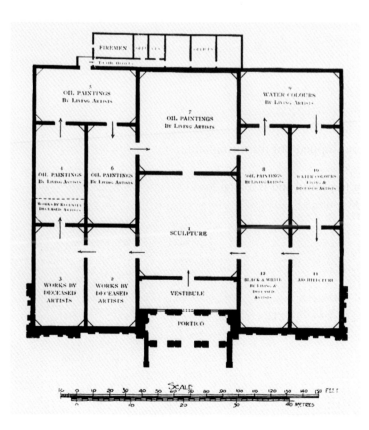

43

Lutyens' first scheme: the pavilion modified

(below) Lutyens' first design, elevation.

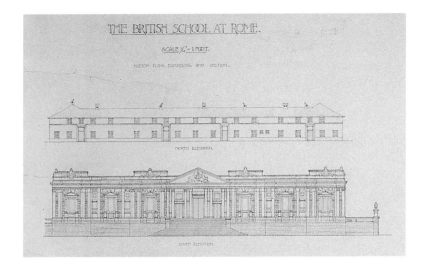

Edwin Lutyens discussing the plans of his first scheme: 'You will see by the plans that we are utilising every inch of the site for the building, that is to say, we have undertaken to commence a building scheme which will, when complete, cover the whole of the available land. We shall begin immediately to rebuild the façade according to a much improved design, which will occupy, when finished, the whole length of the present façade plus the length of the podium walls. We shall however omit from the first contract the end pavilions and the portions of the façade at each end where the podium walls are. These ends will be finished when we begin on the hostel.'

This drawing depicts the first scheme for reusing the existing pavilion structure. The façade design is one bay longer on either side than the pavilion. Other superficial changes on the façade and portico included the substitution of niches in place of the original side entrance doors, and the change of insignia in façade. This scheme dates from between April 1911 and January 1912, when Lutyens went to Rome taking the plans with him.

(opposite, above) Lutyens' first design, sections.

This drawing depicts longitudinal sections DD (through portico, peristyle court and lecture theatre) and EE (on cross axis of peristyle court, looking towards the entrance show the second scheme with entrance hall and very low courtyard and long low lecture theatre. EE is also an interesting section because it shows the Director's room at left with its vaulting and library with lay light. The clerk's area is located just before the library and uses the existing steel roof works, structure of atrium, studios with existing roof work.

(opposite, below) Lutyens' first design, plan.

A detailed plan of the first floor layout including the library to the right and the library entrance vestibule leading from the central square small colonnaded courtyard between the entrance and the lecture theatre to the rear. On the left studio bedrooms are situated off the gallery-like back courtyards. Men are housed on the sides and women behind the theatre. This is the scheme as revised by Lutyens after he 'revisited the site and familiarised himself with the requirements of the institution' and which was considered by the Building Subcommittee on 10 May 1912. Measurements in these drawings can be made in both feet and metres. Unlike the first scheme, this one includes a second floor with the laundry block at the centre of the rear wing and flats with loggias at the two rear corners of the building. The front portion of the design appears to be the same as in the first scheme.

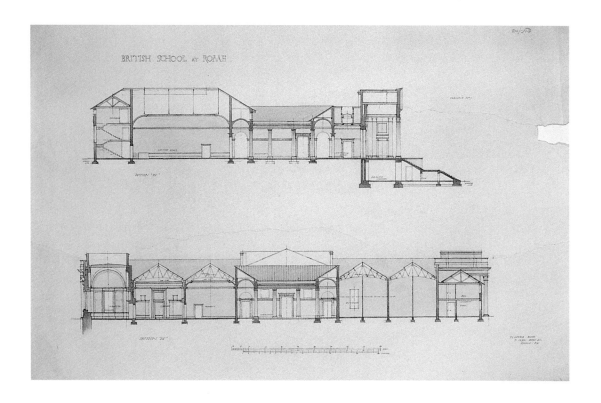

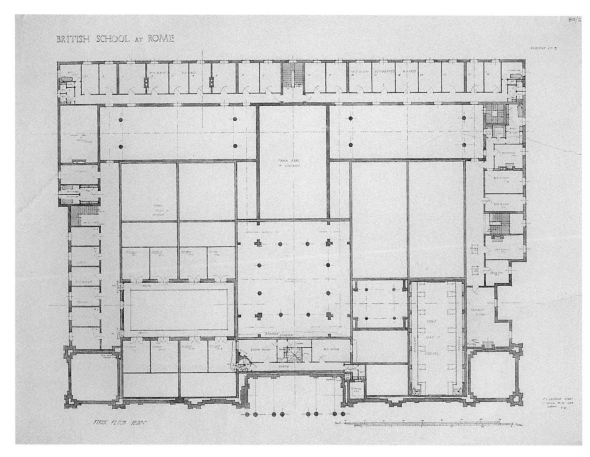

LUTYENS' NEW DESIGN

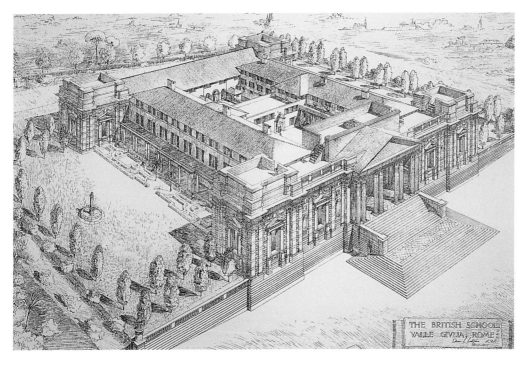

(opposite, above) Plan of first floor.

In February 1913 work was halted on the orders of the 1851 Commissioners. Lutyens wrote: 'I am instructed by the Commissioners of the Exhibition of 1851 to order you to immediately stop all works except the Portico Entrance Vestibule... The intention is to revise by way of modification the wings of the façade and replan the whole of the building at the back.'

He produced a radically new design which no longer sought to reuse the old pavilion. Unlike the first scheme, this was a carefully thought-out project for a residential complex. Beyond the portico an Exhibition Hall is created, with three glass doors opposite the three wooden doors of the portico, more generous than the small entrance hall of the first plan. From the Hall one would have passed into a Doric colonnaded courtyard, which was now reduced in size compared to the first plan. A service wing comprising the servant's hall, kitchen, scullery and pantries separated the formal representational courtyard to the south from the service courtyard to the north. The north side of the first courtyard was to be occupied by a niche commemorating Edward Austin Abbey. Although the central location of the servant's wing resulted in two smallish and relatively unusable courtyards, in terms of planning it did provide excellent access and great proximity for ease of service, whether to the Director's rooms to the west, or to the Dining Hall to the east. In the southern rooms behind the façade, Lutyens now relocated an expanded library to the west, entered directly from the hall. The library was also linked to the suite of rooms for the Director which now occupied the west wing of the ground floor: these rooms were to look out onto the garden through a Doric loggia which would have protected these rooms from the sun and heat. The Common Room was situated to the east, close to the Dining Hall and washrooms.

(opposite, below) New scheme, elevations.

North, west and east elevations of third scheme with details of the studios and of the especially grand side elevation with a Doric portico at the west and a Doric portico with a central raised pediment in the front of the dining room to fill the wall above the double height space where no windows are present. East and west elevations both have loggias, but the one on the east is grander, with a pediment over the central three bays and, in the central bay, an arched opening breaking into the tympanum of the pediment. Behind this is a double-height dining room.

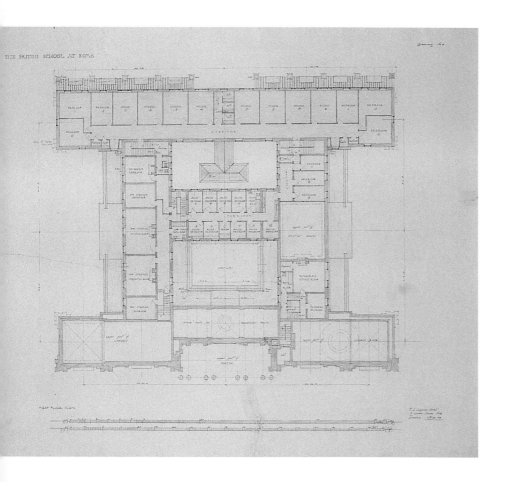

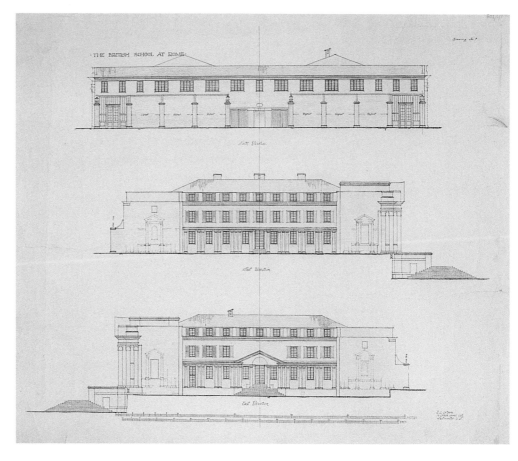

THE NEW SCHEME AS FINALLY BUILT

(above) BSR facade in 1916 (note the trees ready for planting).

(opposite, above) Plan of scheme as built in 1916, with unconstructed areas outlined.

(opposite, below) Sketch of what was actually built between 1920 and 1924, executed on the back of an envelope by an unnamed architect (note the tennis court is constructed, but not the Common Room).

    The final scheme reduced the width of the studio wing and substituted two laterally located corridors for the earlier centrally located corridor, thus providing a solid wall on which to locate a newly proposed patrons' niche. The East Wing, the Common Room, and the linking service wing which would have split the courtyard were set aside for construction in the future.

    After three years of stop-start construction based on schemes which were continually revised, things were in a sorry state, and pressed by the committees who were hoping to finally resolve the outstanding issues and instil some new impetus out at Rome so as to finish the project, Lutyens was finally persuaded to return to Rome, which he did in July 1915. Lutyens complained about the Clerk of Works, Squire, but Rennell Rodd clearly believed that blame for the failure to complete the project lay elsewhere: 'I am seriously considering whether I ought not to resign my connection with the British School... I know I shall be told it is the War and that we cannot expect things to be otherwise. But the building ought to have been completed before the War'. Rodd went on to remark to Shaw: 'Lutyens has been here, in quite a chastened spirit and so far as I can see has done his best to put things into a more hopeful condition... I gather one of the difficulties has been too many counsellors. There is Lutyens and his man: there is Humphreys and his man: there is the Committee and their man, and each dislikes the other, and asserts independence. What we really want is a dictator.'

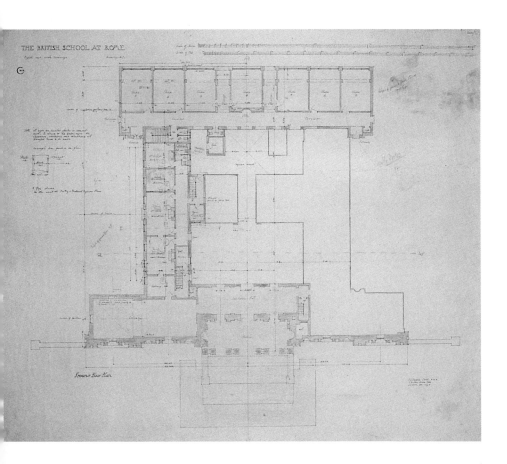

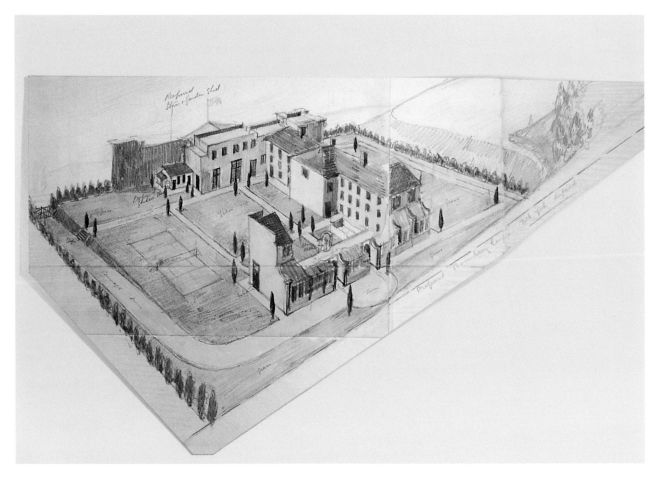

Edwin Austin Abbey (1852–1911)

(left) Bust of Edwin Austin Abbey by Sir Thomas Brock (under restoration by Andrew Wright-Smith, Australia Council Resident 1999).
(below) Lutyens' design of the Abbey niche.

Edwin Abbey was an American citizen, born in Philadelphia, but he worked and lived for the last 30 years of his life in England. Famous for his pen-and-ink illustrations of Dickens, he worked in water-colour, oil and fresco, executing a mural panel for the Royal Exchange in 1904. He was among those consulted by Esher and Shaw in 1910 about the proposed Rome prizes, and took up the idea with enthusiasm.

He was presumably a personal friend of Esher's. His wife (she disliked the word 'widow') Gertrude Abbey, wrote to Esher on 23 June 1913: 'It is my wish to build, in memory of Edwin Austin Abbey, a hostel for the use of students, as part of the British Academy in Rome, that it may be a token of his and my recognition of the hospitality which, during the thirty-three years he lived here, he received in England, especially from the members of his own profession, who not only accepted him as one of themselves, but elected him to membership of various bodies...I wish to present this hostel to England, in the hope that it may, in some way, so aid the activities of the British Academy in Rome, that that institution, in which he took so vital an interest, may one day send out an artist who shall carry on here the work and the traditions of Edwin Austin Abbey.'

Mrs Abbey paid a cheque for £6000 on the last day of 1916. She was however, puzzled by the School's title (2 August 1916):

'P.S. I wonder why the School is designated as "at" Rome? I remember a conversation with Mr. Henry James, about three years ago, on this point and he said that "at" should be used only when referring to small places like Fairford and that "in" should be used for large cities – that you would not speak of living "at" London or Rome or New York, but "in" those places...'

The need to incorporate a bust of Abbey played its role in Lutyens' design. He initially designed an alcove in the centre of the back wall of the studio corridor, but later created a new, and more prominent, location in the courtyard itself.

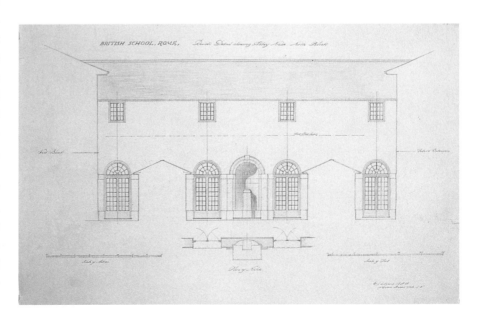

So, between changes of plan, shortages of cash, and delays imposed by war, the project dragged far longer than expected. The need to complete became more pressing when the lease on Palazzo Odescalchi could no longer be renewed, and by the time Ashby and Strong took possession of their building in July 1916, it was at best two-thirds finished. The entire east wing was missing, together with the kitchen block, so that a temporary kitchen had to be set up in the Director's flat, and temporary dining quarters in the first two artists' studios.

In retrospect, the surprise is perhaps that the project survived the outbreak of a world war at all. It was felt to be a matter of national importance to maintain the initiative. The

Annual Report of 1913-4 urged subscribers to maintain their contributions despite the war: 'Although the School was originally founded and is mostly maintained by private generosity, yet it claims by its title as well as its work to be a public institution of high importance. As representing the national interests in a foreign country the School must be prepared to take a leading place in Rome when the war is over, and to exhibit a vigorous life during its continuance.'

Rodd as Ambassador evidently felt the same way; and it may be relevant to note that

TEMPORARY QUARTERS.

Two views of a studio in 1923, in temporary use as a common room.

Since the Common Room and kitchens were not completed in 1916, the School had initially to make temporary use of two studios and the end of the Director's apartment.

The photographs record an artist's studio under occupation as the common room. Prominent is Ashby's collection of Piranesi prints in a special display cabinet.

TEMPLE OF LO SCASATO CIVITACASTELLANA

Lord Esher too was a founder member with Cecil Rhodes of a group intent on furthering the world influence of Britain in the Empire. In the context of European rivalries, the School had become a national cause.

Meanwhile, the first scholars elected under the new 1851 scheme, the painter Colin Gill, the sculptor Gilbert Ledward and the architect Harold Chalton Bradshaw had to make do with the facilities of the Palazzo Odescalchi. At the same time, in 1913, the first Jarvis scholar appointed by the RIBA, Louis de Soissons, arrived. Together with the Pelham, the Gilchrist and the Herbert Baker students, the School now had an impressive group of award holders. And even if they had no hostel, they were already discovering the joys of the sort of collaboration which had been typical of the institution since Ashby took con-

(above) Temple of
Lo Scasato
Civitacastellana,
by Harold Chalton
Bradshaw
(RS Architecture
1913-14).

(right) General
view of Praeneste
restored, 1919,
by Harold Chalton
Bradshaw.

trol. The Villa Giulia Museum (then called Villa di Papa Giulio), next door to the build-ing site of the School, proved a magnet. Bradshaw and de Soissons collaborated in pro-ducing measured drawings of the building.[6] At the same time, Mary Taylor of Newnham, Cambridge, the Gilchrist Student, was working on the architectural terracottas of Falerii held in the Museum. By the following year, Bradshaw was assisting her in a restoration of the Falerii terracottas; and in 1916, Taylor and Bradshaw published their joint work in the *Papers*.[7] Ashby wrote in the preface to the volume that

'the first paper is the result of the collaboration of a student of the Archaeological Faculty with the first Rome Scholar of the Architectural Faculty... Such co-operation may undoubtedly be expected in an increased degree in the future, and may add to our satisfaction in the enlarge-ment of the activities and scope of the School.'

The prophecy was borne out in more ways than one, and when Bradshaw returned to resume his scholarship after the war in 1919 to work on a restoration of Praeneste, it was with Mary Taylor as Mrs Bradshaw.[8]

But numbers of students soon dropped away from the astonishing peak of 80 in 1913-14. In 1914-15, thanks to enlistment, only 14 students (so many!) registered, and Ashby took the opportunity to visit Australia for a lecture tour, spreading the message about the School. By 1915, numbers were down to two, and the Director himself was recruited by his old friend George Trevelyan as a member of the British Red Cross Ambulance Unit, supporting the Italian allies in the bitter fighting around Isonzo: as a Quaker, Ashby was a pacifist, but certainly did not shirk action. By the time the building was handed over for occupation in 1916, only Eugénie Strong and one student, the architect Ernest Cormier, were left. Cormier left for Paris at Christmas, 1916. The Annual Report sadly noted:

'A long Roll of Honour hung in the vestibule of the new School alone represents the students, past and present, at Rome.'

The Roll of Honour, printed in the Report for 1917-18, lists 37 men, starting with the Director, and ending with the School servants, Armando Bonora and Giulio Santi. Miraculously, only four of the list were lost in action, including William Loring, the first secretary of the Managing Committee, and the young Guy Dickins, who had worked on the Catalogue of the sculptures of the Conservatori Museum between 1909 and 1911. But the Great War left a more lingering trauma, figured in the war memorials by Chalton Bradshaw, Gilbert Ledward and Charles Jagger at Hyde Park Corner, Horse Guards Parade, and elsewhere, and in the later death of the sculptor Emile Jacot, who never recovered from his war wounds.

They came back from the war to a changed world, and a changed School. Symbolic of the break of links with the past which had created the School was the death in 1919 of Francis Haverfield, who never recovered from the loss of his pupils at the front. Haverfield's vision of an approach to Roman history informed by archaeology had under-pinned his role in launching the School, and in 1910, with the active collaboration of the School, in launching a sister society in London, the Society for the Promotion of Roman Studies (Ashby and Strong were regular contributors to its Journal, and the formidable Secretary of the Society and Editor of its Journal down to 1940, M.V. (Marjorie) Taylor, was part of the same 1913 vintage of Rome students as Mary Taylor). However, Stuart Jones succeeded Haverfield in Oxford, so preserving the Rome connection, and returned to his

work on the Catalogue of the Conservatori Museum, in which he was assisted in 1920 both by Strong and by the young Bernard Ashmole, holding a Craven Fellowship from Oxford.

But now the School was a residential community. There had always been worries about how archaeologists and artists would react to living at close quarters. Lutyens had reported Eugénie Strong's anxieties:

'Mrs. Arthur Strong is in a very querulous and yah yah mood. I think she thinks our School is going to be too big for her and she is terrified of the rough architectural students. Why she picks out the architectural ones I don't like to think.'

There was initially much discussion over whether the 1851 Commission should appoint an additional member of staff to look after the artists, though the conclusion was reached that an annual visitation by a Faculty member was enough. If they had paid more attention to Ashby's consistent record of interest in art and architecture, his keen photography, and his record of collaboration with artists and architects, they might have been less nervous. The sequence of initial suspicion between artist and archaeologist, followed by growing trust, is illustrated by the letters of the most talented and sympathetic of the new generation of post-war scholars, Winifred Knights. As was to happen again and again in an institution that brought people into unexpectedly close contact, initial suspicion borne of difference gave way on closer acquaintance to respect and enthusiasm.[9]

In fact the mixture of artists and archaeologists flourished. The artists of the early 1920s were an extraordinarily rich crop, with Colin Gill, Winifred Knights, Tom Monnington, and Job Nixon, and even with Barbara Hepworth modestly tagging on as the wife of John Skeaping. But the 'archaeologists' too number some future big guns: Donald Harden, the future authority on the Phoenicians, excavating Carthage for his first time, Charles Oman, the future expert on medieval warfare, exploring the medieval topography of Rome, Arthur Darby Nock starting his work on Roman religion, Jocelyn Toynbee starting to work on Hadrianic art, Humphrey Payne pursuing Corinthian pottery around South Italy, and Ian

MEMORIALS OF THE GREAT WAR

(left) Model for the Guards' Memorial, Horse Guards Parade. The Memorial was erected in 1922, to a design by Chalton Bradshaw (first Rome Scholar in Architecture), with sculptures by Gilbert Ledward (first Rome Scholar in Sculpture). The photograph of the model comes from the BSR Archive.

(belove) Model for the National War Memorial, Brussels, by Charles Jagger.

Charles Sargeant Jagger (1885-1934) was elected Rome Scholar in Sculpture in 1914. Though he was prevented from coming to Rome by the war, he drew his stipend and received regular correspondence from Shaw during his active service in the Artists Rifles and subsequently the Worcesters. He was wounded three times in action and gassed twice.

He wrote to Shaw from the Dardanelles on 30 Oct 1915: 'I cannot of course tell you where I am, but I can tell you that for nearly four weeks I have been under both shell and rifle fire without respite, and I am beginning to feel the want of a change...Yesterday I managed to get permission from the C.O. to go down to the beach for a bathe. It was the first time I had removed my clothes for 3 weeks, or indeed had a wash of any kind...'

He wrote again from Malta on 30 Nov 1915: 'You may have heard that I "stopped one". Well it wasn't altogether correct because it

went right through, probably some beggar behind me had the pleasure of actually stopping it. However my wound was quite clean and didn't turn sceptic, so it is now healing rapidly and I shall be none the worse for it. I am still feeling very "cheap" nevertheless because I have jaundice as well and it is not a pleasant thing to have about you. I was knocked out on the 5th Nov about midnight and have been here since.'

He returned to action, and was wounded again in Flanders, and wrote to Shaw on 15 May 1918: 'I seem to be such a healthy brute that I heal almost before I have been hit. I was wounded twice on the same day – the first one slight and I was quite able to carry on but the second put me out – I got it through the left lung but am already walking about and shall be in town again shortly.'

After the war, he was given an extension of his scholarship in England to execute a war memorial: his bronze relief 'No Man's Land' which was presented by the School to the Tate, subsequently transferred to the Imperial War Museum.

He was elected to the Faculty of Sculpture in 1921, and supported the School until his death in 1934.

The Artist's impressions of Ashby

A sketch of Ashby by Winifred Knights (from letter of 10 January 1921).

Winifred Knights to ner mother, November 1920

'I can't tell you how lovely Rome is Mother. The gardens are so beautiful and all the plants and trees are different...The school is a beautiful building also and so comfortable to come back to English people after all the shrieking foreigners, they are a noisy lot...I'm afraid the painters are rather in the background. It is all archaeology that is the pity of both Mrs Strong and Dr Ashby being archaeologists. Never mind perhaps it is all the better. We shall be able to do what we like. It is very free here especially while Mrs Strong is away.'

13 November 1920

'...the archaeologists get my goat they are all so darned superior, & clever they always talk shop and never never play unless it is college songs on the piano. They are not alive, they are walking with their heads turned the wrong way...'

10 January 1921

'Among the P.P.C.s I have enclosed 3 of Frascati, there are some large villas there with wonderful old gardens, Ashby secured a permesso, and we spent a lovely morning wandering through them... After lunch we went still further into some hills which were once the crater of a high volcano, and we came to the remains of the Roman town, Tusculum, Ashby was quite, quite, happy then, and took off his funny little coat and began running down holes and Roman drains like a terrier. Toward tea time, we came down the hills and stopped at the Jesuit monastery and found some boy priests playing football so imme-

diately our men began playing and then Ashby joined in, playing goal and they had a fine game.'

January 1921

'Ashby has given some good lectures on Roman roads, and the history of Rome, with the lantern. Mrs Strong has started on the Mosaics and Baroque...'

February 1921

'We have been having a gay time since Mrs Strong came back. I am dutifully learning to become a social success. We entertained Lady Otterline Morrell, her husband and daughter, a week ago and a day or so ago Lord Beauchamp and his daughter to lunch... At both lunches I had to go with the guests up into Mrs Strong's room for coffee. I am her pet exhibit at the moment, I can tell you it is a bit terrifying, she is such a flatterer.'

56

PORTRAIT OF STEPHEN AND VIRGINIA COURTAULD by L. Campbell Taylor.

Stephen Courtauld (1883-1967) was, with his brother Sam, heir to a family fortune based on rayon manufacture.

He fought in the First World War in the Artists' Rifles, as did Gilbert Ledward, the first Rome Scholar in Sculpture (1913) and Charles Jagger, second Rome Scholar in Sculpture (1914); their friendship is reflected in the inclusion of several of their works in the collection at Eltham Palace, restored by Courtauld in the 1930s (Winifred Knights, Tom Monnington and H. Wilson Parker were other Rome scholars who made their contribution to the Palace). Courtauld served on the Executive Committee of the School from 1925 to 1939, and chaired a subcommittee on finance from 1927 to 1939.

His gift of £15,000 entitles him to be remembered as the biggest of the School's benefactors before recent times.

Richmond starting work on the Aurelianic walls in collaboration with the Jarvis Scholar in Architecture, Marshall Sissons. All these became household names in their fields.

The numbers of scholarships were augmented by two significant donations. One was occasioned by the will of Bernard Webb, the first architect student of the School in 1901. Dying in March 1919, he left the School (his will still gave the old address at Palazzo Odescalchi) a legacy of £3000, 'for the purpose of a Studentship to be known as the "Webb Studentship" in Architecture or Archaeology and tenable at the said British School at Rome and to be obtained by competition from and amongst bona fide students not exceeding the age of 32 years who have been members of the Architectural Association...' The success of Ashby's enthusiastic marriage of architecture and archaeology shows in his desire to promote students who were architects by training, but archaeological in their interests. The money finally arrived in 1922, and a special committee of architects and archaeologists was formed to select the Webb scholars. Between 1923 and 1984, by which date the funds had dwindled away, a distinguished series of architects held the scholarship, including Geoffrey Jellicoe, Sheila Gibson, Quinlan Terry and Will Alsop.

Microhistory: The Tennis Court

(lright) Landscape with Tennis Court by Winifred Knights.
(below) The tennis court, 1925.

5 November 1912, Executive Committee minutes report a recent visit by Evelyn Shaw to Rome:
'he had obtained from the Sindaco the gift of some additional land adjoining the site of the building, the most considerable piece being a strip of 17 metres wide along one side, which would give room for a tennis-court.'
A tennis court is marked on Lutyens' 1913 plan but was not constructed.

8 June 1920, Ashby to Shaw:
'I have just seen a professional from the tennis club here, and he tells me that a hard court could be done for something like 3000 lire including wire, as the place is already level...'

20 August 1920, memorandum from Strong (in Rome) to Ashby (in UK):
'Court. The rain has now come and the soil is in better condition and the men are making good progress with the tennis court. ...Roller. Remember that you will want a good roller for the court...'

3 Sept 1920, telegram to from Strong to Shaw:
'PLEASE ALLOW PURCHASE ROLLER 900 LIRE UTMOST URGENCY FOR TENNIS COURT UPKEEP'

10 November 1920, Ashby to Shaw:
'Walcot has turned up again and, munificent fellow, has just given me a cheque for £100 to pay for the tennis court, which he said he had always thought of giving. I think it is uncommonly good of him, and if you would send him a letter and formal receipt, I think he will be pleased.'
(The donor is William Walcot, an artist admitted as an associate by Ashby in 1909, and then allowed by him to rent an unoccupied studio in 1919. Walcot was a noted painter of perspectival reconstructions.)

26 April 1922, Shaw to Ashby:
'I see there is a charge in the Accounts for tennis balls Lire 190, and piano hire 50 lire, both of which must be discontinued and in future charged to the students themselves.'

12 May 1922, Ashby to Shaw:
'Tennis – As to tennis balls, there is still an unexpended balance of about lire 1,700 of the lire 9000 that Walcot gave for the tennis court, which is being applied to purchase balls etc. etc. Any item under that account will in future be marked "Walcot a/c" on the sheets.'

16 May 1922, Shaw to Ashby:
'As to the tennis court, I think that as Walcott's [sic] donation was taken into the general funds it should be spent on the court and not upon the balls. The students should supply their own balls.'

The second new scholarship of this period was one in Engraving (the name was only later in 1978 changed to Printmaking). This was probably the coup of Evelyn Shaw. Lord Esher announced to a meeting of the Executive Committee in March 1919 his acceptance of a gift of £15,000 from 'one who wished to remain anonymous – for the purpose of endowing an annual Rome Scholarship in Engraving'. The sum was a very substantial one, two and a half times larger than that given by Mrs Abbey in the School's most memorialised donation. This donor's request for anonymity was so fully respected that the School came later to forget completely one of its greatest benefactors. Shaw's correspondence reveals that the donor was his close friend Stephen Courtauld, brother of the founder of the Courtauld Institute. Stephen remained a devoted supporter of the School, serving for many years on its Executive Committee; his thirties art deco house near Greenwich, Eltham Palace, was full of work by Rome scholars. A new Faculty of Engraving was created to select the scholars. By an irony of historical amnesia, when in the 1980s the 1851 Commission started to withdraw funding for Art Scholarships, they chose printmaking, as the medium most closely related to industry, as the branch they would 'continue' to support, though they had never funded it in the first place. And though the Engraving/Printmaking Scholarship disappeared with the final withdrawal of 1851 funding, the scholars left behind a rich archive of prints, the fullest record of artists' work the School possesses.

The number of scholars was thus rapidly growing in the early 1920s. Both Ashby and Strong emerge as far from remote in their dealings with the students. (Ashby writes to Shaw, 11 March 1920, 'Many thanks for your letter. I am very glad that the art students are happy at the School. Naturally, as far as technical direction goes, I can do far more for the architects than anyone else: & Bradshaw is an exceptionally intelligent and pleasant person.') One only has to observe Ashby's eagerness to get the tennis court constructed, or the battles he had with London over holding dances in the Library, or even his championship of the artists' cause against the unilateral imposition of 'College Fees' by Shaw to see how much he had the interests of residents at heart. The idea that he was temperamentally unsuited to be warden of a hostel was a myth created by London to excuse its arbitrary sacking of a man who understood as few others have done what the job required.

Between 1919 and 1922 new building work was reduced to the level of tennis courts and sheds. But the main building still desperately needed to be finished. There was still no dining room, and two artists' studios had to be used, as we have seen, for the purpose. Accommodation was extremely short, and was only partially helped by the insertion of

Harold Chalton Bradshaw
by Edwin Halliday (RS Painting 1923)

wooden mezzanines in five of the artists' studios in the summer of 1921, so liberating bedrooms on the floor above. In 1922, Harold Chalton Bradshaw, the first Rome Scholar in Architecture, was invited to provide plans for a block behind the blank east façade for a common room on the ground level, and servants' bedrooms above. While Lutyens' plans too had envisaged a Common Room in this position, Bradshaw's Common Room was also intended to serve as

THE BUILDING OF THE COMMON ROOM

(above) Bradshaw's watercolour impression of east end of Common Room.
(right) Bradshaw's sketch of west wall of Common Room with gallery.
(belove) The new kitchen, 1924.

Bradshaw sensibly placed the kitchen under the Common Room/Dining Hall, so obviating the need for the ungainly central block of Lutyens' design. A 'minstrel's gallery' above the entrance to the Common Room was subsequently suppressed by the insertion of a lift in 2000.

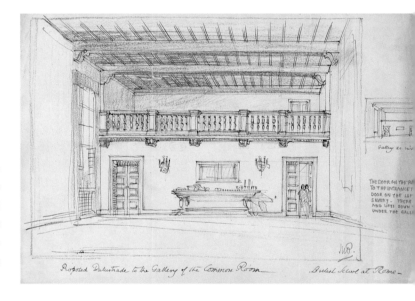

Dining Room, with kitchens below, so removing the need for the ugly kitchen block in the courtyard planned by Lutyens. Finance of £5000 was provided by the 1851 Commissioners, still in generous mood; the Executive Committee report of 1923 drew attention to how much the School owed to the Commission, which put up its annual grant to £1000, twice the grant still received from the government, and

(left) Eugénie Strong.

(below) Thomas and May Ashby.

which calculated the amount previously invested in the building as £45,000, and the capital value of the scholarships it provided as £73,000. Contributing on this scale, the Commission could indeed call the tune, and it did not even bother to call meetings of the Council or Executive Committee on an annual basis.

Building work on the new block started in May 1923, and was finished by the end of 1924. Ironically, it was the prospect of more space that provoked the row that ended the regime of Ashby and Strong.[10] Relations between the two had been placed under immense strain by Ashby's marriage in the summer of 1921 to May Price-Williams. Mrs Strong and Mrs Ashby disliked each other intensely: Ashby (who continued to admire Mrs Strong as a scholar) complained frequently about Eugénie Strong's 'nervous condition and dominating character', while Strong complained about May Ashby's interference in the running of the School.

The School was not big enough for two strong-willed women competing for the position of 'Lady of the House'. Back in London, Esher and Shaw were already weary of the bickering when a new row broke out over who was to benefit from the additional space released by the new building. The temporary kitchens had occupied the end room of the Director's ground-floor flat; Ashby petitioned for its restoration to his quarters. Strong counter-petitioned for the restoration to herself of the bedroom constructed *enfilade* as part of the Assistant Director's flat, and so marked on Lutyens' plans. But that meant reducing the Director to one bedroom, and the Ashbys insisted on separate bedrooms. The investigation conducted in April 1924 by Arthur Smith, vividly confirmed by contemporary photographs, shows Eugénie Strong living upstairs in considerable elegance, and the Ashbys below squashed by his ever-expanding collection of books. The Directors who have, since Mrs Strong's departure, been privileged to live in her apartment, and the Assistant Directors, who have subsequently lived in very much smaller quarters elsewhere in the School, must reflect that however successful she may have been as a Society Hostess, her demands had rather lost a sense of proportion.

Neither Ashby nor Strong anticipated how their row would escalate. Although each of them was appointed on the basis of constantly renewed short contracts, they evidently

HAVING A BALL

Ashby and students at a Christmas party, 1924 (the photograph was given by Ashby to his friend Lugli).

Letter, Evelyn Shaw to Ashby, 20 January 1921:
'I am delighted to hear that the students had a good reception and I am more than pleased to know that you allowed the Library to be used for a dance. After all, the Library is only part and parcel of the School, which is for the use of students and not for outsiders. I am not the least concerned about what out-siders may say. I want the stu-

dents to enjoy themselves on these occasions and to be always happy, and so long as we know that they are not rowdy and that they are well behaved I should not care twopence for the old ladies in Rome. I am more than glad that this reception was held upon the arrival of Mrs. Strong as she I know will have appreciated the natural gaiety of the occasion. Neither of you need be the least nervous about the dancing in the Library; it is a very good thing for the students and for the Library.'

Letter, Winifred Knights, 4 February 1921:
'But no rest for me for Dr. Ashby came in after dinner & insisted on being taught to dance & the task fell to me. He is one of those people who have no idea of dancing & never will have, but he was so keen & I really think he made a great improvement dancing during the evening but I am feeling stiff this morning in consequence.'

Letter, Evelyn Shaw to A.H. Smith, 2 January 1923
'I dislike and suspect Mrs. Ashby's interference in official matters.
I really think Ashby ought to be sacked for allowing his wife to make such a monstrous proposal to the Chairman of the Faculty of Archaeology...
The question of using the Library as a playground would ordinarily be left to the discretion of the Director, but since a definite request has been made for permission to be granted to the Director's wife to entertain in the Library, it should in my humble opinion be refused...'

THE DIRECTOR'S AND ASSISTANT DIRECTOR'S FLATS

(left) Assistant Director's flat.
Eugénie Strong's sitting room in 1922. Behind the curtain at the end is the door to the bedroom claimed by both Ashby and Strong.

Report of A.H. Smith to Executive Sub-Committee, 8 April 1924:
'Mrs Strong at present has Bedroom, Study and Library, and Sitting Room. The Sitting-Room serves the combined purposes of Drawing-Room and Dining-Room, but the Study can be used on occasion as a second sitting-room. The points emphasised by Mrs Strong were that she would like to have room for a piano, to have room for preparations and service in connection with a tea-party, and to have space for occasional ironing, and other similar domestic operations. These are all desirable amenities, but on the whole it appeared to me that even in their absence Mrs Strong was the enviable occupant of a very charming apartment.'

Letter of Mrs Hardiman, Bursar, to Quick, 27 Sept 1923:
'In making the inventory, I penetrated even unto the Directors' flats, and made the surprise discovery that almost all the very beautiful furniture in Mrs Strong's flat belongs to the School, having been bequeathed thereto by Vansittart and Squire.[11] There are very few things in Dr Ashby's flat belonging to the School.'

(right) Director's office and sitting room.
The ground floor of Ashby's flat in 1922. Ashby's flat was effectively part of the School Library long before his collection was formally acquired by the institution.

Report of A.H. Smith to Executive Sub-Committee, 8 April 1924:
'The Office-Library is full, not to say over-full, of books and papers, and not capable of use except as an office and study. The Sitting-Room serves the combined purposes of Drawing-Room and Dining-Room. In addition the room has large bookcases with a somewhat ragged overflow of the Library. I pointed out to the Director that a collector must accept the incidental discomforts of his pursuits, but he replied, with undeniable force, that his Library was strictly germane to the purposes of the School: that it was available as a supplement to the School Library, with a corresponding catalogue, and that consequently there was no sitting-room in the apartment that could be considered private.'

Note from Mrs Strong to Shaw,
with a photograph of herself as Librarian.

imagined that they were settling into their new quarters in the long term. It is poignant to discover Ashby putting his own money in the summer of 1924 into the construction of a pergola outside his study (provoking another fit of pique from Strong): he had no inkling that he was building for his successor. But Shaw had lost patience, and decided to 'sack them both'. Smith as Chairman of the Faculty of Archaeology, technically the employer of the Assistant Director/Librarian, secured a decision of the Faculty on 29 May 1924 not to renew Mrs Strong after the end of her contract in 1925; much concern was expressed about her neglect of cataloguing. An Appointments Sub-Committee was summoned on 30 May 1924, but was not completely clear in its recommendation, suggesting one year's renewal for both Ashby and Strong, and further consideration later. The Faculty met again on 20 June, confirmed its intention to terminate Strong's appointment, and acquiesced in the termination of that of Ashby should the Executive so decide. The Executive met on 24 June, and terminated both appointments with effect from a year's time in the

ASHBY'S PERGOLA

Ashby's Pergola, 1926.
Ashby was constructing a pergola in the summer of 1924 just where Lutyens' plans had foreseen a Doric portico outside the west wing of the building.

Letter of Mrs Strong to Shaw, 30 April 1924:
'He is now building (though at his own expense I believe) a long brick pergola which will give him, so to speak, an extra and very delightful room in Spring and Summer.'

Letter of Ashby to Shaw, 10 June 1925:
'Cost of pergola, lire 1200.
There are 8 brick pillars, and a pitchpine beam to join them above. On this rests the lighter framework to carry vines & climbing roses, which are already growing well. I also paid for the Venetian blinds to hang down the front of it, lire 985.'

Letter of Radford to Shaw, 22 October 1936:
'At present there is a pergola covering the space immediately outside the ground floor windows. This is covered by a thick growth of leaves which obstructs the rooms of the Library and the Director's study so that on sunless days it is almost impossible to work in them without artificial light. The wood of the pergola is beginning to rot... I should prefer personally to do away with the pergola and grow a wisteria on wires up the wall...'

interests of a managerial reorganisation of the School.[12]

The trauma of this decision has rippled through the School's history to the present. In one blow, the School lost two of its greatest scholars. Eugénie Strong was an extraordinary figure, one of a pioneering generation of women scholars. She left a deep impact in Britain on the study of Roman art, and on the development of the School: her contribution outweighs that of many Directors, and it was only because she was a woman that in that period nobody thought of making her Director herself. Yet the personal blow for Mrs Strong was hardly exceptional: she was aged 65 at her retirement, which could be celebrated by a grand dinner at the Hotel Cecil attended by an array of famous names.[13] What she (justly) objected to was the public indignity to which she was subjected.

The dismissal of Ashby at the peak of his powers at the age of 51, when as Rodd appreciated he was unlikely to find alternative employment elsewhere, was a tragedy equally for the man and the institution. He accepted his fate with Quaker dignity:

> 'I do not wish to discuss the circumstances of my compulsory retirement from the Directorship, nor to express any opinion on them. I have not enough knowledge of them, nor do I seek it at this late stage.'[14]

But it broke his heart, for he cared for the School and everything it represented with unqualified passion. He loved the School too much to do or say anything that could

Busts in clay of Eugénie Strong and Thomas Ashby by David Evans (RS Sculpture 1925).

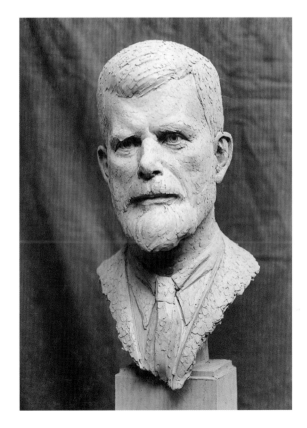

harm it, and continued to live in Rome nearby and work on the topographical dictionary of Rome, and the aqueducts; but he suffered something that would now be called a nervous breakdown, and his abrupt death in 1931 was that of a man who had lost what he had lived for.

The institution equally suffered its own loss of nerve. Its next Directors were all short-term appointments, and though several were later to be men of great distinction, none stayed long enough to make a real impact or to recapture the vision and passion that characterised Ashby. The row that broke out in London over the decision cost Evelyn Shaw dear, and he never again allowed the situation to get out of control. The price of greater control in London was loss of initiative in Rome; that sense of independence and vigour did not return to Rome until after the Second World War. Only in retrospect could one imagine how golden the age of Ashby had been.

Mrs Eugénie Strong
by Tom Monnington.

AFTER ASHBY
1925-1939

AFTER ASHBY
(1925-1939)

THE OFFICIAL LINE on the departure of Ashby and Strong was that circumstances had arisen which 'made it necessary for the Executive Committee to review the whole position of the administration of the School'. The solution was to abolish the office of Assistant Director/Librarian, till that point a burden on the budget of the Faculty of Archaeology, and give the new Director more administrative support. The reality that underlay this excuse was that the weak link in the School's organization was indeed at the level of day-to-day administration. Already by the early twenties, the School had a substantial domestic staff: in April 1925 they numbered 13, headed by the butler, Armando Bonora and his wife Regina (the original team from Palazzo Odescalchi), and including Bruno Bonelli, future prop and stay of the School, as hall-boy,[1] and William Pavey, foreman of the Humphreys building team, who eventually formed a romantic attachment and stayed on. (Three quarters of a century later, the domestic staff stood at 9, though the number of residents was more than double.) Here was the consequence, in terms of workload, of having established a residential hostel. Naturally the management of this staff was a considerable challenge, and the crisis that brought down Ashby and Strong revolved largely round the failure to cope with it.

The weak link lay in the position of Secretary or Bursar, the English officer given charge of the staff and the accounts. In early 1922, Miss Helen York had the post, but left in May on the official grounds that it was more of a housekeeper's job than she liked, though Ashby confided to Shaw that 'she found Mrs Strong rather difficult during the last week or so'.[2] Her successor, a New Zealander called Gordon George, was an unmitigated disaster. He came from Oxford with glowing references as 'a gentleman of tact and taste', but by the summer of 1922, in the absence of Ashby, was embroiled in a spectacular row with Mrs Strong, in the course of which she called him 'a cad and a bounder', and he wrote to London alleging assault, and to the Embassy in Rome alleging that her nervous condition was due to an addiction to cocaine.[3] He was also acutely disliked by the staff, and Armando

68

probably spoke for others in losing his temper and accusing George of not even being English. In October, he was dismissed by Strong, and London sent out Shaw's right hand man, Stanley Quick, to investigate. George probably sealed his fate with Quick by saying that he should report to Ashby, not to London, and confidentially admitting that members of Council asked why Lord Esher had entrusted so much power to Evelyn Shaw; but Quick had the good sense to focus on the accounting not the personal side, and confirmed the dismissal on the basis of gross incompetence. George tried to take the School to court, but was paid off. Mrs Strong had the satisfaction of reading in the papers some months later of the arrest of an 'Inglese degenerato' called George Gordon, apprehended on the shores of a lake near Florence in the act of perpetrating 'atti innominabili' upon an 11 year old boy. 'Cad and bounder' was perhaps in retrospect mild.

A replacement was found in Forsyth Gray, but within a month, Ashby and Quick found him dead drunk in his office at 10 a.m., and dismissed him. Stanley Quick stayed on three months in the School sorting out the mess with the domestic side; the tragedy is that this

THE BSR EXHIBITION OF 1926.

The sculpture section of the BSR exhibition in Rome includes David Evans' portraits of Eugénie Strong and Winifred Knights. Mrs Strong wrote in protest to Shaw (31 March 26): 'It has come upon me as a surprise that the B.S.R. Exhibition this year takes place as early as next week; I heard it quite accidentally yesterday. I therefore write in order ... to ask you not to allow that portrait of me, by the sculptor Mr. Evans, to be exhibited. I do not object to its look of age, or even of illness, but I dislike the coarseness of the head and the puffy and utterly dull look...It was not Evans' fault, it was mine for having sat when I was dead tired and really ill.' Not only did the exhibition go ahead with the bust, but a version cast in bronze was kept in the London office at least until 1959, when Evans died, and his widow offered the School a copy, which was refused. The School's copy has been subsequently lost.

Garden Designs

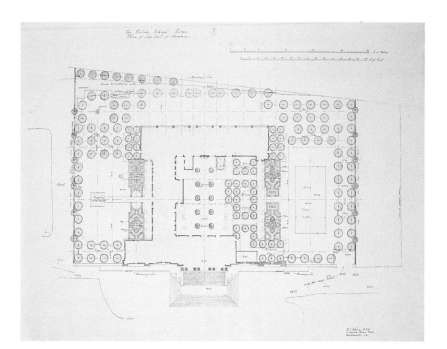

(right) Lutyens' garden design.

The original planting pattern provided by Lutyens foresaw pollarded limes marking the spaces where architectural elements had not yet been constructed. It also provided a circular fountain on the central axis of the Director's garden. Both these elements, along with the loggia along the west front, were dropped.

(left) The Director's garden in 1924.

Ashby had constructed a garden with wide gravel paths between an elaborate symmetrical system of beds. They required heavy maintenance. In times of financial shortage, Smith was to propose abandoning this garden and sacking the gardener, Camillo Tabacchiera (seen here amongst his beloved beds):

'The gardener, Camillo, is an obstinate old man of doubtful honesty, to whom English ideas of what a garden should look like are abhorrent. Nor will he produce lettuces and so on, as an offset to the expense.'[4]

(below left) The Cortile looking west in 1922.

Before the East wing was constructed in 1937, the Cortile formed a continuous open space with the eastern strip of land and tennis court. The Cortile had a singularly unimaginative design of four rectangular beds divided by gravel paths. The one advantage was that the Abbey wing, being south facing, enjoyed a lot of sunshine.

(right) The Cortile in 1927.

Only after the Sisson/Skeaping fountain had been put up in 1926 did the cortile acquire its still existing pattern of beds, which centre on the circular feature created by the fountain.

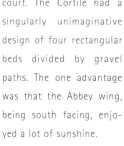

eminently sensible and sympathetic man could not stay where he was needed and effective, but had to return to Shaw's side in London. He found a new Bursar in the wife of one of the Arts scholars, Violet Hardiman. She wrote a stream of long confidential letters to Quick, ensuring that London was fully abreast of every internal friction that arose. By October 1923, a major row blew up between her and Ashby (Quick filed the correspondence as 'during earthquake of Oct 1923'). The friction was over May Ashby's 'interference'. Not all of it seems unreasonable in retrospect: the Director's wife can hardly be blamed for entering the kitchen to discover why the bread tasted of cat, and on finding the cat asleep in the bread basket, and the kitchens full of flies and rubbish, drawing the conclusion that appropriate standards of hygiene were not being observed. Ashby concluded Mrs Hardiman, though excellent as an accountant, was not competent as housekeeper. She offered her resignation, which Shaw refused, insisting that Ashby give her a free hand with the domestic side.

Violet Hardiman continued until the expiry of her contract at the end of August 1924, and a new Bursar was sent out by London. Kate Luke as an experienced school matron was perhaps more like the housekeeper figure Ashby felt was needed. Alas, she arrived early to learn the ropes, and even in that time quarrelled bitterly with her outgoing predecessor, who publicly accused her of being 'a cheat, a liar'. Eugénie Strong, by now embittered by her own dismissal, was alarmed to discover Miss Luke incapable of the most elementary multiplication, and without a word of Italian. She dipped her pen in venom and wrote to Quick:

'I am sorry for Miss Luke & like her so much, a sweet gentle English nurse and matron, thrown in the midst of this difficult Italian life. She will make a good pair with Bashmole, as he was always called here. They will be equally innocent of any foolish babbling in foreign tongues or of the wicked ways of 'foreigners', & make the School truly British as it doubtless should be.'[5]

Kate Luke survived until September 1925, keeping up the stream of 'confidential' letters to Quick.

The saddest thing is that London was so enormously well informed about all these petty squabbles in Rome that it came to dominate their picture of the School – as if Ashby and Strong were not in the full flood of academic productivity, and the scholars flourishing, one of the finest crop in the School's history. Lord Esher knew far too much about it all (Quick, his old aide,

Violet Hardiman, bust by David Evans.

addressed him confidentially as 'Chief'), and it brought him close to despairing of the School:

'The position is this. One after another, Secretaries, Directors, Asst Directors, have been swept out. There seems to be no finality. And these removals have always been the outcome of "chatter". Where is it going to end?

…More and more I regret we founded this School at Rome, which has been, from the beginning, a constant source of anxiety.'[6]

If Esher had stuck to the Annual Reports and left domestic affairs alone, he would have been prouder of his creation.

BERNARD ASHMOLE (1925-28)

Ashby's successor was chosen precisely to sort out this mess. Even if Roman gossip could not yet recognise in the young Bernard Ashmole the scholar of international standing he was rapidly to prove, the Committee could:

'As regards Ashmole, he is a little over thirty years of age – married to a charming woman- & has one small child. He is said to be the coming authority on classical sculpture & already enjoys a reputation among the learned… which ranks high above that of Mrs Strong. He is at present with Hogarth at the Ashmolean. He was the man I originally mentioned to you as being in a sense ideal for the job: but when first approached he would not look at Rome, chiefly because, as a former student of the School, he felt the atmosphere of the place was so disheartening that no human being could set things right. Since he has learnt that there is to be a clean sweep he has changed his mind & is prepared to accept…'[7]

Ashmole was surely the choice of Arthur Smith, as Chairman of the Faculty of Archaeology, who had examined his B. Litt. in 1923; as Ashmole recalled, their careers were curiously inter-related, since Smith was to be his successor at the School, and he was to succeed (though later) to Smith's Keepership of the Department of Greek and Roman Antiquities at the British Museum.[8] But he was also in a sense a protégé of Eugénie Strong, who had invited him to join the Capitoline Museums catalogue project in summer 1921, and whose suggestion it was that the sculptures of Ince Blundell Hall should be catalogued, which he undertook in 1922-24.[9]

Ashmole evidently saw his calling as cleaning the Augean stables. His autobiographical account of his Directorship focuses on improvements made for the benefit of students. Catering problems were solved by replacing the cook, who proved to have been on the take. Plumbing problems were solved by replacing furred up pipework. The archives reveal rather greater challenges. There was a crisis over the staff in October of 1926, when Ashmole returned from leave to find the School in ferment, with tales of a maid having an affair with the nightwatchman, and Sidney Cooper, Miss Luke's replacement as Bursar, and the Butler Armando equally unwilling to intervene. Ashmole took this as the opportunity for a new start. The erstwhile hall-boy, Bruno Bonelli, was promoted to

Assistant Secretary (later Bursar) with charge over the Italian staff. That meant firing Armando Bonora, who by 1926 had already clocked up 25 years of service, and was bitter to be sent packing at the age of 49. But Ashmole regarded him as 'benevolent but inefficient'. In any case, Bonelli proved the perfect choice, and for the next 46 years ran the staff with formidable smoothness, avoiding all the turmoil that had marked the reigns of the English Bursars (or at least ensuring that no word of them filtered above stairs, let alone to London). Cooper was replaced by an English nurse, Miss Marjorie Deane, and by an Italian accounts clerk. It was tough on both Bonora and Cooper, but London let Ashmole act with a free hand as they never allowed Ashby. By the end of 1926, the domestic staff numbered 17, including four maids and a chauffeur. It was a big team, outnumbering the scholars.

Ashmole also performed a more lasting service to the scholars. It had been a firm rule of Shaw's that married scholars might not have their wives in residence; up to 1923 they were required to reside outside the School in Rome, and from 1924, in the interests of 'corporate spirit', required to reside in the School but without their wives. The appointment of Mrs Hardiman as Bursar was, among other things an ingenious way around this rule, which gave much distress, since the Bursar had residence in the School. From his arrival on, Ashmole tried to persuade Shaw to allow wives to reside, on the grounds that they did so anyway even when forbidden. Shaw and Esher resisted, but Ashmole with some help from Rodd wore them down. An nice illustration of the absurdity of not appointing married men emerged. R. A. Cordingley, the architecture scholar, married Madeleine Tardieu, Eugénie Strong's trusty assistant librarian, but Shaw forebade her to move in.[10] In January 1926 the Committee caved in: with the happy result that Winifred Knights remained in residence after the end of her scholarship, thanks to her marriage to Tom Monnington, and Barbara Hepworth came into residence as wife of John Skeaping.

Ashmole used his expertise in sculpture to the School's lasting benefit, thanks to his contact with John Marshall, the dealer in Antiquities who acted for the Metropolitan

BERNARD ASHMOLE by Reginald Brill (RS Painting 1927).
Brill's portrait shows Ashmole in the Director's office, contemplating the classical sculptures on which he was an authority.

ASHMOLE'S SCHOLARS

(above) Bernard Ashmole with the scholars of 1928.

(left) Group in cortile c. 1928 by Edward Halliday (RS Painting 1925).

The group in the photograph, taken in summer 1928, are on the lawn to the south of the Abbey wing where later the East Wing was constructed. In deck chairs are Bernard and Dorothy Ashmole (centre) and Ian Richmond (second from right). Dorothy Hatswell is in the foreground on the lawn, Edward Halliday standing at the back with a moustache. The painting by Halliday is set in the same position, looking towards the Abbey bust. Dorothy Hatswell holds a bird cage.

Museum, and friend of E.P. Warren and Beazley. It was in gratitude for advice given by Ashmole over what emerged as a group of forgeries by Dossena that Marshall paid for the fountain that became the centre piece of the cortile, which, by an exemplary collaboration, an architect, Marshall Sisson, and a sculptor, Skeaping, did together (had Skeaping's wife done the carving, it might have been another story). Marshall also donated to the School one of the forgeries, the feet of a running female figure in archaic style. Marshall died not long afterwards, in 1928, and his executor, E.P. Warren, gave the School the choice of his library – Ashmole selected 691 volumes, and two large bookcases. The Library also acquired his collection of photographs.

Ashmole's three years were too brief to be marked by the launch of any archaeological (or other) projects, such as were the glory of the Ashby years. It is doubtful whether, without the support of an Assistant Director or any other academic figure, and constrained to act personally as Librarian, he

THE MONNINGTONS AND SKEAPINGS.
Barbara Hepworth came to Rome to accompany her then husband, John Skeaping. Ashmole's liberal approach brought her
into residence from outside the School. Tom Monnington met
Winifred Knights (who had previously been engaged to Arnold
Mason) while at the School; she was enabled to stay on as a
wife when she married Monnington.

would have found time himself to do so, and when he decided in January 1928 to return to London,
it was because he felt that 'my archaeological work is so far in arrears these three years that it would
not be fair to University College to neglect it any longer'.[11] But they were good years for the students.
The gay atmosphere that he generated is reflected in his memories of fancy dress parties and bonfires.

More importantly, his Directorship was marked by the creation of scholarships in the Faculty of
Archaeology, History and Letters. Ever since the creation of Rome Scholarships by the 1851
Commission, there had been a disparity between the Arts Faculties, the prime function of which

THE ERECTION OF THE FOUNTAIN IN 1926
The fountain was put up in 1926, designed by the Jarvis scholar,
Marshall Sisson, with sculptured reliefs of deer by John Skeaping. Sir
Philip Sassoon refused to pay for it, judging it 'devoid of elegance or
beauty'; Ashmole admitted it 'rather severe, but... none the worse for
that'. The 9,500 lire (£79) it cost was given by John Marshall. The garden was laid out a year later.

(left) Skeaping deer.

Skeaping tried out his deer for the fountain in several formats, as sketches and as sculptures in the round.

(below) Painting of Cortile by Marjorie Brooks.

Marjorie Brooks was Rome Scholar in Painting 1930-32. She married the Architecture scholar, William Holford. The original painting was presented to the School in 1981.

was to select scholars in their disciplines, and the Faculty of Archaeology, History and Letters, which as the surviving remnant of the original School, raised money from subscribers, and paid for the Assistant Director/Librarian, the library, and archaeological projects. There was nothing left to endow scholarships, though the gap was partly filled by the studentship funded by the Gilchrist Trustees, and by the Craven fellowship and Pelham studentship from Oxford. But since the end of the Great War, the old language of 'students', those admitted to the School as a privilege but funded by external sources, had been eclipsed by the language of 'Rome scholars', and the Faculty of Archaeology badly felt the lack of its own. Part of the 'reorganisation' on the dismissal of Ashby and Strong was to relieve the Faculty of the expense of paying for the Librarian, while its income was boosted by the donation of £3000 as an endowment for book purchase, thanks to the generosity of an anonymous benefactor (actually the Treasurer of the Faculty, William Russell, who was later to buy the Ashby collection). The boosted income allowed the Faculty to launch its own Rome Scholarship in Archaeology (in fact open to all disciplines) from 1928, the first holder being R.C. Carrington, who worked on the society and economy of Pompeii.[12] Three years later, a second scholarship, in Medieval Studies, was launched, its first holder, Geoffrey Barraclough, to be a future Chichele Professor at Oxford.

Apart from Rome scholars, a significant number of future stars were working at the School in the Ashmole years: Russell Meiggs, as Pelham student, was laying the foundations of his future great tome on Ostia (though it was to be transformed by the excavations of the fascist period, and he continued reworking it until 1959), Jocelyn Toynbee was working on Hadrianic art, Togo Salmon on the Roman colonisation of Italy, and Ronald Syme on the reign of Domitian. Among others admitted in this period were three future Directors, Ian Richmond, Colin Hardie, and Ralegh Radford.

The buzz of those years was later recalled by Togo Salmon:

'Apart from the excitement of studying the past in the place where it happened, there was the grand opportunity for getting to know their European opposite numbers and even for meeting the great savants. In 1927 Julius Beloch was regularly to be found at work …in the magnificent library of the German Archaeological Institute…; Emile Mâle was at the Ecole Française…; Ettore Pais was lecturing on Roman history in the University of Rome; and Giuseppe Lugli, already known as an up-and-coming topographer, was Secretary of the Romanian Academy… Flinders Petrie and Randall MacIver worked daily in the BSR library for weeks on end. All of this was most exhilarating.'[13]

THE ASHMOLES BY PARKER AND EVANS

(below left) Bernard Ashmole by H.W. Parker, 1928.
(right) Dorothy Ashmole by D. Evans.

Harold Wilson Parker was Rome Scholar in Sculpture 1927-29. Parker made commemorative busts of both Bernard Ashmole in 1928 and Ian Richmond, a year before he became Director in 1930. The bust of Bernard Ashmole was bought for the School.

Dorothy Ashmole was sculpted by David Evans, but the bust was cordially loathed by the couple, who destroyed the plaster original:

'Evans…was a realistic sculptor of pedestrian talent, and Dorothy's portrait was lifeless… Neither of us liked it… One evening therefore at dusk we carried it to a far corner of the garden where there was some hard paving, the intention being that I should throw it as high as possible into the air, when it would fall and shatter into a thousand pieces. We did not know that the plaster had been reinforced by hessian, and the head, instead of shattering, fell with a dull thud still in one piece. I then took a spade and, whilst it seemed to be looking at me reproachfully and more like Dorothy than before, battered it into a shapeless mass which we then interred, both feeling curiously like murderers.' (Autobiography, 47f.)

ARTHUR HAMILTON SMITH (1928-29)

When Ashmole returned to the Chair of Archaeology in London, he put forward the name of Richmond for his replacement.[14] Shaw took soundings, including Mortimer Wheeler, and concluded Richmond still needed a couple of years to mature, and would then be ideal.[15] A stop-gap Director was found in A.H. Smith. Just retired from his Keepership in the British Museum, and a founding member and Secretary of the original Managing Committee of the School, member of the new Executive Committee from 1914, and Chairman of the Faculty of Archaeology of 1922, he had played a key role in the downfall of Ashby and Strong.

However devoted he may have been to the cause, a retired Museum keeper of notably old-fashioned sentiment was an odd choice of Director. He was something of a disciplinarian, and the artists did not appreciate his periodic lectures about gentlemanly behaviour, including proper dress. Nor did he like Ashmole's liberal policy on wives. He was much irritated to discover that the new Assistant Librarian, Miss Hatswell, was following her predecessor's example in marrying a scholar, the painter Edward Halliday. He swiftly reversed Ashmole's liberal permission for artists' wives to reside in the School. As the

A.H. Smith with his scholars, 1929.

A.H. Smith twice served as stop-gap Director, in 1928-30, and in 1932-33. This view, taken in summer 1929, of Smith and his wife surrounded by scholars perhaps illustrates the success of one of his policies: 'I have been trying, with partial success, to raise the standard of dress, in which there seems to be a tradition of slovenliness' (letter to Shaw, 19.1.29).

Marriage of an Artist (Halliday's studio)

Edward Halliday is portrayed by fellow scholar Robert Lyon (RS Painting 1924) ascending the mezzanine of his studio. Dorothy Hatswell is washing plates in the foreground. The marriage of the two gravely provoked Director Smith (letter to Shaw, 3.8.28): 'Miss Hatswell proposes in a lighthearted and irresponsible fashion to marry Halliday, and ignore her obligation to Rome. She has been so casual about it that I do not know what they contemplate as their future programme. But if she carries out what seems to be her plan of not relieving Miss Hutton now, I should strongly deprecate her presence later at the School as a student's Bride. '

THE CHRISTMAS ENTERTAINMENT OF 1928

The occasion was recorded, with surprising enthusiasm, by Mrs Smith: 'Then the show began, which was so good we feel you ought to hear of it! ... the hall was prepared for the great thrill of the evening. Stage, chairs, and everything else disappeared – The great sheets of paper with the swags on were let down, & the whole room was a vast *panorama of Rome*. We were each given a "tessera", & had to sign our names, & pass through a turnstile, & then we found ourselves gazing at Rome, & being pestered by a guide – Mr. Carrington – dressed to the part. When all were in, the Guide showed us round. His "talk" was very clever – a skit on the Lectures the Director had

been giving. The large Latin inscriptions over the ruins were topical (but the Latinity was not of the Arch. Faculty). A row of statues, Vestal Virgins, were portraits of our daughter, Miss Nathan, Miss Cameron, & Miss Hands. Over the mantelpiece was the famous Nile statue (subject of a recent lecture) – the Nile A.H.S. & the cubits students. All the big monuments were represented – & hills- & hill towns. It was all the conception of Mr. White, who drew out the sheets in his studio, & gave them to folk to colour – & they never saw it up as a whole till the day.' (Mrs Smith to Shaw, 27.12.28)

(above) Common Room as 'set' viewed to west. The 'stage set' prepared by the artists for the Christmas celebrations of 1928 transformed the dining room. The inscription to the right, on a mock triumphal arch, alludes to Smith's paternalistic and oppressive regime: 'To the most Paternal Director of the School, because he wished for the suppression of the barbarians, but deprecated the suppression of individuality'. The inscription on the left refers to 'a loquacious woman who with incredible benevolence insinuated herself into everyone's business'.

(below) Common Room as 'set' viewed to east. The far end of the hall had to the left four Vestal Virgins: the first 'administered the electric lantern well', the second is noted for her 'long lurid tongue', the third says 'The Camerons are coming', the fourth is the Senior Vestal. Above the fireplace is Smith as the Nile, surrounded by his students as cubits of the Nile flood.

Committee recorded:

'the present Director, after a few months experience of the system, had come to the definite conclusion that the presence of wives, who had no serious occupations, exercised an undesirable and disturbing influence upon the corporate life of the School which was not designed to accommodate married couples.'[16]

The Committee therefore decided to ban married men from competing for or holding the Scholarship. So much for the Cordingleys, Skeapings and Monningtons – or the Hallidays.

But Smith meant well (he knew he was only holding the fort for Richmond), and with the passing of time came to fuss less about discipline, and to learn more about the unique nature of the School. His enthusiastic report on a series of 'after-dinner discourses' in 1930 shows the scales falling from his eyes:

'One of the first of the series was by Cecil Brown, on "Pure Form". It gave rise to a wonderful discussion, not yet ended. You would think perhaps that the Painters might not want to listen to the Historians, or the Archaeologists to the Architects, but they seem to enjoy it very much. Each in his turn plays The Professor, and afterwards likes to go on "Professing" with the happiest results. I think they are having more pleasure in each other's company on this account than they ever had.'[17]

Smith's was no exciting regime. He surely merits the epitaph he penned in the opening sentence of his second Annual Report (1929-30):

'The past year has not been marked by any event of outstanding importance.'

But at least he made London happy, at what was to prove a critical turning point.

Ian A. Richmond by H.W. Parker (1928).

IAN RICHMOND (1930-32)

In January 1930, Esher died. If his control of the School had been verging on the despotic, it was benevolent. 'The Chief' felt passionately about the institution which owed so much to his personal initiative: he was as delighted to hear that all was well (as when Gertrude Smith wrote ecstatically describing the Christmas entertainment) as he was distressed when squabbles seemed to bring it down. His natural successor as Chairman was Rennell Rodd, and the Chairmanship of Rodd with the Directorship of Richmond brought a sort of second flowering of the Ashby vision.

Ian Richmond came to Rome first as Gilchrist student under Ashby in 1924, intending to work on the Roman house, but swiftly changed his subject to the Aurelianic Walls. His delayed assumption of the Directorship allowed him to finish his monograph on the Walls, which remains a classic.[18] From the first he showed a particular enthusiasm for collaboration with architects. In 1924-25 he was working with the Jarvis Scholar, Marshall Sisson, on a restoration of the gate to the Praetorian Camp (with results published in the *Papers*).[19] By the next year he was collaborating again with Sisson on the Porta Appia, and with R.A. Cordingley, Rome Scholar in Architecture, on the Mausoleum of Augustus, in those days before Mussolini's intervention still embedded in the urban fabric and far harder to restore (this too published in the *Papers*).[20] He was elected lecturer at Queen's University, Belfast, but returned the following year for four months, still finding time to help Anthony Minoprio, Jarvis Scholar, on his restoration of the Basilica of Maxentius, and G.A. Butling, Rome Scholar, on the Temple of Hadrian. Minoprio too published his results in the *Papers*,

THE BASILICA OF CONSTANTINE

The Basilica of Constantine: Actual State viewed from the Sacra Via[21] by Anthony Minoprio (Jarvis Student 1925).

'Our hosts for the next two years were the Director, Bernard Ashmole... and his charming wife, both of whom were always most friendly and helpful. The principal duties of the Director were to keep the School running smoothly, to give advice and help to Scholars when they needed it and to maintain contact with other institutions and the authorities in Rome. We met daily for lunch and dinner in the Common Room but apart from this and occasional games of tennis, I don't think I took up much of the Director's time...

In the winter of 1925, one of our archaeologists, Ian Richmond, suggested I might undertake, with his help, a reconstruction of the Basilica of Constantine...This was a project which appealed to me greatly and, under Richmond's guidance, I began to measure and draw the "actual state" of the impressive brick and concrete remains...I soon realised how lucky I was to have the benefit of Richmond's remarkable knowledge of Roman brickwork and construction, his acquaintance with the historical sources in the libraries and his ability to deduce and state lucidly what must have been the original form of the building.'[22]

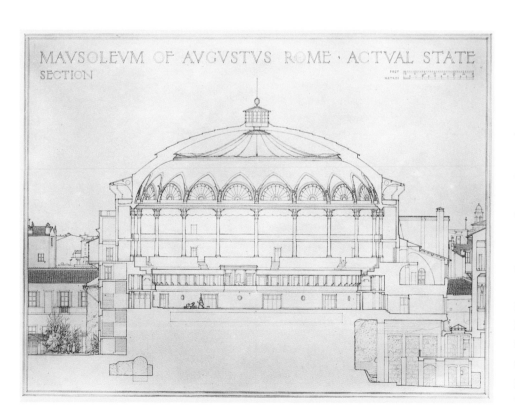

CASTRA PRAETORIA · ROMA · A·D·XXIII · PORTA DECVMANA

Restoration of the gate of the Praetorian Camp by Marshall Sisson (Jarvis Student 1924).

The Mausoleum of Augustus: actual state, south elevation[23] by R.A. Cordingley (RS Architecture 1923), who became Professor of Architecture at Manchester University in 1933.

Richmond to Shaw, 29.10.30: 'You will be glad to hear of a signal honour paid to me the other day. On the 28th, the Duce, accompanied by officials of the Governor of Rome, opened a group of monuments belonging to the Municipality. I was the only foreigner invited, especially because of my work with Cordingley on the Mausoleum; and when it came to describing that monument, not only was our work handsomely mentioned in the pamphlet and in the speech, but I myself was singled out and called forward to see and admire what they had done. A nice piece of policy for both parties, but very gratifying to myself, for my own sake and the school's – a real personal tribute.'

The fascist excavations made the city extraordinarily exciting. Togo Salmon recalled the period thus: 'When I arrived in 1927, the Largo Argentina was completely boarded up. But some weeks later we were invited to a peepshow behind the fence, and G.Q. Giglioli and A.M. Colini conducted us around the four temples of the Area Sacra. Subsequently we had similar privileged treatment at the Forum of Trajan and the Forum of Augustus and even at the Vatican, this being the period when the main approach to St Peter's was being systematised and the old Piazza Rusticucci eliminated... And it was now that the mass of structures near the Capitol were cleared away to make room for the via dei Fori Imperiali. The re-erection of the Ara Pacis Augustae in the Campus Martius, however, came after 1929; during my student days Augustus' tomb nearby still served as a concert hall, and BSR personnel regularly attended the performances there.'[24]

MAVSOLEVM OF AVGVSTVS ROME · ACTVAL STATE
SECTION

by which time Richmond as editor seems to have suppressed the acknowledgement to himself legible in the draft.[25] Similarly William Holford, Architecture Scholar in 1930, was to publish with Richmond the town-plan of Roman Verona.[26] The Committee rightly thanked Richmond in the Annual Report (1926-27) for the help he had given the Director. It is obvious why he seemed such a natural successor to Ashmole.

Richmond's appointment went down extremely well in Rome. He was seen in many quarters as a return to the Ashby tradition. He let it be put about that his term of appointment would be for some time – short-term appointments win little respect in Rome.[27] And he was curiously gratified that he was seen with favour by the fascist regime. Mussolini had already begun work on the Mausoleum of Augustus, and Richmond was singled out among foreigners by an invitation from the Duce to attend a ceremonial at which his paper with Cordingley on the Mausoleum was extolled.[28]

But his key diplomacy was internal. Immediately on arrival in October 1930 he threw himself at once into healing the wounds of the past. He at once went to pay his respects to both Ashby and Strong, finding the former much easier than the latter:

'Ashby is very friendly, with me: but I think it still definitely hurts him to come to the School, so I have not pressed that side of it, but developed all I can outside, going excursions with him and discussing problems. Mrs. A. also came to tea with my parents and was very cordial. The other lady [Mrs. Strong], I believe, I could have in the School to-morrow. She works a good deal in the Library, and I see enough of her to keep the peace: also, I find that I can always master her by laughing at her, which is a great solace.'[29]

Mrs Strong he humoured, mostly because he knew that her negative gossip was dangerous to the School. Ashby he treated with profound reverence. He did persuade him to visit the School for lunch, but understood his man in proposing a collaboration in the study of the via Aurelia.[30] The thaw between Ashby and the School was cut short by Ashby's death in May 1931, and Richmond was deeply shaken:

'I am so upset to-day by the news of dear old Ashby's death that I am feeling quite wretched and ill. It is a loss of a dear friend and valued colleague.'[31]

But he swiftly appreciated that he could now play a vital role in securing Ashby's library and papers for the School.

'Of course the personal loss is lamentable, and I will not dwell on it, though you will understand me well enough when I say I loved him very much indeed personally and revered him professionally. And there is no doubt my presence here was already smoothing out old difficulties, and that we should have gone on together from strength to strength. Yet there are fortunate things in the situation, if one looks for them; namely that my book got out just in time to be well reviewed by him, and to mark me out as his successor, however unworthy and conscious of my unworthiness; and that people have been greatly cheered to think that the School was in the hands of one of his old pupils, and that the rift was in the process of being mended, as everyone clearly saw… The next question is of the disposal of the books and priceless library… I can tell you, in a word, that nobody is in closer touch and happier touch than I am personally, and that I have every chance of pulling the best out of the situation.'[32]

The importance of Richmond's diplomacy for the future of the School, and specifically of the Library, cannot be overstated. The Ashby collection is the core of the Library, defines its direction, its distinction and its possibilities. Richmond's moving farewell in the Annual Report is a call to the School to understand the Ashby vision:

'The tradition which he built, in nearly twenty years' faithful service, is now ours to enrich or mar. It was too valuable a thing to lose, too fresh in the writer's mind not to supply the obvious model to emulate. But the chances of keeping it up have been enormously increased by the action of his widow, Mrs Thomas Ashby, who has enabled the School to acquire, with the generous help of our Treasurer, Mr W. Russell, his whole collection of books and photographs, and has placed in the custody and at the discretion of the Director the equally valuable collection of prints and MS. notes. Here is a mine from which scholarship should be greatly enriched, while the value of the topographical section of the Library places our collection of works on Roman and Italian topography in the first rank.'

Richmond foresaw that financial pressures were likely to force the foreign institutions in Rome to specialise in their collections:

'It is clear, that with the acquisition of Dr. Ashby's collection of Italian topographical literature, the British School possesses a nucleus for such a specialised collection; and it must shortly become a matter of policy whether this is not to be kept up to date, at the expense of other subjects of special interest to this Faculty…'[33]

Richmond's policy remains valid seventy years later, and only the age of computerisation would allow the *Unione* of Roman Libraries to move towards such a policy. Equally prophetic, by curious quirk of fate, was his vision of the physical surrounds of the Library. The sudden accession of 4000 books brought a space crisis, and Richmond grasped that the west wing, housing the Director's flat, was the natural direction for expansion:

'Our eventual object must be the worthy housing of our topographical library in wider quarters, and, while various methods of solution are possible, that which seems to commend itself most warmly, on grounds of economy and planning, is a remodelling of the wing containing the Director's study. Visions of an aisled hall with alcoves, of greater content than the present Library, shall be conjured up in better times: for the present, we are content to await in faith both them and a kindly Maecenas.'

If the fulfilment of the prediction has had to wait till a new millennium, it would not have been possible if Ashby and Richmond had not had both vision and faith. And had Richmond not won the confidence of May Ashby in those brief months before her husband's death, it is improbable that the collection would have ended in the School's hands at all, for the bitterness was great, and none of Ashby's successors before Richmond (above all not Smith) had extended a hand of friendship to him.

The wonder is that Richmond arrived in the nick of time; the tragedy is that he left too soon. Having persuaded May Ashby to sell the School the entire collection of books, he found a donor in William Russell, long Treasurer of the School and benefactor, in the past too, of the Library, who first loaned and then gave the mere £2000 requested.[34] But Richmond was also playing to acquire the other half of the Ashby collection, consisting of prints and drawings. He persuaded Mrs Ashby, who was returning to England, to let him house them in the Director's apartment, and was well on the way to acquiring them. But William Russell died within the year ('Russell's death is a great blow, for one wonders where we shall find such another'),[35] and Richmond's negotiations were cut short by his own premature departure. Neither Smith nor even Hardie stood much chance of talking Mrs Ashby round, for all she cared about was that her husband should be loved and revered. So the School lost the a collection of prints, that was so closely linked to Ashby's books, to the Vatican.

If Richmond's regime was a return to Ashby, his handling of the administration was a distinct improvement. He found himself on arrival supported by two English members of staff, both non-academic: the Bursar, Mrs Hutton, and the Assistant Librarian, Miss Hands. He grasped that without a second academic to look after the Library, the Director would be both overwhelmed by administrative burdens, and intellectually lonely. Mrs Hutton developed a tumour, and he persuaded her to put her health first and resign:

'You may congratulate me upon being the first Director for ages who has ever brought off a resignation without a row!!'[36]

For all the tones of a triumphant Roman general, he was right in believing that he was slaying a dragon that had troubled the institution too long. Instead of appointing a new Bursar, he gave full responsibility on the staff control side to Bruno Bonelli, and got the Committee to allow him an academic Librarian: Richard Crooke was appointed, from October 1931, and proved a success. In early 1932, to his relief, Miss Hands resigned her position

THE GROWTH OF THE LIBRARY

(above) The Library in 1917.

(left) The Library in c.1924.

The entire building history of the School has been marked by the inexorable growth of the Library, its greatest single asset. On the move from Palazzo Odescalchi in 1916, it had already grown to 10,000 volumes. The Library was designed for 25,000 volumes. By the early thirties, Richmond estimated its size at 23,000 volumes – Hardie in 1935 thought the number more like 30,000. At that date, 130 periodicals were acquired, by purchase or exchange, each year, and 250-300 monographs. The Ashby Library alone comprised 4,000 volumes, and the Churchill Library 1,600.

RICHMOND AND HIS SCHOLARS.

Mural frieze by Marjorie Brooks. In the top
panel, Richmond is borne into the heavens on
a cloud supported by Miss Hands and Mrs
Hutton. In the central scene, the artist is the
tall figure third from the right. In the bottom
scene, her future husband William Holford is
second from the right, a book in one hand and
a bottle in the other.

as Assistant Librarian, and her replacement,
Miss Esmé Sturch, had a dual responsibility
as Secretary to the Director and Library
assistant. So the administrative posts were
halved, and the academic ones doubled.

But Richmond was cut off in the fullness
of his promise. Throughout the winter of
1931-32 he suffered from acute health problems – a strange mixture of dermatitis,
rheumatism, scepcis, arthritis and bladder
problems.[37] By the early months of 1932 he
was on the mend; by April he was back in
good spirits, having come out of a bout of
depression;[38] by June the last traces of arthritis were gone, though he was still off alco-
hol;[39] and by August, back at home in
Yorkshire for the vacation, he could declare
himself to be flourishing mightily.[40] Yet on
19 September he sent a letter that fell like a
bombshell: his specialist had advised him
'two things: absolute rest and freedom from
responsibility now, and no lengthy return to
the Italian climate in the future'.

Poor health had been used as an excuse
for premature retirement so often in the
School's history that people were bound to
speculate that other, more scandalous,
motives lay behind this precipitate change.
The complete absence from the archive of
Shaw's normally abundant correspondence
in the critical weeks does nothing to allay
suspicion; and the fact that Smith, who
leapt into the breach by returning to Rome
for the next few months, could only answer
the solicitous enquiries of everyone as to
Richmond's health with vague evasion pro-
vokes suspicion mixed with indignation.[41]
The one lesson Shaw and Smith had learnt
from the Ashby debacle was to bring about a
resignation, in Richmond's own words,
'without a row'. The loss was wholly the
School's, and Richmond went on to a career
of luminous distinction as an archaeologist
of Roman Britain.

COLIN HARDIE (1933-36)

The choice of a successor took a few months; meanwhile Smith held the fort again, nobly from an altruistic point of view, disastrously for relationships with Mrs Ashby, since in no time he was demanding to have the Ashby prints removed from the Director's apartment, and appalling Richmond with the prospect: 'if A.H.S. goes and ruins what yet may be done by writing a cold letter to Mrs Ashby…She hates him enough already, without that!'[42] He also took a hand in the search for a new Director, scotching the chances of Russell Meiggs, easily the most promising applicant, and the closest to Ashby in interests, by describing him as 'for an Oxford don…rather "common"'.[43] The critical quality in a Director is to care about the School and what it stands for; Meiggs was the ideal person to carry on the Ashby tradition, and he was also, as Shaw came to appreciate too late, 'very much admired by the artists of his time'.[44] Instead the choice fell on Colin Hardie, a young Classicist from Balliol. Not only was he, at 26, distinctly young for the job; his commitment was untested.

Hardie's first challenge was to secure the rest of the Ashby collection. No sooner arrived in February 1933 than the experts were advising him that the prints, valued at £800, were an unique collection, unparalleled in either Vatican or State libraries.[45] Mrs Strong was urging him of the importance of securing the topographical prints, 'in order that, as she said, we might lay the Ashby ghost by forming this memorial to him'.[46] But though he was later to claim that Monsignor Tisserand had somehow outwitted him in gaining them for the Vatican, his letters at the time tell a story of mishandled diplomacy:

> 'I expected my letter to Mrs Ashby to disturb her to some extent but I did not expect the explosion to be so violent.'[47]

> 'Mrs Ashby's last letter to me disgusted me finally. She is sarcastic about things I never said. But I won't answer her…'[48]

And though Eugénie Strong found a benefactor to pay, the widow of Comm. John Gray, an old

COLIN HARDIE by Douglas Bisset (RS Sculpture 1934-37).

Bisset impressed the Faculty of Sculpture, who believed that he had made excellent use of his Scholarship, and the Director, C.A. Ralegh Radford, who believed him to be a very competent craftsman and an assiduous worker. In Colin Hardie's last year as Director Bisset executed a portrait bust of him, the clay model of which is seen here. Bisset also executed a portrait bust of the next Director, C.A. Ralegh Radford. Bisset went on to eventually become Head of the Sculpture Department at the City and Guilds of London Art School.

Hardie's proposed transformation of the facade.

member of the British-American Archaeological Society, and therefore a friend of Ashby's, who offered 20,000 lire to the Library in memory of her husband; Hardie, shocked that this recently widowed lady should 'add a mass of sob stuff about her husband', failed to follow through on the offer.[49] Hardie's real concern was to get the bulky print presses out of his flat, not to secure the collection.

Hardie liked little of what he found in Rome. He found the cook Gaetano D'Angelo 'rather old & feeble', and Domenico Bosio (a war cripple) 'oldish & rather fussy',[50] and within three months had sacked Gaetano, Camillo the gardener, and four others.[51] More bleakly, after his first five months he wrote a series of astonishing reports outlining the School's failings. He invited the Faculty of Architecture to consider whether there was any point sending architects to Rome. The argument for collaboration with archaeologists no longer had weight since there were no archaeologists in residence. Reconstructions and measured drawing seemed to him a waste of time. They would do better to spend far more time in travel, and far less time in Rome, where the company scarcely beckoned:

'The community here is a very small one and lives for a long period at very close quarters. Its members are not selected with any view to their being congenial and are, in fact, often not. They get on each other's nerves, whether they belong to the same or different Faculties.'

Set, if you will, against Hardie's bleak vision that of an architect of his day, William (later Lord) Holford, for whom the relationships between architects and their fellow scholars were 'co-operative, argumentative and critical, but… always stimulating'.[52]

Shaw suppressed Hardie's report, as he did a draft letter by Hardie to the *Times*. In this he managed to question whether there was 'good reason for Englishmen to come to a city no longer the centre of European art and not even of Italian', attacked the building for losing its southern aspect to the façade, rubbished its position across the Borghese gardens as 'cut off from the city', suggested that archaeologists these days prefer to go off to Spain, Crete, Palestine or North Africa, and suggested that living conditions, with bathrooms shared by both sexes were 'such as would shock the authorities of any University'.[53] Such criticisms have been voiced before, and will be voiced again; rarely by the voice of the Director in person, let alone in public.

But Shaw was weary of sacking Directors, and continued to back Hardie. Two years later Hardie was still insisting that the façade was a waste, and that the School should be completely remodelled, inserting rooms to enjoy the southern aspect. His accompanying sketch is a wonderful fantasy of what the School might have been.

The major problem faced by the School in the thirties was coping with the fascist regime. The most brutal impact was financial: once the gold standard was abandoned in 1931, the pound fell in value against the lira by 30%. At least Hardie, as a good Scot, knew how to make economies, sacking staff and winding down activity. Then there was the problem of the building boom of fascist Rome. Parioli was becoming a fashionable area, and buildings encroached all around. By late 1932, the School of Architecture had already sprung up to the west, and Smith sketched it in all its horror.

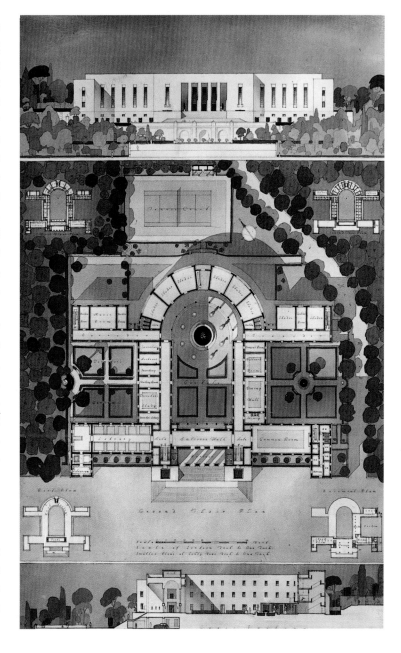

Greater cause for concern was the prospect of private houses being built on the plot to the north of the School, threatening to block out light from the artists' studios. There were protracted, and ultimately vain, negotiations with the Governatorato to persuade them to ban building on the site, or to acquire the land and give it to the School, and with the 1851 Commissioners to buy it. Hardie was right to suggest it would have made a fine plot for a Director's house, unrealistic to suppose the School could ever afford it.

But the time was slipping away when Britain could count on the enthusiastic support of the Italian authorities. Crisis point was reached with the Italian invasion of Abyssinia in October 1935; the League of Nations, led by Britain and France, condemned the invasion and

Alternative scheme for School by Philip Hirst (RS Architecture 1936).

Philip Hirst is a fascinating example of an architect steeped in the classical tradition, who collaborated in restoring a number of classical monuments, yet whose vision for an alternative BSR was entirely in the idiom of the fascist architecture of the 1930s.

THE SCHOOL OF ARCHITECTURE as neighbour.

Letter of Smith to Shaw, 7 October 1932: 'I write this from the drawing room looking out of the window, not at the charming country view, but at an enormous School of Art, which (so we hear) is hastening completion, for opening by the Duce on Oct 28. Happily the screen of trees, planted along our margin, for such an eventuality, is well grown, and in a few years will be effective. The coming visit has also made them hastily put the road in front of us into order, which no effort on our part could accomplish.'

A month later, Smith reported: 'The School of Architecture now cuts off about 25 degrees of sky from the lower rooms on the west of the School, and I think my successor must consider the removal of Dr Ashby's pergola which further darkens these rooms. In the meantime, I have only clipped the wistarias.' (Report to Shaw, 10 November 1932).

imposed sanctions. By November 1935, anti-British feeling was running so high that Carabinieri had to be stationed outside the School.[54]

> 'Anti-English feeling is being fanned assiduously, and English words are disappearing from the streets. "Old Scotland" (a tailor) is no more. Anderson no longer sells "photos" and there are no more "tea rooms". They are going to fantastic lengths, and their Archbishops are inciting the faithful to the holy war.'[55]

Eventually the School closed, to the horror of Mrs Strong, who wrote a vehement letter of protest to the Faculty and cancelled her subscription for the first time since its foundation.[56] But it gave Hardie and his Librarian, Ellis Waterhouse, the excuse to take a long break from the School, and for the first five months of 1936, Hardie travelled in Greece, Israel and Syria, expressing happiness ('I am enjoying life very much') for the only time in his Directorship.[57]

Meanwhile the Governatorato taught the School a small lesson in relations with the host country. In April 1935, they informed the School of their intention to construct a new road (now via Cancani) to the east of the School, linking up to the via delle Tre Madonne, recently renamed via De Notaris, so giving access to the building plots to the north of the School. By no coincidence, it emerged that one of the land owners there was Bottai, the Governor of Rome. The road was to be routed across the easternmost part of the School's plot, so shaving off the tennis court.[58]

Diplomatic representation was made through the Embassy, and it seemed that the threat was off. But by the time Hardie returned in June 1936, the threat was far worse: the new plans routed the future via Cancani diagonally across the tennis court. Hardie went to call on his neighbour, Bottai, who gave him a lightning audience ('extremely rapid in the fascist style'), but agreed to change the routing to save the tennis court.[59] Bottai won both ways: he had fired a diplomatic warning gun across the School's bows, and secured an access road to the building plot which he was doubtless able to sell at great profit. The School lost the light to the artists' studios, a strip of land to the east, and counted itself lucky not to have lost its tennis court.

It would be hard to guess from Hardie's bone dry correspondence that there was any artistic or academic life in the institution in his regime. But Ellis Waterhouse, whom he appointed Librarian, finding Crooke short of intellectual interest, was on his way to a distinguished career as an art historian, and published his *Baroque Painting in Rome* with the School. Another young art historian who started visiting regularly in these years was Anthony Blunt, as a Fellow of Trinity, Cambridge. He spent five months in 1933-34 studying baroque decoration, and returned the following year, coinciding with Guy Burgess. Blunt always remained a devoted supporter of the School. Then there was Bertha Tilley, working on Virgil's Latium, Tom Dunbabin, working on Sicily, Dale Trendall, working on Paestan pottery, and John Ward-Perkins, studying the monuments of Rome.

Confronted with such rising stars, Hardie complained there were no archaeologists in the School. Indeed, there were too few scholarships. But a windfall came his way, still dropping from the tree of the Ashby legacy. Signora Rivoira died in 1933 leaving the School a legacy of £2000 to support a scholarship in medieval archaeology, in memory of her husband. Commendatore Gian Teresio Rivoira was the distinguished architectural historian whose *Lombardic Architecture* Rushforth translated into English, and whose *Roman Architecture and its Principles of Construction* thanks 'my friend Thomas Ashby... whose knowledge of the facts and literature of Roman topography, unrivalled in the English-speaking world, has been freely placed at my service'.[60] The Rivoiras never forgot Ashby's School, though the School has contrived to forget them. Rivoira scholars include Peter Brown, historian of late antiquity, Martin Harrison, Professor of Roman Archaeology at Oxford, Katherine Dunbabin, Roman archaeologist and art historian; with Paul Roberts (now of the British Museum), the fund expired in 1989.

C.A. RALEGH RADFORD (1936-45)

The search for Hardie's successor revealed that the post, underpaid and overstressed, was losing its appeal. Various Oxford dons were sounded out, including Russell Meiggs and A.H.M. Jones, but none were interested. Eventually Ralegh Radford, an experienced archaeologist and friend of Mortimer Wheeler, working as Chief Inspector of Ancient Monuments in Wales, was prevailed on to come out in a hurry, since Magdalen insisted on Hardie taking up his fellowship in October. Radford was supported by Dale Trendall as Librarian, already emerging as the authority on Paestan pottery; when Trendall returned to his fellowship at Trinity, Cambridge in 1937, he was replaced by James Craig, who was deflected by the war into the diplomatic service.

After the black days of the Abyssinian crisis, things were looking up, and the devaluation of the lira added an effective £1000 to the School's income. The most pressing issue, which Hardie had already highlighted, was the completion of the building. Pressure came from two directions. On the one hand the Library was ever expanding, and since the accession of the Ashby collection, still no additional space had been created. On the other hand, available space was diminished by the crisis of the Common Room ceiling. An alarming sag in the beams showed that it was structurally inadequate; not only had ferro-concrete been substituted by the builders for the steel specified by Bradshaw in 1924, but it was not even properly made. (The Italian engineer described the construction as a 'flower-basket'.)[61] After much discussion in 1936, the School took the easy way out, and rather than replacing the beams, simply demolished the walls of the servants' rooms above, so depriving itself of valuable space.

By 1937, with everything looking more hopeful, the Committee decided to embark on the construction of the fourth wing to the east of the cortile. Chalton Bradshaw adapted the scheme which he had already drawn up at the time of the building of the Common Room for a wing with two floors; he now added a third floor and did his best to give the appearance of symmetry with Lutyens' west wing. Executive responsibility was handed over to the Embassy architect, Ettore Rossi, who drew up detailed drawings (Radford was to complain that as work progressed, he modified the plans continuously without seeking approval from the School).[62] Costs were estimated at £4,500, and the 1851 Commission, still in supportive mood, provided a loan of £2,500, half of which was supposed to be matched by appeal, but was later converted into an outright gift. Work started in the summer of 1937 and was complete by Easter 1938.

The opening ceremonies were not held until January 1939. They cast a fascinating light on relations with the fascist regime. There is extraordinarily little hint in the School's business correspondence of any antagonism to the regime. On the contrary, when Radford was approached by the Gruppo Universitario Fascista with a view to participation in an exhibition, Shaw urged collaboration:

'I think you were very wise in arranging to send

Ralegh Radford by H. A. Freeth, RA.

Hubert Andrew Freeth (RS Engraving 1936) married Ralegh Radford's secretary, Roseen Preston.

(left) East wing under construction, 1937-38.

(below) The new east wing as complete, 1939.

a few examples of our art students' work to the G.U.F. We must not be left out of these movements and I am sure that, if the exhibition does not entail special preparation which might interrupt normal study, the School should be represented at future exhibitions of foreign students' work under the auspices of the Fascist Party.'[63]

The same enthusiasm marked the British participation in the Augustan Exhibition of September 1937. The Director returned a month early from his vacation to be present at the ceremony, and wrote back a glowing report:

'The Augustan Exhibition yesterday was most successful. England was better represented than any foreign country & the English alone had brought addresses which were formally presented to the Organizer Giglioli after the ceremony. I think he and his collaborators were very pleased.'[64]

Not a hint here of the possibility of ideological problems. We may recall that Aubrey Waterfield's candidature for the Directorship had been blocked in 1936 because of his antifascist views. Corrado Ricci, the man behind Mussolini's archaeological programme, was elected an honorary fellow of the School in January 1939 (succeeding to Boni and Lanciani). Eugénie Strong's enthusiasm for the Augustan Exhibition (as for the rest of the archaeological programme of the regime) was spelt out in her articles; yet this implies no support for fascism, and one of her visitors at via Balbo recalls her making merry at the absurd requirement by Mussolini that all University staff marry to increase the population.[65] Not everyone in the School can have been happy even with acquiescence: it is not hard to guess what Anthony Blunt and Ronald Syme, both regular visitors in this period, must have thought. But probably Togo Salmon was not far out in suggesting that the students rarely aired their views of fascism: 'I doubt if any of the BSR students approved of

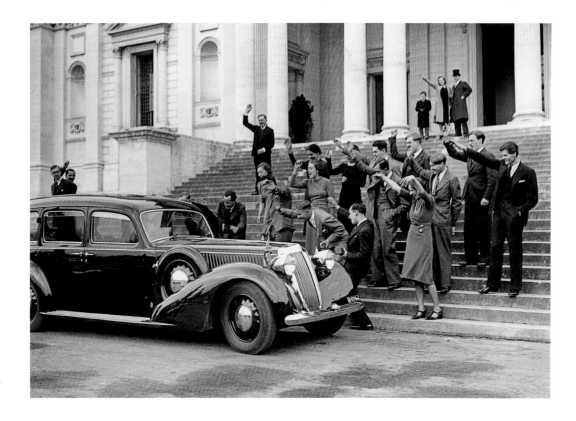

FAREWELL TO CHAMBERLAIN.

Mrs Barbara Craig (née Chapman) recalls that the visit was engineered through the artist Hermione Hammond, a close friend of the Chamberlain family. She identifies the figures (from the left) as: James Craig (Librarian, her future husband); Raymond Cowern (engraver); Ralegh Radford; Hubert Freeth (his wife had him change his name to Andrew); unidentified; Barbara Chapman; unidentified; Anne Newland (painter); Roseen Preston (Secretary, future wife of Freeth); Alex Wylie (architect); Una Fitzhardinge (Pelham Student); unidentified; E.H. Crosbee; William Tocher (sculptor); Godfrey Davis (RS Classics); Hermione Hammond (painter); Frank Archer (painter); unidentified; Albert (Pont) Pountney (sculptor); at the top of the steps are Polly Bevan (Assistant Librarian), her little brother and father).

THE VISIT OF NEVILLE CHAMBERLAIN AND HALIFAX, 1939.

Radford to Shaw, 13 January 1939: 'The Prime Minister and the Foreign Secretary today visited the School at 3.30 and stayed about 35 minutes. They saw the Common Room ground floor of (the) new wing, four of the studios and library & all the students were presented to them. Both seemed very interested... The visit was private & informal and only the staff & students were present.'

it; I suspect that they had difficulty taking it seriously. Some of them may have been quite content with the way it prevented any public disorder. But to this day I have no idea as to what were the political views of my companions at the BSR.'[66]

Radford therefore engineered as an opening ceremony for the building an official visit from the King of Italy (or H.M. the King Emperor Victor Emmanuel III as, after some exchanges with Shaw, he was allowed to style him).[67] The ceremony was preceded by a brief visit from the Prime Minister, Neville Chamberlain, and the Foreign Secretary, Lord Halifax, on 13 January 1939; in this sense the School was contributing to their policy of appeasement.

The opening of 24 January, unlike the informal visit of the British Prime Minister, was a major event. Sir Rennell Rodd, as Chairman of the Executive Committee, returned to his old hunting ground. Evelyn Shaw too came out in person, accompanied by his young daughter Pamela. There were also three Chairmen of Faculties, all Rome scholars: Harold Chalton Bradshaw (Architecture), Tom Monnington (Painting) and Gilbert Ledward (Sculpture). The King was accompanied by the new Governor of Rome, Principe Colonna. Shaw followed up the visit by an exceeding warm personal note to Colonna.

But the School needed to cultivate these links to survive. The issues of the road to the

THE VISIT OF KING VITTORIO EMANUELE III, 1939.

'H.M. the King Emperor Victor Emmanuel III of Italy was present on the opening of the new east wing of the British School at Rome on the 24th January, 1939. The King was met on the front steps of the School by the Chairman of the Executive Committee, Lord Rennell, and C.A. Ralegh Radford, then proceeded at once to the Dining Hall where the royal visitor and official guests were seated. A short speech followed from the Ambassador concerning the new building wing. The King was then taken to view the new Common Room, and the Library, where he was presented to other representatives of the British School, after which he departed.'

Philip Hirst (RS Architecture 1936) recalled the visit: 'Early in [1939], members of the School's Art Faculty visited us in Rome, among them Chalton Bradshaw, Sir Evelyn Shaw, accompanied by his daughter, and Tom Monnington. One evening the faculty invited the scholars to a party in the town. Sir Evelyn declined to join us, preferring to retire early, but kindly gave Monnington a generous fifty pounds and told us to go and enjoy ourselves. When I asked where we were going, Tom Monnington said he remembered a very good night spot from his days in Rome, the 'Florida'. I tried to tell him that it had changed somewhat since then and was now a 'high class house', where one could drink and dance with the numerous female partners available, not quite the place to arrive with a mixed group of students. However, he was determined, so several carrozze were summoned and we drove down to the Florida, where we created quite a stir by arriving with our own partners. After a bottle or two of Champagne and a dance we left and drifted down to the 'Bibliotheca', a pleasant night club. On the way back one of our girls, a painter, fell into the Skeaping fountain in the Cortile and 'bent' one of the goldfish, which remained 'bent' for as long as I remained at the School.'[68]

east, and the building plot to the north, continued to raise much anxiety, and contacts with the Municipality oscillate between reassurance (the buildings to the north would only be 'villini signorili', small and low) and threat (a Royal Decree now gives permission for 'ville comuni' of many storeys).[69] In the event, both road and neighbouring houses were constructed during the war, and Radford was shocked to find on his return in October 1944 how badly the studios were overlooked by their new northern neighbour.[70]

Building issues dominated Radford's tenure. Despite his archaeological competence, there was no chance of a significant School project in Italy. The suggestion coming from the Faculty of Archaeology, of which Ashmole was now Chair, was to join with the School at Athens in the excavation of the Roman villa at Knossos; Shaw had to stamp very hard on this diversion of the School's activity.[71] The alternative scheme was to return to Ashby's work on Malta; a plan which looked very promising because of the enthusiasm of the colonial government of the island, and which fitted neatly with the presence of a former Rome Scholar, John Ward Perkins, in the Chair of Archaeology at Valetta. But the plan was cut short by war.

It comes as a surprise to discover how buoyant the mood of the School was on the verge of international conflict. Not only was building undertaken, and archaeological activity planned: new funding was coming in. Shaw made a successful approach in 1937 to the Government to review the annual grant, which had stood at £500 since 1906, and had the sum raised to £1000, and responsibility transferred to the University Grants Committee. At the same time he was pressing for new scholarships, hoping to persuade Harrison Woodward to pay for a new Medieval Scholarship, and to get Sam Courtauld (brother of Stephen, still Chairman of the Finance Committee) to fund one in Art History.[72] In the event, neither idea came off, but a deal was done with the Trustees of the Edwin Austin Abbey Foundation that in future Abbey Major Scholarships in Painting should be awarded by the Faculty of Painting, and held in Rome. It is no coincidence that the most distinguished painters since that date have been Abbey Scholars, for the Faculty treated it as their prime award.

Radford can be remembered by the School, as he was recommended by Shaw, as a highly competent administrator:

'He thinks for himself and can be relied on to make the best of any job he undertakes. I have been with him when he entertained the King of Italy and when he has scolded a servant or examined the complicated plan of an Italian engineer; he is at home in all these things, and none of his distinguished predecessors have shown greater aptitude for business and departmental administration.'[73]

IL DOPOGUERRA
1945-1974

IL DOPOGUERRA
(1945-1974)

AS WAR CLOSED ICY FINGERS AROUND ITALY, the School's activity froze, and nature as if in sympathy wrapped the gardens in a blanket of snow, captured by the camera of Bruno Bonelli, who at first was able to report back to Radford. But there were still matters to attend to. The eastern perimeter wall giving security from the long-disputed new road was only built in early 1940. There were still some signs of life, and a relative of Mrs Strong was given permission to use the tennis court in March 1940.[1] But the situation rapidly became more dangerous. Eugénie Strong decided to see the war out in Rome, but the fascists expelled her from her flat in the via Balbo, and in May 1942 Radford consented to her moving into the Director's flat for safety. Shaw however felt it inadvisable, especially given the number of her visitors.[2] Eugénie died on 16 September 1943, and left the School she loved as her sole heir. When the two wills, English and Italian, were tied up in 1946, the estate was worth £4,699 to the School, in addition to her furniture and her library. The money was put to a Library Endowment Fund.

Bruno Bonelli kept the School, now surrounded by a full perimeter wall, hermetically sealed, with the aid of the porter, Valeri, and the nightguard, Cavaceppi. After initial thoughts of entrusting responsibility to the Dutch Institute, it was placed under the formal control first of the American Embassy, later of the Swiss Legation. When the Allies reached the Valle Giulia, there were several old friends of the School among British ranks. The first visitor was the Rome Scholar in Classical Studies of 1938, who had been turned down for enlistment in 1939 on the grounds of poor eyesight, Capt. Geoffrey Davis of the Intelligence Corps.[3] He knocked on the door early in the morning of 5 June 1944, and found the anxious Bruno Bonelli at home. Together, they unfurled the Union Jack.[4] But Ralegh Radford, still in name Director, was also with the army in Italy, after working at Bletchley and then being sent out to North Africa in May 1943. He reached the School in October 1944, found the building in excellent repair apart from problems with the roof, and found the Swiss Legation had been enjoying the tennis court.

(above and previous)
Views of BSR under snow,
winter 1939.

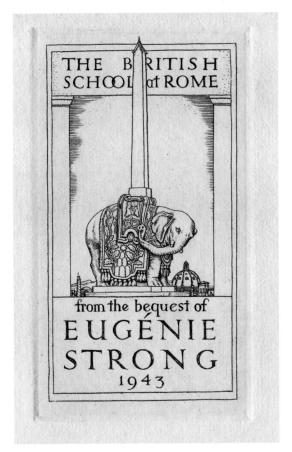

(above) Eugénie Strong bookplate, designed by Robin Austin (RS Engraving 1922).

(above right) The Embassy staff at the VE Day Celebration (photo Teresa Cullis).

(right) Bruno Bonelli, Bursar.

For a while, the School had unusual occupants. There were negotiations with the Army over using it as an Army School of Art (the British Army had not forgotten the cultural outreach which led it to employ the first Rome Scholars in Sculpture, and to have Ashby lecture to the troops in North Italy). In the event, it was the British Embassy staff who in July 1944 moved in. One of them, Teresa Cullis, recalls:

'The Ambassador's secretary, Kate Witherow, was in charge, and the day-to-day running was in the hands of the incomparable Bruno Bonelli, a tower of strength and ever-smiling help to us all, as he was to generations of staff and students. There were, I think, 15 of us, cypher officers, secretaries, archivists, telephonists, consular clerks and the bag lady (diplomatic bags, of course)… From early December a studio was used by Edward Ardizzone, then serving in the army as a war artist. His *Diary of a War Artist* describes how he got lost in the Villa Borghese on his way to the School to see Professor Radford… Another occupant of a studio for a time was a singer called Harry Beard, who had lived in Rome before the war and knew its musical world well…'

Radford was able to be present in the School on and off until October 1945, thanks to his presence in Rome on military duty. But another officer also present thanks to his role as Director of the Allied Sub-Commission for Monuments and the Fine Arts in Italy was Radford's successor.

JOHN BRYAN WARD-PERKINS (1945-1974)

Rarely has a Director been chosen with less hesitation than was Ward-Perkins, and rarely has anyone come to the post with better qualifications. Educated at Winchester, like Ashby, he had excavated in his schooldays under J.N.L. Myres, one of Ashby's Oxford tutors. He came to the School first in 1934 as an Oxford Craven Fellow, and guided by Ellis Waterhouse embarked on the study of architectural ornament. In 1936 he was appointed Assistant at the London Museum under Mortimer Wheeler, whose close friend he was to remain, at the time the Institute of Archaeology was being created with Wheeler as its Director. After gaining considerable experience of excavation in Britain and France, Ward-Perkins was elected the first Professor of Archaeology at the University of Malta in 1939, where he spent six months. He so gained close knowledge of an island which from Ashby through Radford to the present has woven in and out of the School's history.

John Ward-Perkins.

On the outbreak of war, Mortimer Wheeler set about recruiting a light anti-aircraft battery, to become a regiment, the 42nd Mobile LA. Ward-Perkins was among the original recruits, and by 1942 was in action in North Africa, missing El Alamein only because of a motor accident. If some of North Africa had to be viewed in passing from a military vehicle, his secondment to reconstitute the Antiquities Commission for Cyrenaica and Tripolitania gave him a thorough preview of what was to be his next major research area. His extraordinary understanding of terrain was formed in a field that was military as well as archaeological.

Promoted to Lt.-Colonel, he took command of Wheeler's regiment during the Allied advance up Italy, and only after victory was he detailed to conduct a survey of war damage to Italian heritage. The 34-year old officer evidently made a significant impact upon his Italian colleagues. It was still remembered 50 years later how he had been received in mud-splattered uniform by the

From the War Damage Photograph Collection.

(above) Palestrina (Praeneste) where bombing exposed the sanctuary of Fortuna.

(right) German troops packing up art works for safety.

Accademia dei Lincei, and delighted them by his slip in proclaiming, 'Sono molto grazioso'. Grateful he was, gracious they doubted. The eulogy of his friend Massimo Pallottino is worth repeating:

> 'As an eyewitness and participant in the exciting cultural events of the immediate post-war period, I cannot forget the image of the young English officer who, veteran of an African adventure that made an indelible impression on his character and scientific interests, was put in charge of the Sub-Commission of the Allied Government for Monuments and Fine Arts, and in that function contributed decisively to the rescue of Italian cultural heritage.'[5]

Little wonder that even Shaw regarded him as having 'superlative claims' to the Directorship.[6] Radford too was a friend both of Wheeler, with whom he excavated in Brittany in the summer of 1938, and of Ward-Perkins: on his appointment in June 1945, Radford described him as 'a personal friend of mine of some years standing'.[7]

He arrived finally to take up his appointment in February 1946 with his wife Margaret, whom he met during his North African 'adventure'. Over the next three decades he formed and rebuilt the School, with unflagging vigour, with a confident habit of leadership formed by military command, and with a sureness of vision unmatched by any Director except Ashby. The aftermath of war stamps his activity not just in the incidental sense that he came back to archaeology from the field, but that it provided a new answer to the question of what Britain was doing in Italy. The Allied officer took a lead in the work of post-war reconstruction, in rebuilding bridges with Italy and the entire international community represented by the Academies of Rome.

Of this the clearest symbol is the Unione, the union of foreign and Italian academic institutions in Rome. The British School has always operated very consciously in the context of other national institutions. An explicit argument rehearsed by all involved in its foundation was the sense of national prestige lost if Britain could not offer an institution to match those of the French, the Germans, the Americans, and progressively a host of other countries including all those of Scandinavia. But this argument was competitive rather than collaborative. Already Lutyens had pointed to what he saw as the weakness of this approach: if only resources were pooled in one 'world wide library', vast savings could be made, and, as he put it, 'The saving in Bibles and *Who's Whos* would keep a student'.[8] (His point neatly exposes its own limits: even if academic libraries stocked Bibles and *Who's Whos*, each nation would still need its own version – these are the very volumes on which no economy would be possible!) But collaboration is a very old tradition among these institutions. The German Archaeological Institute started as an international 'Istituto di Corrispondenza', and throughout the last century an important function of the Academies

Aerial photograph of Ostia (from the RAF Collection).

has been to enable scholars of different origins to collaborate with each other, not compete. Already Richmond had grasped the vision of institute libraries having a complementary function to be encouraged by increasing specialisation; and already in the thirties a 'Camerata' had been founded of regular meetings of students from different academies to read papers and discuss their research (even Smith grasped the benefits of this).

The Unione was founded in the immediate aftermath of the war in the precise circumstance of the need to recover from Germany the four great German Libraries which had been removed from Italy in 1943: those of the German Archaeological and Historical Institutes, the Biblioteca Hertziana, and the German Art-historical Institute in Florence. The international community had been deprived of the best resources, especially in Roman archaeology and art history, and the initial idea was to run them jointly from the Unione as a pooled resource. Fortunately, the arguments for restoring them to German control eventually prevailed, and at a time when Germany could have no political presence in Rome, its vigorous contribution to its academic presence ensured that bridges were swiftly rebuilt. These libraries remain an especial glory of Rome, and on them the international community continues to lean heavily.[9]

The Unione developed to become a forum for common concerns of the foreign academies, and thanks to the inclusion of Italian and pontifical institutions, a mechanism for nesting foreign institutes formally into local structures. Long after Ward-Perkins, its greatest triumph is the creation of a Library Union, URBS (Unione

Kate Whiteford (Sargant Fellow 1993) *Ostia* (one of series of prints inspired by the aerial photograph collection).[10]

Romana di Biblioteche Scientifiche) which by providing a common computer catalogue to its members enables precisely the specialisation which Richmond foresaw, and enables the avoidance of waste on *Who's Whos* that Lutyens feared.

A close ally of Ward-Perkins in creating the Unione was the Swedish Director, Eric Sjöqvist. It was with Sjöqvist too that Ward-Perkins carried out his first excavation in Italy, in December 1946, at San Salvatore in Spoleto, together with the local Superintendent, Enrico Josi. Richard Fraser, the architecture scholar, was recruited to draw the plans, renewing the collaboration of archaeologist and architect that reached a peak with Sheila Gibson.[11] As an excavation it was 'modest', but it was a significant step towards the future. Not since the eighteenth century when Gavin Hamilton and Robert Fagan were active had the English been given licence to excavate in Italy, and it was an assumption spelt out in the foundation of the School that excavation in Italy could not be its mission. But at Spoleto the way towards the future, of collaboration with the Italian authorities, was first tried out.

Among the positive by-products of the war was the application of air-reconnaissance photographs to archaeology. Ward-Perkins' military experience led him to understand the enormous value of the detailed aerial documentation made by the RAF. He rescued from destruction the enormous collection of photographs for the School in 1945/46, and over the next ten years, with some financial support from the Unione,[12] had them indexed and related to the 1:500,000 maps of Italy. Eventually, in 1974, the collection was consigned to the Italian state Fototeca Unione; it had played a critical role in drawing attention to the archaeological importance of aerial photography. The photographs had occupied an entire room of the School throughout Ward-Perkins' Directorship: the room was then renamed, a little eccentrically, the Wilson Room, in honour of one G.E. Wilson, a recently deceased friend of an occasional visitor, J.G. Adshead, who donated £300.

Ward-Perkins' prolific activity defies detailed narrative, but what above all he deserves to be remembered for is his success in engendering collaborative research activity on a sustained scale such as not even Ashby aspired to. Of course he was a busy administrator, every bit as effective as Radford; of course, like most other Directors, he had to worry about the fabric of the building, including the construction of a Library Extension in 1962-63. Of course he gave up his share of time to the scholars and artists, without perhaps being as popular as Ashmole, or so willing to

HUGH LAST AND JOCELYN TOYNBEE on the steps of the School, Christmas 1946.

Teresa Cullis writes: 'Towards the end of the year (1946) Professor Hugh Last arrived to give the inaugural lecture. I have two memories of him, apart from the lecture. He, the Director, Jocelyn and I were in a very small group taken round the new excavations in the Roman cemetery under St Peter's. To follow them round, share their wonderment and hear the discussion was indeed memorable. The second is entirely frivolous. Professor Last was with us for Christmas, and we were still running the hostel side of the School. We decided that for Christmas dinner everyone should wear a party hat. We provided a sailor hat for Professor Last, and it suited him very well.'

throw himself into other people's projects as Richmond – rather, he recruited everyone to his own projects.

His long Directorship was marked by two major and sustained archaeological projects, in North Africa and South Etruria.[13] In 1947 he visited Tripolitania and Malta in February. He was scanning precisely the same horizon as Ashby had done, and landed upon the very territory Ashby had been trying to secure a firman for just before the Great War:, Lebda, or Lepcis Magna. He also enlisted the first Rome Scholar in Classics to arrive after the war, Joyce Reynolds: her project was on the Social Background of the Equestrian Order, but she soon found her subject overtaken by the definitive publication of Pflaum, and turned to Ward-Perkins for advice. She was soon swept by his enthusiasm into the publication of the Inscriptions of Roman Tripolitania that established her as the leading British epigraphist of her generation (the book appeared with admirable speed in 1952).[14]

The choice of Libya was confirmed by the appointment in 1948 of Richard Goodchild, since 1946 Antiquities Officer for the British Administration in Tripoli, as Librarian (Assistant Director was still in abeyance as a title). Soon they were excavating at Sabratha with 25 students with the assistance of Kathleen Kenyon (July-September 1948). Olwen Brogan, long Secretary of the Faculty of Archaeology, was another who joined the excavations. Another important collaborator was Jocelyn Toynbee. Hugh Last, as one of the literary executors of Eugénie Strong, had asked her to edit the unpublished Strong manuscript on the History of the Vatican, and to complete the revised edition of Roman

Wadi El-Caam - the beginning of the Leptis aqueduct.

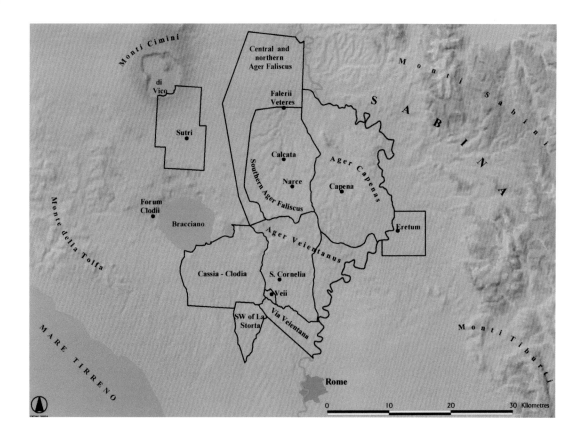

Map of South Etruria with principal survey areas marked.

Sculpture. Toynbee was perhaps a little deflected, and co-authored with Ward-Perkins a book on the newly excavated Shrine of St Peter beneath the Vatican,[15] a famous study of the Hunting Baths at Lepcis,[16] and much work on architectural ornament.

By the early 1950s, Ward-Perkins was ready to wind up Tripolitania and move on to a new challenge. By January 1952 he was reporting Tripolitania completed, though Goodchild was opening up a new field of activity in Cyrenaica with excavations at Benghazi. Goodchild was appointed Director of Antiquities in Libya, and left in November 1953 after five years of exceptionally fruitful collaboration; in his place was appointed Spencer Corbett, the architect to the Lepcis expedition, and the first ARIBA since Ashby to hold office in the School. Corbett was still working in Cyrenaica in 1956, but resigned in 1957 to collaborate with Richard Krautheimer on his famous Corpus of Christian Basilicas. (Corbett was succeeded by Michael Ballance 1957-62, and only then was the title of Assistant Director, in abeyance since Strong, restored.)

The Libyan project both exploited the opportunities created by the war in North Africa, and was the culmination of a tradition of archaeology in the School which, frustrated by the lack of opportunities in Italy, aspired to make the entire Western Mediterranean its field. It ended, by no coincidence, with the withdrawal of British forces from Libya. But the mood was changing rapidly in Italy, and not least because of the supportiveness expressed by the Unione, an era of active collaboration with foreign archaeologists was opening up. By the 1950s, the Americans were allowed to dig in Cosa, and in the Regia in the heart of the Forum, the Swedes in Etruscan sites around Viterbo, the French at Megara Hyblaea. The British School Survey of South Etruria, though less dramatic than these in terms of results produced by excavation, has outstanding significance as a sustained and profound study of landscape over time, breaking new ground in archaeological method.[17]

'During the autumn and spring the Director and a group of students undertook a number of field trips into the Campagna north of Rome. Although this area is rich in antiquities (many of which are disappearing as the result of land-resettlement schemes), it has been strangely neglected in recent times, and it is hoped

Ward-Perkins in the field recording an inscription.

Relaxation in South Etruria.

that it may be possible to follow up this work in the near future.' (Annual Report 1954-55)

The interest in the Campagna Romana and the awareness of a rapidly disappearing ancient landscape is pure Ashby, though Ward-Perkins was even more effective than Ashby in recruiting others to the cause. The new project starts quite suddenly in the autumn of 1954, with the arrival as Rome Scholar in Classical Studies of Martin Frederiksen, the Australian whom many came to see as the most brilliant ancient historian of his generation. Inspired by Ronald Syme at Oxford, his declared intention was to study 'Methods of enlistment of the governing class from c.100 BC to about the death of Trajan', abbreviated to 'Novi Homines' ('New Men'). It is less easy for those outside the field to sense how alien the sort of archaeological survey undertaken by Ward-Perkins was to the text-based studies of social mobility that had become the central concern of Roman history: the deflection of Joyce Reynolds from the equestrian order to the inscriptions of Tripolitania was forgivable because the new project was epigraphical, but from Frederiksen onwards suspicion grew in Oxford that Roman historians were being diverted in Rome to archaeological irrelevances. Later (in 1962), by contrast, Peter Wiseman was to arrive studying 'Novi Homines', and resisting diversion added study of Roman Roads as an extra string to his bow.

The project grew swiftly. In 1955-56 the territory around the Etruscan city of Veii (Ager Veientanus) became the focus; in 1956-57 it was Ager Faliscus, the territory of the Falisci round Falerii Veteres (Civita Castellana) where Harold Chalton Bradshaw had worked in 1919; in 1957-58 the Rome Scholar in Classical Studies, Guy Duncan, was put on to Sutri and its territory, while the Rome Scholar in Architecture, Roloff Uytenbogaardt, was given the medieval hill-town of Calcata (an influential architect in South Africa, he became the great champion of the School's link to his country after Herbert Baker); in 1958-59 Leslie Murray-Threipland was excavating the north gate of Veii; in 1959-60 Barri

(above) Tim Potter and his daughter Belinda, 1998.

(right) Potter's excavation at Narce, 1968.

(above) Via Clodia - in the woods above S. Liberato.

(right) Tomb cover on M. La Corte, Narce.

(left) Pot washing on the front portico.

(below) Molly Cotton at Francolise, 1962.

Jones, Rome Scholar in Classical Studies, was put on to Capena; in 1960-61 Charles Daniels was given the early medieval papal estate of Santa Cornelia near Veii; in 1961-62 Joanna Close-Brooks embarked on the excavation of the important iron-age cemetery of Quattro Fontanili at Veii; in 1962-63 William Harris, Rome Scholar in Classical Studies, was put on to the via Cassia, while Sheila Gibson, the Bernard Webb Student in Architecture, surveyed at Forum Clodii near Bracciano; and the site of Eretum, on the opposite, east bank of the Tiber, was identified and ear-marked for Robert Ogilvie.

As the project grew in ambition and tempo over the years, the names both of Rome Scholars recruited and archaeological friends brought in from outside became too many to list in full, even in the Annual Reports, but each year brought significant new faces: Lady Wheeler excavating at Veii in 1964-65 and at Santa Rufina the next year; Tim Potter, Rome Scholar, starting with Sheldon Judson at Narce in 1965-66; Mario Torelli and Mary Ann Meagher studying Etruscan pottery from Veii in 1966-67; David Whitehouse (Rome Scholar in Medieval Studies for 1963) studying medieval glazed wares from Lazio in 1967-68, while Nancy Hirschland (later Ramage) was looking at Etruscan bucchero. By the late 60s, the expansion of the project slowed down, and in 1969-70 the

Excavation at Gravina, 1973.

classical side of the project was declared 'within reasonable sight of completion': attention was shifting increasingly to the new project in Apulia.

Lists of names do nothing to convey the excitement and fun of this project. It represented an extraordinarily effective utilisation of the always scarce resources available to the School, by using the people there to study what was on the doorstep. It involved close collaboration with Italians, especially in the excavation of Quattro Fontanili, and won profound respect in the Italian archaeological community. It was admirably broad in chronological range: one could argue that the really important results were not classical at all, but prehistoric (Potter at Narce), protostoric (Villanovan Veii), and medieval (Santa Cornelia, Santa Rufina etc).

The contribution to the understanding of pottery, especially local wares, was profound. It was at this period that the 'Camerone' came into being as the School's archaeological workshop. The area above the dining room originally designed for servants' bedrooms had been stripped of internal walls in 1935 to avoid the collapse of the ceiling. The ceiling was finally strengthened in summer 1951, and the space above released for book storage for the overflowing Library. But it was not until 1958-59 that it was equipped as a workroom and turned over for archaeological use. The book overflow was finally cleared out on the completion of the Library extension in September 1963, and in 1967 the room was officially renamed the 'Margary Room' in recognition of the generous donation (in 1962) of £5000 by I.D. Margary, the authority on Roman roads, though customary usage prevailed, and the name of 'Camerone' ('large room') survived. There first Anne Kahane and then, from 1965, Molly Cotton presided over the fervour of activity generated by the recording and analysis of tens of thousands of potsherds collected and other material processed.

The Libyan project occupied Ward-Perkins' first eight years; the South Etruria Survey lasted 20 years and was far from finished even when he left. Individual elements of the project were published with great efficiency as they were completed. It took the cheerful self-confidence of Tim Potter to spin an energetic and readable interim synthesis. In his own words:

'I have to say that it is a matter of deep regret that John Ward-Perkins, diverted by so many other tasks, did not go beyond the *Ager Veientanus* volume, and produce a more general account of the South Etruria survey. He certainly wanted to, and when I was asked to write something – by Donald Bullough, former Scholar and Acting Director of the School, after giving a lecture at his University, St. Andrews – I naturally sought Ward-Perkins' permission. It was a conversation held in 1977, on all fours, at his house just outside Cirencester where, following lunch (and the requisite brief *siesta*), he was weeding the lawn. 'Don't write the book I want to write', he remarked, somewhat acerbically, to which I replied (correctly) that 'I couldn't'.[18]

There is a sense in which the School is still writing that book, and the legacy it owes to Ward-Perkins is the vision of what could be achieved by co-ordinating the efforts of numerous volunteers over a long period of time and by careful recording building up a database of information of lasting value.

But he was indeed distracted by other commitments. Apart from his own major publications on Roman architecture, on Roman city planning and on the imperial marble trade, there were more archaeological projects in the air with every season that passed. It was the age when the fame of an archaeologist depended more on activity in the field than tidy completion of publications. From 1963-64 onwards there was increasing interest in Apulia, starting with the excavation of the medieval castle of Lucera by Barri Jones and David and Ruth Whitehouse that produced large quantities of majolica, developed for a decade by Alistair Small and others, particularly Joan Taylor (another friend of Mortimer Wheeler), in fieldwork around Gravina, first at the iron-age site of Botromagno, then extending interest to Cozzo Presepe and elsewhere.

All this archaeological activity is enough to create the impression that nothing else counted in the School, and certainly it stamped its character on the institution. But in fact they were busy and flourishing years on a wide front. One reason for a shift of emphasis towards archaeology was the gradual substitution of the British Academy for the 1851 Commission as the dominant source of annual funding. The original Treasury grant of

The Library extension, 1962-63.

Proposal from the 1950s for a new building east of BSR, on site of 1960s extension to the Galleria d'Arte Moderna.

£500 only rose to £1000 just before the war, when the 1851 Commission were paying £4,500 for Arts scholarships and upkeep. After the war, the Treasury was persuaded to go up to £3000, and the figure steadily rose, struggling to keep pace with inflation. From 1950 the Treasury routed its grant through the British Academy; and the fact that Mortimer Wheeler was Secretary of the Academy until 1969 meant that the claims of archaeology, and the voice of Ward-Perkins in particular, were heard with great attention. The growth of the archaeological activity of the School is part of the growth of archaeology as a university discipline in post-war Britain, and the growth of Schools and Institutes abroad under the wing of the Academy is part of that pattern.

At the same time, the 1851 Commission was beginning to distance itself. In 1947 Evelyn Shaw reached 65 and retired as Secretary to the Commission, and as Honorary General Secretary to the School. He received his knighthood, and joined the Executive Committee in his own right, serving on it (amazingly) for the next 23 years. He was replaced as Secretary by his understudy, W.D. (Digby) Sturch. Through the early fifties, the Academy and the 1851 were roughly on a par as sources of income: so in 1950 each provided £5000, in 1959 the Commissioners gave £6,250 to the Academy's £10,000. But the sense that the 1851 called the shots had gone.

Indicative of the change is that when money was needed for the Library extension, the School went out to appeal for the first time since 1912, when Esher had threatened to pull out if there was any talk of public appeal. Brigadier Maurice Lush, retired MD of Shell, Pakistan, and Ward-Perkins' commanding officer in the Italian campaign and firm friend, was appointed in 1960 to run the appeal without fee. They asked for £25,000, raised £18,000, and since the extension when finished in late 1963 cost £14,500, there was a surplus with which to endow the Library. Contributions came both from academic institutions and from the world of industry and banking.

The extension was designed by Anthony Minoprio (Jarvis Student 1925, one of Richmond's collaborators), who came in this period to have a role like that of Chalton Bradshaw in his day. A forgotten fragment of School history is that in the early 1950s, the Committee had been dreaming of a very different solution to its space problem, the construction of a new building on the far side of via Cancani. The matter got as far as approval from the Comune, but was blocked by the Italian Foreign Office, which asked for a similar concession to the Italian Institute in London. Minoprio had already made sketch plans for the new building when the word was received that the site was to be given instead to the Gallery of Modern Art for an extension. They put up what must be, despite fierce competition, the most grotesquely ugly building ever erected in the School's vicinity, but never completed or put it to use: its replacement by a new extension designed by Diener and Diener is one of the most cheerful prospects the new millennium has to offer to the School.

The real moment when change comes to a head is the late sixties. The post-war generation had come of age, and in all fields challenged the wisdom of its fathers. The artists rejected the classical in every sense, and Rome could seem irrelevant, if not actually a symbol of what was to be rejected. The archaeologists were now looking for theoretical approaches and scientific method, and classical archaeology was the branch of the discipline least responsive to these demands. The School in 1968 may not have been exactly a hotbed of revolution –Sir Anthony Blunt was probably the most subversive presence– but it was next door to the seat of Italian student unrest, and the vivid description of the riots at the Faculty of Architecture by Tim Potter from his vantage point on the School's roof bring home the turmoil of the times (see end of chapter).

Where Ward-Perkins stood on all this was made clear by his request to the Executive Committee in 1970 that all students should sign undertakings to abstain from political activity, a request prudently deflected in favour of a Directorial pep-talk.[19] It was getting distinctly harder for the veteran of Monty's campaigns to understand the demands of the long-haired generation, and the young Tony Luttrell, who replaced Michael Mallett as Assistant Director (1967-73), felt he was out of touch (however unwelcome the message). The revolution

Evelyn Shaw.

touched the 1851 Commission too, which established a Review Committee in 1969 under Lord Robbins, author of the report which revolutionised the universities in the sixties. The traumatic findings were reported at the meeting of September 1970:

> 'with the development in recent years of industrial design as a recognised discipline there were now other ways in which the Commission could probably more appropriately employ their funds in accordance with their Charter than with the maintenance of the Rome Scholarships.'[20]

By uncanny coincidence, the 88-year old Sir Evelyn Shaw missed this meeting, and sent his resignation, on grounds of health, to the next. He had lived to see the 1851 set their hearts against everything he had laboured for.

But there were good reasons. First, the initiative of Lord Esher was scarcely justified by the Charter of the 1851, which specified the promotion of industry; and in a new world that was rejecting the classical and promoting industrial and scientific innovation, this was no trivial incompatibility. Second, the conditions which drove Esher, the sense that British Art could make a vital contribution to the British imperialist cause, had gone, with the passing of the Jaggers and Ledwards and war memorials. Third, the British Art establishment, about which even in 1910 Shaw was expressing acute suspicions, was now so modernist as to be scarcely compatible with the 1851 ideology: just as in 1910 classical art seemed a bulwark against modernism, so in 1970 they turned to technical drawing and industrial design. Finally, the School had ceased to be their baby. Under the tutelage of the British Academy it had come of age, and entered a different world of research-driven funding.

The Commission was very graceful about its withdrawal: it continued its funding for six years at the same level, and let inflation do its work. It staged its withdrawal over so long (until 1996) that the School had by then completely replaced the support for Art Scholarships from other sources, and experienced no crisis. What should remain is a deep institutional gratitude for the 85 years of support that gave us our building, and enabled the institution to grow and flourish in a way otherwise impossible in those early days before the availability of other arts and research funding.

There is much else too for which Ward-Perkins deserves to be remembered: we can pick out music and gardening. Joyce Reynolds recalls that 'at least one student who had clashed with him was won over by the sound of his playing at the piano',[21] and many recalled with pleasure the Christmas parties and carol singing. The love for music led to a broadening of the School's cultural activity, and between 1946 and 1950 the School hosted a series of Mendelssohn scholars or other award winners from the Royal College of Music: Jocelyn Lubbock, Malcolm Arnold and Stephen Dodgson. The singer Harry Beard who took a studio at the end of the war was perhaps behind this; he remained an occasional visitor, and on his death in 1971 left a small endowment of £1000 towards a Music scholarship. This tradition was to be revived in 1998 when Jaguar Italia started sponsoring a scholar from the RCM.

As for gardening, everyone remembers that Ward-Perkins had firm views on how exactly to extract a weed, and Tim Potter was surely not the only one to conduct an interview on all fours. John and Margaret loved the garden, which flourished under them: the photographs are testimony. They also followed Bernard Ashmole's example in commissioning a fountain from a sculptor. In October 1962, Glynn Williams, holder of a scholarship from the Gulbenkian foundation, was invited to erect a fountain in the Director's garden

The Director's Garden

The Director wrote to the Faculty of Sculpture (18.6.1962) recommending Glynn Williams' request for a grant to carve a fountain for the vacant site at the N.W. corner of the School's garden:[22] 'The site is one that cries aloud for something of the sort, and will do so even more when we have the formal terrace over the new Library extension at the opposite end of the axis. Clearly the proposal must stand or fall on the Faculty's opinion of Williams' suggested design and of his ability to carry it out. Perhaps, however, knowing the site well, I may be allowed to add that the scale and material (a local stone) do seem to me to be right and that in the setting one probably does want some sort of compromise with tradition rather than a purely avant-garde piece.'

View from the Pincio by Eric Hebborn (RS Engraving 1959).

'Following the instructions given to me by Bruno and Augusto, I strolled through those magnificent grounds with their shady walks of old ilex on my way to find Via Margutta and David. I passed a lake, a riding school, fountains and statuary. It was sunset as I made my way towards the Pincio, and emerging from the dark lanes flanked by trees and shrubs framing the marble busts of Italy's patriotic heroes, I was suddenly faced with a ravishingly beautiful view of central Rome silhouetted in purple against a vibrant sky of crimson and gold.' (Hebborn, *Drawn to Trouble*, p.186).

at the cost of £400; since February 1963 the rounded figures of his inverted couple have defined one axis of the garden.

How art fared in these years is the topic of a later chapter; but it is worth adding a word here on the Director's relationship with the artists. Eric Hebborn, who came to fame as a master forger, recalls with great affection and respect his years as Scholar in Engraving (1959-61). Recalling complaints of the day from among the artists that the Director ought to be an artist, he thought 'the then Director, John Ward-Perkins, an excellent head of the School, who did his very best to understand and help the artists'. In his own case, that meant handling the scandal that Hebborn was cohabiting with Gianni, a young man he had picked up in the Borghese gardens. He persuaded the Director that Gianni was his life model, but had to take to bed when assailed by migraine attacks:

'At this the Director gave me a stern look and said: "Very well, Hebborn, but be careful, people *will* talk you know." That evening there was a knock on my studio door. I hastily dressed, and opening the door only slightly, so that the visitor could not see my naked model posing with a full erection, I came face to face with Margaret Ward-Perkins. The thoughtful woman wanted to know how Gianni was feeling, and would he care for some aspirin.'[23]

One sign of the thoroughness with which the Director undertook his responsibilities towards artists are his reports to the Faculty on the progress of each scholar. Perceptive and pointed, they show he kept in close touch with their activities. Of Hebborn he had this to say:

'A gentle, thoughtful sort of chap, who seems to know where he is going and has on the whole made good use of his time. For a short time after Christmas he got into rather bad company; but that situation has now sorted itself out, and I anticipate no further trouble.'

In fact the endless agonising of the Fine Arts Faculties over how to support their scholars was resolved in this period by the appointment of practising artists as Advisers, resident for three or four months each year: Derek Hill, Scott Medd and Heinz Inlander for a succession of years in the 1950s and 60s gave valuable support. The Arts in this period were boosted further by an important legacy, the last crop of fruit from the Ashby tree. In 1924 the Bursar, Mrs Hardiman, reported to Shaw:

'A friend of Ashby's is working for a week or two for two or three hours each morning in a spare studio, and will be charged with Service in proportion to what the students pay. He has come down from Florence, on account of his health, and is staying at the Hassler in Rome. His name is Sargant.'[24]

Francis William Sargant (1870-1960) was evidently much taken with the School. He was a bachelor of some substance, working as a sculptor in Florence (the Tate has his 'Carlino') and shortly afterwards indicated his intention of leaving his Florentine properties, which consisted of four villas, to the School.[25] A fifth property was added in 1928.[26] The obstacle was the inheritance tax of 30% imposed on foreigners, and the possibility was explored of registering as an Italian Ente Morale to escape this tax. The option was abandoned when it emerged the School would then fall wholly under Italian law.[27] Sargant continued to visit, and artists would periodically visit him in Florence. After the war, he resumed contact: he had been forced to sell three of his four properties to pay taxes for the Abyssinian war,[28] but now proposed to leave the School his London property, consisting of two studios at 19-21 Cheyne Row, in memory of his sister, the fresco painter Mrs Mary Sargant-Florence (to whom Cheyne Row had previously belonged).[29] On his death in 1960, their value was estimated at £10,000.[30] Sargant's idea had been to offer studio space to returning Rome scholars, but in the event they were let (among other tenants was a film studio called Town and Country Productions). Finally sold in 1985 for £265,275, the capital is now the largest single element in the School's endowment, funding the Sargant Fellowship.

Another legacy that falls in this period was that of a German art historian, Jacob Hess (1885-1960). Thrown out of Italy at short notice in 1938, he was helped in London particularly by Fritz Saxl at the Warburg, and by Ellis Waterhouse, former Librarian of the School. In the late sixties he approached Ernst Gombrich at the Warburg to offer them his flat near the Vatican, in via Ostia; but finding they could not think of maintaining a flat in Rome, contacted Ward-Perkins. The flat was left to the School 'in grateful memory of the financial, scholarly and moral support which I received in London between 1938 and 1947'. He died in 1969, and the flat was used for many years by senior visiting scholars, until it was finally sold in 1996 for £100,000 to help finance rebuilding the studios.

The Ward-Perkins years neatly define a generation and its passing: the generation that set about rebuilding Europe after the trauma of war, but which found itself overtaken by a younger generation that had not known the war, and demanded more radical change. Ward-Perkins was vastly respected in Rome, as had been Ashby; and like Ashby, he left the School an intellectual legacy, a vision, and an accumulation of primary research on which future generations will draw.

THE RIOTS OF 1968

Tim Potter, letter to family, 1 March 1968 (7.00pm): 'All is quiet after a day that was the most horrifying and sickening that any of us can remember. By the time you get this – and it's widely believed that not all is over – you will probably have heard the bald outline. This is an eyewitness account...

I went up onto the roof with a camera. Then, gradually, through the trees one could see the students gathering, until they numbered about a hundred. Not all were students, either; many were far too old, and they grouped to talk. Suddenly, three buses of police came round the corner, and stopped in front of the students. A road block was set up, and then the buses moved down to the west side (the architectural faculty side) of the British School steps, right underneath us. Photographers, motion camera men and police cars appeared. All was quiet, in the face of this show of strength. I went to the Camerone for coffee, and we then heard a loud chanting. Rushing back, we were in time to see a great march of students, men and girls, with banners, round the corner of the Gramsci. They must have numbered over two thousand. They occupied the road in front of the Faculty. Then eggs began to fly. Donning steel helmets the police charged. Missiles – stones, sticks and batons – began to fly. Attack and counter attack followed, and students spreading like a wave in the face of the opposition, and then reforming to attack again.

At this point memory blurs the horrors that followed. The police, though outnumbered had the upper hand. All the time there was a continuous din, from chanted and then hysterical slogans – fuori, fuori! – to frenetic instructions from police commanders. From the left, a police station wagon raced towards the faculty. Stones smashed its windows, it skidded to a halt, its occupants ran, and yelling students seized it. In no time, an oily cloud of smoke began to rise, and soon it was a blazing wreck. Bloody students and police were helped by friends to safety, the baton fell, the stone was thrown. The students charged again at the Faculty, scenting victory, and meanwhile others attacked police

sheltering behind the three buses parked beneath us. Under the cover of this a military Fiat 500 was systematically smashed and burned, right beneath us. Some students persuaded newly arrived firemen to leave alone the burning wreck. Others pushed a non-military car to safety. An ambulance arrived, a militant student tried to prevent its passage. Others, more sensible, let it through; its need was great. Then the buses were pushed into the open road, and two of them smashed and burned. The third with wounded policeman, escaped.

I then heard the first pistol shot. At the same time, students – men and girls – all clutching clubs and stones, rushed the faculty. The police fell back. An entry was forced, and in front one could see some students inciting others to calm down. Some negotiation followed. There was a round of applause, breaking in on a sudden silence. Then, too suddenly, the police appeared, and rushed the talking students. The rumour flashed round of a policeman's death. The students ran, but some too slowly, they were seized, both men and women, some beaten with batons, some punched, many dragged off into the building. Others retired, supported or limping. Black smoke obscured the sun. We watched, with grandstand view, unable to do anything...'

NEW CHALLENGES
1974-1995

New Challenges
(1974-1995)

Just as the end of the Ashby regime left the School uncertain of where to head, so the passing of Ward-Perkins' long and confident regime ushered in an era of questioning and reassessment. So much that could be taken for granted as shared values in the immediate post-war period was now in crisis: modernism in declaring war on the classical and the traditional put the whole 'relevance' of Rome under question. Archaeology was coming into its maturity as an independent discipline, no longer happy to be seen as the 'handmaiden of history': classical archaeology proved sluggish in catching up with either the new theoretical approaches or the scientific techniques pioneered by the prehistorian. Schools both of art and of architecture rejected their own classical traditions, and with them the most obvious reasons for coming to Italy to study the art and architecture of the past. Amid such existential anxiety, the School was plagued by financial crisis, as inflation rose to record levels of 20% per annum, and sterling weakened towards its low in 1986.[1] Though the School owes its successes to many factors and the efforts of many people, it can do little to counter the debilitating effect of a weak pound. All these problems were compounded by the progressive withdrawal of financial support by the 1851 Commission. But the salutary effect of crisis was that the School was forced to rethink its identity and potential rather in advance of its continental counterparts, which enjoyed undiminished government funding throughout this period, and was able to emerge from its lean years with a renewed sense of purpose and vigour.

David Whitehouse (1974-84)

At his retirement, John Ward-Perkins was the oldest Director apart from Arthur Smith, and had accumulated all the advantages of *auctoritas* and deep respect in the Roman community that a long-serving figure enjoys. In appointing David

Whitehouse as his successor,[2] still in his early thirties, the School merely reverted to its long-standing tradition of appointing young men – but left him with the challenge of a very hard act to follow. Whitehouse was no new-comer. Rome Scholar in Medieval Studies in 1963, he had played an active part in School projects in South Etruria and particularly in Southern Italy, establishing himself as a respected expert on medieval glazed pottery. In particular he contributed significantly to the new project of the early seventies at Tuscania, where the medieval rubbish pits produced rich material for study. He broadened his scope to early Islamic archaeology, directing excavations at Siraf in Southern Iran, and becoming Director of the British Institute of Afghan Studies at Kandahar. He brought more experience to his new job than most of Ashby's successors.

If Ward-Perkins' great strength had been to get a large number of scholars to contribute over a period of time to an ambitious theme of wide importance, a reaction now set in to diversify. That is immediately visible in the grant-giving policy of the Faculty of Archaeology, which instituted a new policy of Grants in Aid of Research, which supported a wide range of archaeological projects across Italy, though none of them very substantially. It answered the mood of the day, when archaeology was increasingly supported by 'mosaic funding', gathering small bits of support from several funding sources, none of which had to commit too much, and all of which felt they were supporting a large and diverse range of projects. But the corollary was that the School was unable to get up steam for any single major project itself.

One feature of the new projects on which emphasis was laid was collaboration with Italian archaeologists: a new generation of Italian scholars had arisen by the seventies, in universities, museums and Superintendencies of Antiquities. They looked more for partnership than the hitherto largely autonomous activities from the foreign schools. But another important change was the shift in focus away from the core classical period to the transitional period from Late Antiquity to the Middle Ages, a period which for historians too was producing some of the most exciting new work.

Soon the School was engaged in excavation at Gubbio, where the

HRH Princess Alexandra and David Whitehouse, 1976.

medieval castle at Monte Ingino served to watch over the route between Perugia and the mountains of the Marche. It proved a successful collaboration with local authorities and the University of Perugia. The use of new scientific approaches was exemplified by Graeme Barker's study of the faunal remains. Next, in 1976-77, came a rescue excavation of medieval and classical remains at Otranto, in partnership with the University of Lecce. Above cemeteries and buildings of the classical era lay an exceptionally rich sequence of Byzantine and later medieval deposits, revealed in a major excavation directed by Demetrios Michaelides. Another new project in 1977 was near Anguillara on Lake Bracciano, at the imposing tower-like structure of the Mura di S. Stefano. After Frank Sear (Rome Scholar 1970) and Margaret Lyttleton surveyed the standing structures,[3] excavations revealed the sequence from a second century AD Roman villa through to a fortified structure in late Antiquity, and a church in the early Middle Ages.

Just as the achievement of the South Etruria survey had been to show how patterns of settlement shift over time, and the patterns gradually established in classical antiquity are transformed in the middle ages, so Whitehouse's excavations threw focused light on a period of transition. The excavation of the Scola Praeconum on the Palatine in 1978 examined a classical Roman structure transformed into a late antique church. A huge dump of domestic debris was recovered including bones and pottery, which proved a valu-

(above) Mura di S. Stefano, Anguillara (from BSR Archive collection).

(right) Axonometric reconstruction of Roman villa at S. Stefano by Sheila Gibson.

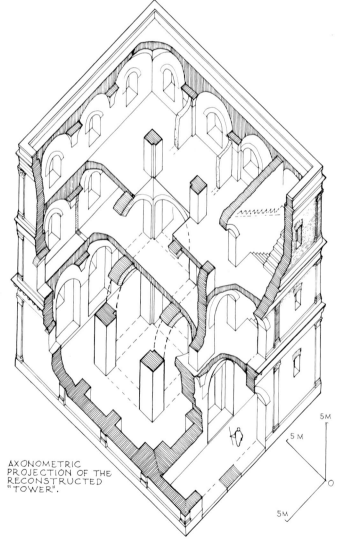

AXONOMETRIC PROJECTION OF THE RECONSTRUCTED "TOWER".

(left) Farfa Abbey.

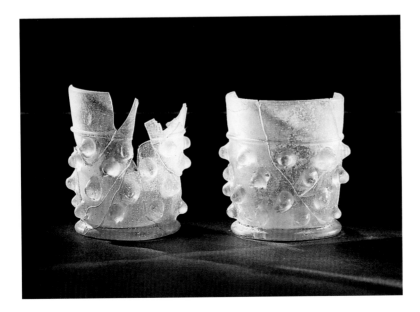

(above) Excavation at
Farfa Abbey, c. 1981.

(left) Medieval glass
beakers from Farfa.

Molly Cotton, Sir Angus Ogilvy, Sir Alan Campbell, HRH Princess Alexandra and
David Whitehouse, 1976.

able source of evidence for the economy and food-supply of fifth century Rome. Finally, the Abbey of Farfa became the major focus of activity of the late seventies and early eighties. Excavations, in collaboration with Charles McLendon of Yale University, revealed the structures of the earlier monastery, sacked in the Lombard invasions, and refounded under the patronage of the Carolingian emperors. Farfa was, as it proved, a significant forerunner of the much larger-scale excavations of the Carolingian Abbey of San Vincenzo al Volturno a decade later.

The limitation of all these projects was that they were underfunded, and that the drive to remain active in the field hampered publication of results, which became a burden for future Directors. A strength was that they built up the Camerone as a centre of study of the finds, especially ceramics and bones. Molly Cotton, long since recruited by Ward-Perkins, and put in charge of the Camerone in 1965, continued to reign, with the title from 1976 of 'Honorary Director', much loved until her death in 1983, when she left the School in her will £20,000 for the Camerone. She was always generous with her private wealth in support of Italian archaeology, and had set up the Cotton Foundation in 1972. The Camerone became a vital meeting place for specialists, Italian as well as English, and the study of ceramics and faunal remains became one of the School's recognised strengths, on which Graeme Barker was to build as director.

If archaeological policy was to broaden the School's appeal beyond the classical, other initiatives, particularly in the hands of the Assistant Directors, aimed to give the School a new relevance in the changing educational scene. Tim Cornell (Assistant Director 1975-77) launched a new series of research seminars for scholars; the programme grew rapidly, and 1976-77 was described as 'the busiest year for a long time' with many lectures, seminars and conferences. Cornell was replaced by Demetrios Michaelides (1977-78), under the new and strange title of Director's Assistant; in addition to his excavations in Otranto, Michaelides took on as Cotton Fellow the cataloguing of the papers of Thomas Ashby and Eugénie Strong, the first sign that the School was awakening to the importance of its Archive. His work paved the way for the brief experiment of an archive Research Fellowship, held by Jill Franklin (1980-82), followed by the appointment of a member of the Library staff, Valerie Scott, as part-time Archivist (1982).

After a series of unsuccessful experiments with 'administrative assistants', the Assistant Directorship was re-established in 1980 with the appointment of Amanda Claridge, to become the School's longest serving Assistant Director (1980-94) since Eugénie Strong. A Rome Scholar (1973), she had collaborated with Ward-Perkins in the notably successful Pompeii exhibition of 1976. She brought to the School a deep knowledge of Roman material culture, from marble to construction techniques, combined with a formidable talent for imparting her knowledge to others. Coincident with her arrival was an undergraduate summer school organised by David Shotter at Lancaster University, where a notable contingent of Italian archaeologists was assembling, including Tim Potter, Hugo Blake, John Wilkins and Ruth Whitehouse. The summer school proved a major success, and the School took it over as a core activity, under Amanda Claridge's direction. Many generations of undergraduates drew inspiration from her deep knowledge of the topography of the city and her understanding of its fabric.

Among the spin-offs of the Summer School was a new field project with a long future ahead of it. A visit to the presidential estate of Castelporziano on the coast just south of Ostia brought Amanda Claridge's attention to the extensive remains of Roman buildings, a peripheral Roman settlement called the Vicus Augustanus, now lost in the thick undergrowth of the woods of a former royal hunting park, and better known to wild boars than to scholars. Over the following years, in collaboration with the Superintendency of Ostia, survey of standing structures and trial trenches have cast a fascinating light on a more modest side of grandiose imperial urbanism.

The longest-standing complaint of the scholars appointed to run a research institution has been from the very start that they find themselves overwhelmed by administration. It

Amanda Claridge at the Arch of Septimius Severus.

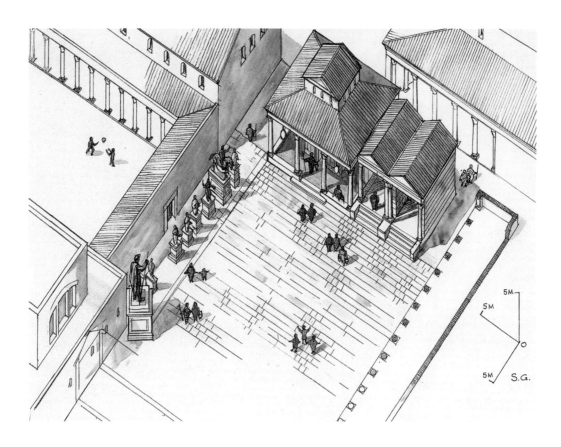

Reconstruction of the Forum at Vicus Augustanus by Sheila Gibson.

Castelporziano, general view of excavations.

is impossible to consult the serried ranks of files left in the Archive by past Directors and Assistant Directors without conceding that the problem is a formidable one. David Whitehouse's valedictory Annual Report observed that his years 'were marked by a notable increase in the burden of administration' thanks, among other factors, to the increasing complexity of Italian law and bureaucracy. Italian bureaucracy has always been a labyrinth; the real problems have always derived from an institution trying to do too much with too little resource and too few staff. Financial pressures resulting from inflation were compounded by a serious outbreak of fraud within the staff, halted thanks to the alertness of Tim Cornell.

But the worst blow was the confirmation of the intention of the 1851 Commission to discontinue their funding. The visit of HRH Prince Philip as President of the Commission in 1980 did nothing to deflect them from the view that, worthy though the activities of the School might be, they did not correspond to their own chartered purposes. Funding was cut back to the Architecture and Printmaking Scholarships, on the grounds that only these disciplines could learn from Italian design methods and practice and so benefit British industry. But stay of execution was granted from 1982 to 1986 to allow the School to pursue alternative funding. Equally serious, notice was given to leave the offices in 1 Lowther Gardens with effect from 1986.

As ever, in the darker days of the School's finances, hope was brought by the generos-

The visit of HRH Prince Philip with David Whitehouse and Demetrios Michaelides, 1980.

Presentation of Honorary Fellowships in 1983: (from left) David Whitehouse, Lucos Cozza, Tom Bridges (Ambassador), Paola Pelagatti, Dale Trendall, Adriano La Regina and Ferdinando Castagnoli.

ity of long-term supporters through their legacies. Molly Cotton's legacy much benefited the Camerone. Equally important, J.P.V.D. Balsdon on his death in 1977 left the School as heir to his Library and one third of his residual estate (amounting to £18,988, a sum which grew to ten times the value by 2000). Dacre Balsdon, Tutor in Ancient History at Exeter College, Oxford, was an assiduous visitor to the School in the post-war period. Famed as a wit and raconteur, and known to the wider public for his popular books on Roman history, on themes ranging from the Emperor Gaius (Caligula) to Roman Women, he served devotedly on the Faculty of Archaeology (1953-72), as its Chair (1959-63), and as member of the Executive Committee (1960-73), playing a significant role in the appeal for the Library Extension of 1962-63. The fund was used to create the Balsdon Fellowship, so adding to the provision of scholarships a position for a senior scholar (or indeed, for a period in the late eighties, a senior artist).

David Whitehouse is justly remembered for the excellent contacts he cultivated with his Italian colleagues. He both invited them to lecture at the School and participate in conferences, and himself frequently lectured in Italian institutions. A symbol of the importance he attached to these vital relationships was the revival of the institution of Honorary Fellowship, one originally invented (though vainly) as an expedient to offer a sop to the sacked Ashby and Strong. A ceremony in May 1983 marked the closeness of the School's ties with four Italian scholars, Lucos Cozza, Paola Pelagatti, Ferdinando Castagnoli and Adriano La Regina, together with a former member of its staff, Dale Trendall; and the friendships have long continued.

Even in its hardest years financially, the School has proved remarkably resilient. Scholars and visitors benefit, whatever the worries in Committee meetings back in London. For all the fluctuations, there are underlying continuities. Each generation of scholars pays tribute to the role of the domestic staff in keeping everything running with seeming effortlessness and in creating a welcoming environment. Bruno Bonelli's retirement in 1972 marked the passing of an epoch – a service of 50 years since his initial appointment by Ashby. Yet the tradition of devoted service was continued in the appointment of Tommaso Astolfi as his successor, and the line-up of staff at the visit of the Duke of Edinburgh in 1980 shows the same team as nearly twenty years later. One figure in the

HRH the Duke of Edinburgh meets the staff:
(from left) Raffaele Veronesi, Peppino Parente,
Tommaso Astolfi, Rino Ramazzotti, Giuseppe
Fioranelli, Antonietta Scaccia, Anna Argeni.

(above) Anna Argeni.
(above reght) Anna Fazzari.
(right) Luciana Valentini with Lucos Cozza.

background, that of Anna Argeni, represents another symbol of continuity and devotion: maid to the Ward-Perkins family from 1946, she lived on in the School long after her retirement, until her death in 1994, loved by the students even as they feared her rebukes for rowdy talking in the cortile on summer nights. Continuity was also represented by Anna Fazzari who started at the School as Assistant Librarian in 1946, going on to become the elegant and efficient School Secretary until 1976. Another vital figure who spanned these years, indeed the two decades covered by the chapter, was Luciana Valentini, who as Librarian from 1973 to 1989 was the School's first, and much respected, full-time Librarian, releasing the Assistant Director from what had become too large a responsibility.

When David Whitehouse left at the end of January 1984 to take up his new appointment as Director of the Corning Museum of Glass, the fort was held for the next six months by Donald Bullough, Professor of Medieval History at the University of St Andrews, and a central figure in the School's committees through his service on the Faculty of Archaeology (1966-83), especially as its Chair (1975-78) and on the Executive Committee (1975-95). An expert on the age of Charlemagne, he followed a Director who had excavated one major Carolingian Abbey at Farfa, and was followed (if at an interval) by one who excavated another (at San Vincenzo). Bullough was deeply involved in a whole series of major questions the Committees in London had been agonising over, like the reform of the School's constitution consequent on the withdrawal of 1851 Commission support and the proper administrative structure for the School, so that his brief tenure resulted in a better-informed view in London. Warm appreciation was expressed in the Annual Report:[4]

> 'His energetic and punctilious stewardship has been important and influential at a transitional moment in the School's affairs; and his period of office was a happy one for the students, artists and academics, in the School at the time. Aided by the Assistant Director, Amanda Claridge, he turned what could have been a moment of weakness in the succession of Directors to one of strength.'

GRAEME BARKER (1984-88)

The choice of Graeme Barker as successor gave a welcome prominence to prehistory at a critical moment. Since Eric Peet's and Thomas Ashby's work in Sardinia and Malta, the importance of the prehistoric period in the School's range of archaeological activities had at least been acknowledged. The South Etruria project too, concerned as it was to read the transformation of landscapes from the prehistoric to the medieval periods, had acknowledged its importance, and Tim Potter's excavations at Narce (for which Barker studied the faunal remains) explored a site most active in the Bronze Age and Iron Age. But it is one thing for classical archaeologists to take an interest in the earlier period on the horizon of their own, another for a mainstream prehistorian immersed in the theoretical and methodological debates of the discipline to set the agenda. Prehistory was by now where the new thinking in scientific archaeology was coming from; and though Barker started as a classicist and held the Rome Scholarship in Classical Studies (1969),

HRH Princess Alexandra with Graeme Barker and Amanda Claridge, 1987.

as a member of the Department of Prehistory and Archaeology at Sheffield, he came with the perspective of one of the key centres of the 'new archaeology'.

Barker had already established a reputation for innovative work in Italy, particularly through the Sheffield project in the Biferno valley in the Molise. In one sense this continued the Ward-Perkins tradition of landscape survey; but it asked different questions about environmental history, and had a particular focus on long-term landscape change from prehistoric times to the present day, for example on the relative effects of people or climate on erosional trends in the valley. Equally, his ambitious project in Libya in collaboration with Barri Jones for the Unesco Libyan Valleys Survey, while returning to an old BSR stamping ground, did so in the context of scientific and environmentalist approaches. He was also involved in a project in central Tuscany around the deserted medieval village of Montarrenti, in collaboration with Riccardo Francovich at Siena.

Barker was able to re-energise the School's long tradition of landscape archaeology with a focus on long-term process, human use of the environment and subsistence economies. He launched a number of new projects: most important a field-survey (jointly with Tom Rasmussen at Manchester) around Tuscania in northern Lazio, where the School had already undertaken a number of important excavations. If the idea of reading changing patterns of settlement from the scatter of pottery that rises to the surface with ploughing was familiar, his insistence on systematic sampling gave the survey a more sci-

Field survey around Tuscania.

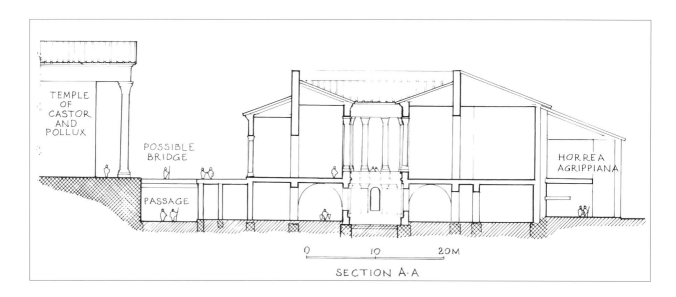

Santa Maria Antiqua: conjectured reconstruction of the Caligulan atrium by Shiela Gibson.

entific aspect. On a smaller scale, he investigated the difficult archaeology of upland settlement in the Cicolano mountains above Rieti, using ethno-archaeological studies of the 'archaeological signatures' left by the present-day farmers and transhumant shepherds using the mountains on a seasonal basis to help understand the evidence of ancient settlement found by his archaeological survey.

The focus on Landscape Archaeology led to a notably successful conference organised with John Lloyd in 1988 on Roman Landscapes that brought together an international team of survey archaeologists working throughout the Mediterranean. Bringing together together British, Dutch, French, Italians, Spanish, and North American scholars, it led to a significant publication (*Roman Landscapes: Archaeological Survey in the Mediterranean*

Region, 1991), and pointed the way to the later and more ambitious Populus project and its five volume publication.[5]

The School was equally active in supporting a range of important projects by UK archaeologists, like the study of the settlement of the Gubbio basin by Simon Stoddart and Caroline Malone, Tim Potter's new South Etruria project at the Mola di Monte Gelato, John Moreland's survey of the land round Farfa, and John Lloyd's survey of the Sangro Valley. In Rome itself, the School was able to participate in the major reassessment of the Forum Romanum launched by Adriano La Regina as Superintendent thanks to Henry Hurst's excavations within the church of Santa Maria Antiqua – by one of those almost irrational continuities that mark the School's history, this was the very church which was the object of the first study by the first Director published in the first volume of the *Papers,* though this time it was the Domitianic brick and concrete building, not its early medieval successor, that was the focus of interest.

The nerve centre of this archaeological activity was the Camerone. Molly Cotton's legacy allowed its extensive refitting, and subdivision by partitions into activity-specific areas (though the name of 'the Big Room' was too historical to drop). The new archaeological laboratory allowed not only traditional study of ceramics, but minute examination of the fabrics of pottery through 'thin-sectioning', and study of biological and environmental remains with the assistance of the bone and seed collections. Investment in the Camerone also symbolized a commitment to post-excavation study. The work thrown up by a dig in terms of studying finds is no less than the digging itself, and is the most common reason why excavations are only published long after the event. The re-equipped Camerone assisted in a programme of clearing some of the School's formidable backlog of publication, starting with the excavations at Otranto by Whitehouse and Michaelides, co-ordinated by David Wilkinson,[6] and going on to the South Etrurian sites of Santa Cornelia, Santa Rufina and San Liberato, taken on by Neil Christie.[7] The new series of Archaeological Monographs that came to flourish under Richard Hodges comes out of the desire to clear a backlog, and to gather the fruit of crops long sown.

If Barker's central contribution was as a committed archaeologist, he was not negligent of other aspects of the

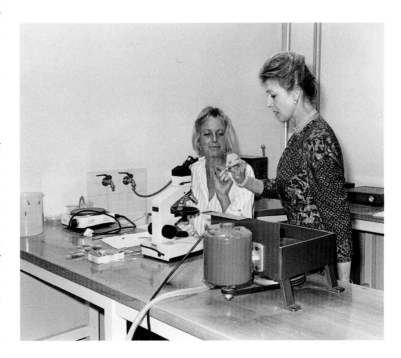

Helen Patterson shows HRH Princess Alexandra the newly acquired thin-sectioning machine in the re-equipped archaeological workshop, 1987.

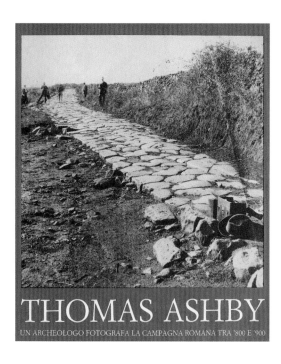

Cover of the Ashby *Campagna* volume.

School's diverse activity. His first Annual Report logs over 70 social events in the first nine months, and notes a threefold increase in the number of visitors to the School, bringing the total to 371. Behind these statistics is the hard slog of the administration of the institution. Barker was also the first to grasp the importance of giving the School's artistic activity greater prominence, raising the profile of the resident artists, and collaborating with the British Council over high-profile visitors like Gilbert and George. Here lay the seeds of the future Gallery programme. There were several lectures by distinguished academics that attracted considerable crowds, notably one by Moses Finley shortly before his death. Barker also launched in 1986 the first exhibition of Ashby photographs of the Roman Campagna (*Thomas Ashby: un archeologo fotografa la Campagna Romana*), the first fruit of Valerie Scott's work in the Archive, and of her determination to awake the School to its wealth and importance.

But while the School buzzed with activity, the London committees grappled with the implications of change. The blow of partial withdrawal of 1851 Commission funding was greatly softened by the success of the British Academy in persuading the Department of Education and Science to increase the level of funding. The annual grant was raised to £500,000 in 1987, and the Secretary of the Academy since 1983, Peter Brown, was duly thanked. Oddly enough, the major implications of the divorce from the 1851 Commission were not financial. The biggest crisis was caused by the need to find new office space from October 1986; only at the last minute after much searching was a new home found in Regent's College (the former Bedford College), and that significantly less spacious than the premises at 1 Lowther Gardens from which the School had been so watchfully run since 1912. The move took place on 27 October 1986, during a thunderstorm, as the minutes recorded portentously.[8] There was a problem of staff, since the School's secretariat had simply been identical with that of the Commission, and now new personnel had to be found, bidding sad farewell to Anthony James, the successor of Evelyn Shaw and Digby Sturch, and Kathleen Stedman, the successor of Stanley Quick and a series a loyal secretaries.

Above all there was the problem of the accumulated effects of three quarters of a century. The administrative archive, in immaculately ordered and labelled filing boxes, had to be housed. But there was also the matter of a major collection of works of art. Evelyn Shaw had been insistent on his scholars leaving their work in the School's office, and others had gradually added to the collection, like the families of the architect Harold Chalton Bradshaw and of the architect Lord Holford and his painter wife Marjorie Brooks. A magnificent series of architectural drawings, many of them reconstructions of

Roman buildings published in the *Papers*, included 81 items in heavy oak frames, which were consigned in 1985 to the RIBA. The decision was taken to sell the paintings and sculptures, and they were auctioned by Sotheby's in October 1987. By cruel chance, the date of the auction was two days after the collapse of the market on 'Black Monday', and only £45,372 was realised. The Fine Arts Faculty was hoping to use the proceeds to build a new studio in place of the garage; in the event, refurbishment of the existing studios was to prove more urgent. In its haste to sell off its family silver, the School omitted to keep an inventory, let alone a photographic record, of the works disposed of, and a significant chapter of the history of British art between the wars was dispersed.

The move from Lowther Gardens also triggered constitutional reform. The whole system of Council, Executive Committee and Faculties had been set up by Evelyn Shaw as a result of the negotiations of 1910-12. The system was designed to present a public front of support by the Establishment in its serried ranks, with over a hundred scholars, artists, representatives of learned societies and institutions, serving on committees, but the reality of power concentrated in Lowther Gardens. The system was regarded by the British Academy (with considerable justice) as grossly overweight, and as failing to provide unambiguous lines of authority. An interim reform was carried out in 1986, by which the four Art Faculties, of Painting, Sculpture, Printmaking and Architecture, were replaced by a single Faculty of Fine Arts (which was indeed what Shaw had originally proposed), though the separate selection panels for each discipline survived. At the same time, Council, which till then had played a purely formal role, became the real source of authority, while the Executive Committee had its role reduced to that of a Finance and General Purposes Committee. Of course, that implied a change to the Charter, and discussions started over the wording of a new Charter. In the event, it was not finally brought before Privy Council until 1995, by which time the reforming genius of Roddy Cavaliero had intervened.

Presentation of Honorary Fellowships to Fausto Zevi and Maria Luisa Veloccia Rinaldi by Ambassador Sir Derek Thomas.

RICHARD HODGES (1988-95)

As Graeme Barker left for a chair of Archaeology at the University of Leicester, another recruit was found from the same power-centre of Sheffield. Richard Hodges had already been active in Italian archaeology since the 1970s with a project in Molise, initially part of the work of the Sheffield team with Graeme Barker and John Lloyd in the Biferno Valley. The medieval settlement in the region, and specifically the spread of fortified strongholds or 'incastellamento', had already been studied by Chris Wickham, a theme to which Riccardo Francovich was also making vital contributions. The invitation of the Superintendent for Molise, Bruno D'Agostino, took Hodges to the stunning site of San Vincenzo at the source of the Volturno river. Between 1980 and 1986 a series of campaigns revealed the spectacular complex around the crypt church built in the ninth century by Abbot Epiphanius and decorated with an outstanding fresco cycle.

The conspicuous success of the excavations at San Vincenzo, which as Director he was able to pursue with more sustained vigour, and much more substantial resources deriving from a regional grant, mean that for many in Italy the name of Hodges (and indeed of the School) will remain closely associated with this site. Between 1989 and 1998 excavations brought to light the vast abbey-church of San Vincenzo Maggiore built by Abbot Joshua from AD 808, its dimensions exceeding those of Farfa or Monte Cassino, and almost reaching those of Old St Peter's in Rome. Despite the Arab sack of 881 (vividly tes-

Richard Hodges and Don Angelo Pantoni at the excavations of San Vincenzo al Volturno.

tified by layers of burning and Saracen arrowheads) and complete demolition in the twelfth century, rich remains were found buried in the workshops with glass kilns, and then of the beautifully frescoed annular crypt modelled on St Peter's.

With the support of substantial funding from the European Union aimed at the creation of an archaeological park, the School was able for the first time to develop a major excavation project on a scale to capture international attention. This idyllic but forgotten backwater deep in the Molise emerged as one of the most imposing centres of Carolingian Europe. Around the project grew a team of highly professional archaeologists, based on the Camerone, who were able to pursue many other projects in addition which raised their own funds: Cathy Coutts, Sally Martin, Andrew Hanasz, Oliver Gilkes and Federico Marazzi were only the nucleus, with numerous other specialists contributing, especially Sheila Gibson for architectural reconstruction, Helen Patterson on the pottery, Gill Clark on the bones, Martine Newby on the glass, and Sally Cann for drawings. The team was able to take on sites in Rome (at the British Embassy at Porta Pia, and at the gates of the American Academy on the Gianicolo), on Elba (iron-working near the hermitage of Santa Caterina), Sutri (a cemetery at Prati di San Martino), as well as returning to earlier School projects at Farfa and Gravina di Puglia. The success of the team was capped by a new project at Butrint in Albania, a location of such stunning beauty as to dim even San Vincenzo,

Perspective reconstruction of the Monastery of San Vincenzo al Volturno by Sheila Gibson.

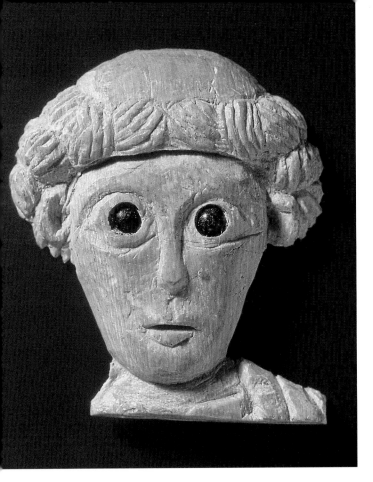

Ivory monk's head with glass eyes, ninth century.

Fragmentary fresco face.

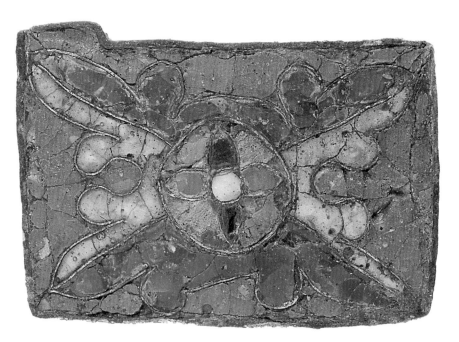

Cloisonné enamel,
ninth century.

though too far from Rome to remain under the School's control.

This scale of fieldwork reached a level to which the School at Rome, with its tradition of landscape survey, had not previously aspired, though one more familiar to the Athens School with Sir Arthur Evans' work at Knossos. It arose not from the chance of being at the right place at the right time, but from the conscious desire to raise the public profile of the institution. The crisis of 1986 and the departure from under the wing of the 1851 Commission had brought new thinking to the institution: it must look beyond its usual sources to raise the level of funding necessary to fulfil its ambitions. To this challenge, Richard Hodges brought an energy and dynamism that marks him apart from most Directors. He understood, embraced and fully achieved the challenge of raising external funding at a level to match the core grant from the British Academy:

'We saw obvious advantages in this strategy. By undertaking sponsored activities we hugely enlarged the prominence of the School. And an activity-led strategy offered the only means of generating sizeable Appeal monies in order to undertake the capital works which had hitherto been deferred because of the lack of an endowment. As a result, the School in recent times has pursued two parallel paths. First, we have embarked upon a programme to modernize and refurbish the School, directed by the School's architects. Second, we have staged a great range of activities: large-scale archaeological excavations funded by sponsors; a new arts programme based around a gallery that we created in 1990, the steady ordering of the archives, and constant events in both academic and public fields.' (Annual Report 1994-95, p.5).

Excavation of annular crypt of San Vincenzo Maggiore.

The logic of the strategy is clear: since the government grant alone cannot sustain both the fabric of the School building and the full range of its activities, the institution must engage in activities conspicuous enough not only to justify its grant, but to attract external sponsorship. The more sponsorship you attract, the more funds can be achieved, and the more conspicuous the consequent activities are, the more funds can then be attracted. The ball was set rolling by Graeme Barker, but the energy of Richard Hodges allowed a quantum leap from which the benefits are still felt. The Appeal was initially launched in 1990 by Sir Alan Campbell, former Ambassador to Rome, one of a distinguished line going back to Rennell Rodd who have served the School notably; the torch was taken on in 1992 by Caroline Egerton, wife of

HRH the Prince of Wales with Lady Egerton, 1994.

Campbell's successor Sir Stephen Egerton, and the most talented and successful fundraiser from whom the School has ever benefited. The initial target of two million pounds was not met until 1999, and the slog was long and hard; but the more the pace of activity gathered, the more realisable the School's ambitions became.

The fabric of the building desperately required attention, as became clear when a former Architecture Scholar, Robert Adam, paid a visit and produced a comprehensive report on its condition. The first urgent need was to restore the façade, the original and most expensive element in the School's construction, which was by now dismal and crumbling. With the vital support of Robert Jackson, who as Undersecretary of State for Higher Education appreciated the need for extraordinary funds, a refurbishment was carried out in 1994. Plans for more ambitious additions to the building had to be set aside as critical health and safety issues emerged in the studios, and in the entire wiring system. It was to take until 1998 to sort out these basic problems, but the funds would never have come in without the programme of activities.

The public activity by which the School most claimed attention, alongside that of the archaeology programme, lay in lectures, conferences and exhibitions. Lectures by speakers of the calibre of Richard Rogers, David Chipperfield, Colin Renfrew, Barry Cunliffe, Joseph Rykwert and Michael Foot attracted packed audiences, while a series of conferences like Oswyn Murray's *In Vino Veritas* made the School a notable centre of academic exchange. There were also musical events, like the avante garde group Bow Gamelan who combined welding percussion and fireworks in their performance on the front steps (1991), or the Durutti Column concert against the backdrop of the projection of a slide by printmaker Michael MacDonough, *Delicatessen*, which dramatically transformed Lutyens' façade (1992).

A key role was played by the Gallery programme. In 1988 Hodges appointed Rome based American artist Susan Kammerer as Arts Liaison Consultant, with Vesna Hardy (wife of Malcolm Hardy, then Arts Officer at the British Council in Rome) looking after the press contacts. This aimed to give the resident artists and architects a higher profile within the Rome arts scene in a period in which the city was centre to important art movements such as Neo-Expressionism and the Transavantgarde. Their advice led to an exceptionally successful and well-attended Mostra (Annual Show).

In 1990 Marina Engel became the School's Arts Adviser supported by Jacopo Benci as Technical Assistant (though his support to the artists went much further). She brought to the post the experience she had acquired working as curator for commercial and non-profit art venues. Her new Gallery programme opened on 22 November 1991, with an exhibition and lecture by Art & Language, followed in tight succession by Helen Chadwick, Howard Hodgkin, Anthony Gormley, Michael Craig-Martin and Hamish Fulton. Later years were to see Rachel Whiteread showing before her award of the Turner Prize, Mona Hatoum carpeting the Gallery with translucent marbles, and Bridget Riley display the colourful geometry of her abstractions. Over a decade and under three Curators (Engel, Alison Jacques in 1996-97, and Cristiana Perrella from 1998 onwards). The Gallery shows and lectures have

Michael MacDonough, *Delicatessen* projected on BSR façade, 1992.

Anthony Gormley, *Learning to Think* exhibited in BSR Gallery 1992.

Rachel Whiteread, *Untitled (floor)* exhibited in BSR Gallery 1995.

reflected recent developments in contemporary British art, thus stirring interest in the Roman public, and the resident artists undoubtedly benefited from this interest.

The Art programme thus demonstrated an entirely new way in which the wedding of Fine Arts and Archaeology that had first taken place in 1912 could benefit the School, though it was no more than a modern transformation of Rodd's perception that the School could only grow stronger by uniting diverse cultural activities under a single roof. The energy of the School flows from the continuous dialogue between the traditional and the contemporary. If archaeologists and historians may risk becoming cut off from the present by their concern with the past, the confrontation in Rome with artists at the cutting edge of questioning the contemporary world is refreshing and inspiring; and if contemporary artists fall under the suspicion of throwing away too easily the wisdom of the past, in Rome they find enthusiasts for the past who can re-engage their interest. There is no contradiction in a School that on one hand puts on shows of conceptual art and video, and on the other organizes exhibitions of photographs a century old. The School neither embraces traditionalism nor modernism: it creates a forum in which the two can meet in fruitful dialogue.

Part of that dialogue was the School's rediscovery of its own history. The way was pointed by the Ashby Campagna Romana exhibition in 1986, to be followed by others on Ashby's Rome in 1989[9] and Ashby's Lazio in 1994.[10] But a major new impulse was brought to the Archive by the final closing of the London Office in Regent's Park in 1991 and the transfer of the administrative archive to Rome. United at last with the archives of the Ashby and Strong collections, the richness and coherence of the archive began to emerge. Architecture Scholar Hugh Petter was able to draw on this archive in 1992 for his book, *Lutyens in Italy*, which told for the first time the detailed story of the building of the School. Richard Hodges himself became interested in the story of Ashby, and the Archive allowed him to reconstruct a vivid biography. Contact in 1992 from the nephew of Winifred

LUTYENS IN ITALY

The building of the British School at Rome
Hugh Petter

Hugh Petter's book on Lutyens.

Knights, Martin Palmer, led to collaboration with Paul Liss and Peyton Skipwith in a memorable exhibition of the work of this most attractive of the School's early artists, and so later to an exhibition of her husband Tom Monnington. To re-examine your roots is not to bury yourself in the past: it has helped to liberate the institution and give it a new self-image and self-understanding.

The relationship with the past and tradition is a theme that also was of deep concern to the Prince of Wales. The Summer School of the Prince of Wales Institute of Architecture was hosted by the School in August 1991 before going on to Viterbo, thanks to the involvement of Robert Adam in the Institute. In the following September, the Prince came in person to open the exhibition of James Hakewill drawings from the School's collection, *The Twilight of the Grand Tour*.[11] Richard Hodges went on in 1995 both to run the Institute of World Archaeology at the University of East Anglia, continuing to run the Butrint project, and to be Director of the Prince of Wales Institute.

HRH The Prince of Wales with Richard Hodges.

THE ARTIST SCHOLARS
1913-1939

THE ARTIST SCHOLARS
(1913-1939)

by Alistair Crawford

*'I have never imagined
a more beautiful place,
it hardly seems real'*

PERHAPS IT IS THE WEIGHT of history that is Rome that lies just outside the door of the British School that makes each year of art scholars seek out their predecessors. Or maybe it is the uniqueness of the building itself, an oasis in the sun, so complete as if there was nothing outside that door. Just as all who visit are drawn to the legacy of Thomas Ashby, the artists inevitably seem to be drawn to the beginnings, to the first twenty years or so, as if those early artists had got it right, laid down the rules of engagement that, if adopted, would make their time spent here equally productive. Today we can see more clearly their unique contribution to art, perhaps the most significant was their invention of a distinct period of British Art situated in Italy. They became the inspiration and the aspiration. Visit the school today and you may well find their hero, Piero della Francesca, still walking the corridors.

The School grew out of the tradition of the Grand Tour, and you could argue that it was founded at the end of it. Yet most British artists continue to want to visit Italy as a rite of passage. In the eighteenth/nineteenth centuries artists frequently came and stayed for years and years, selling their wares to the annual migrants from the north. Artists, in spite of constant denial, are highly influenced. All art is based on art, but influences simply attach themselves, they cannot be prescribed by a curriculum. The story of the art scholars, from the first in 1913 to the last before the closure on the declaration of war with Italy in 1939 is a noble yet curious one. As you would expect from such an establishment institution (one taken over in 1911 by the very heart of the empire) the scholars who passed through its doors did go on to contribute to society, to art, some with much distinction, almost all as teachers of artists and many became influential principals of art schools. References in the press repeatedly recognised the product as well made, conservative, certainly never controversial nor too modern. The real success, clearer now with the passage of time, was that some artists consistently managed to make their own way against the tide.

(above and previous)
Thomas Monnington,
Piediluco.

COLIN GILL (1893-1938)

(right) Colin Gill's studio, 1920.

(below) Allegory (1920-21).

Inaugural Rome Scholar in Decorative Painting in 1913. The tenure of his Scholarship was interrupted by the First World War, when he was sent to France in 1915, from which he was invalided home in 1918, having just obtained the rank of captain. He completed his tenure in 1919-21. The photograph shows Gill's studio in 1920, when he was working on *Allegory*, but at a phase before he inserted Winifred Knights into the composition (standing figure with birdcage to left). Note too that mezzanines had not yet been inserted into the studios. He was praised by the Faculty of Painting for his 'eminently scholarly faculty'.

Gill maintained his fondness for the School, and a year before he died in 1938, he visited Italy again, staying at the School.

The British are nervous of artists and much prefer to support less controversial projects such as buildings. That a British institution set up abroad originally for the study of history, letters and archaeology would wish to welcome artists is unique. In that it still provides artists' scholarships today is something of a little miracle and, it has to be said, the result of a few self-sacrificing individuals. Artists were included in the plan of 1899 but it took until the reorganisation in 1911 when the 1851 Commission took control to provide the fine art scholarships. No doubt the original plan envisaged that the Royal Academy Gold Medal Travelling Scholarship to Rome, founded in 1771, would transfer from its host, the British Academy of Arts in Rome, to the new School, but the RA was never to

provide financial support.

The British Academy in Rome grew out of Joshua Reynolds' visit in 1752 when an 'English group' was formed for the benefit of visiting artists. It became associated with the formation of the Royal Academy in 1768. With the patronage of George IV, it gained formal status in 1823, largely brought about by Keats' friend Joseph Severn. The 1820s to 40s were to be its most influential period. Unlike the French Academy, it never obtained adequate funds, nor did it succeed in becoming incorporated into the Royal Academy. With a small collection, cast room and library, by the time of the foundation of the British School, it had became essentially a life class at 53b Via Margutta. In 1912 the Academy amalgamated with the School but soon after members voted to annul the agreement. Since they had no money, their unofficial re-emergence was ignored by the 1851 Commission and eventually the agreement was revoked in 1929. In 1936 the Academy was 'suspended indefinitely' in the face of persecution from Mussolini's black shirts and all its records and acquisitions 'lost'.

It is inconceivable today with our modularised and regulated factory outputs from our universities for an institution to set up three Faculties, Painting, Sculpture, and Printmaking, consisting of around 30 distinguished artists of the calibre of George Clausen and John Singer Sargent to look

after the interests of a mere *three* new scholars per year, a maximum of nine students. If it may be thought a scholarship lasting three years abroad for a few promising artists is excessive if not actually counterproductive, add to that anything from three to six years prior 'apprenticeship' at an art school, no wonder they could all draw well. The aspiration was the long established and well endowed French Academy at the Villa Medici with its *Prix de Rome*, a title soon used unofficially by British commentators (and recipients) for the BSR 'scholarships'. That such provision could be made for so few; there were only 56 awards from 1913-38. The School was set up with imagination and vigour but in true British tradition with virtually no money. Eugénie Strong as Assistant Director was paid a miserly £100 (it rose to £125), less, even before the deduction of living-in expenses, than a scholar's annual grant of £200 (it rose to £250). The first scholar, Colin Gill (1892-1940), cousin of Eric, arrived in 1913 when the new building was still not ready, then the First World War intervened (he left for service). The next did not come until 1919, then the School closed in 1935 when students were sent elsewhere and closed again in 1936-37 with 1938 as the last cohort until after the war in 1947.

We are also looking at a history of our own attitudes and moralities, for example, the slow decline of misogyny: firstly no women scholars, then special segregated quarters for the first female student, Winifred Knights, in 1920, and finally the arrival of the inconceivable marital bed

ALFRED FRANK HARDIMAN RA (1891-1949)

Alfred Hardiman's studio in 1920.

Hardiman studied sculpture at the Royal College of Art and then at the Royal Academy Schools, and won the 1920 Rome Scholarship in Sculpture. Hardiman brought his wife, Violet, out with him to Rome, but they were required to live out. However, Hardiman's wife settled in very easily and was employed as Secretary in 1923, so giving her a room in the School. Thanks to his wife's job, Hardiman spent a fourth year at the School, in order to complete his seven-foot bronze figure of "Peace". After the completion of his tenure the Faculty of Sculpture felt that he had 'more than fulfilled the promise displayed in his earlier work.' Indeed, he went on to be commissioned for work in St James', Piccadilly, a portrait head of Cecil Rhodes, for Rhodes House, Oxford, and a controversial Memorial to Earl Haig in Whitehall. Hardiman was Hon. Secretary of the Faculty of Sculpture since 1925 and a member from 1929 until his death in 1949.

WINIFRED KNIGHTS (1899-1947)

(above) Winifred Knights' studio in 1920.

(right) Marriage at Cana (1923) by Winifred Knights. Rome Scholar in Painting 1920-23, Knights studied at the Slade School of Fine Art, winning the scholarship to Rome by her painting 'The Deluge'. During her scholarship, she painted 'The Marriage at Cana', set in the Borghese Gardens. It was later presented by the British School to the National Gallery of New Zealand. In 1922 Knights met Thomas Monnington, who was himself just embarking on the first year of his Rome Scholarship in Painting. They were married in 1924 at the British Consulate in Rome. Knights maintained her close relationship with the British School at Rome by joining its Faculty of Painting in 1933, a relationship which was ended by her untimely death in 1947. After her death the Faculty of Painting wrote of Miss Knights (Faculty of Painting Report 1949, p.16): 'The works she produced during and since her Scholarship were few in number, but of exquisite quality, and the exceptional beauty of her drawings has placed her among the outstanding artists of her generation. The School has lost in her a remarkable personality and a devoted friend.'

(See *Winifred Knights 1899-1947*, published by the Fine Art Society and Paul Liss in association with the British School at Rome (1995).)

THOMAS MONNINGTON, PRA (1902-76)

(above) Allegory (1924-26).

(right) Sketch for *Allegory.*

Rome Scholar in Painting 1922-25. A pupil of Henry Tonks at the Slade, the Faculty had doubts about his quality, and at first awarded only a probationary scholarship, confirmed in 1924. He married Winifred Knights during his tenure: she appears in many of his studies, including the figure to the right in *Allegory.* The setting of the painting is Piediluco in Umbria where they spent their honeymoon in summer 1924. After his return from Rome became member of the Faculty of Painting, becoming Chairman from 1948-67; also a member of the Executive Committee from 1945-72. In 1966 he was elected President of the Royal Academy.

(See *Sir Thomas Monnington 1902-1976*, exhibition catalogue published by the Fine Art Society and Paul Liss in association with the British School at Rome (1997).)

(the word partner was still an economic term) on the Directorship of Ashmole in 1925, who had the bravery to argue against Lord Esher who demanded that there should be 'no wives!' The atmosphere in those early years, under A.H. Smith, was more akin to a library, nay a monastery, where students were not encouraged to be heard or seen. Even at breakfast and lunch when they had to eat their food propped up on the armrests of the spread out armchairs, or when compulsorily dressed for dinner, conversation was often at a minimum, once likened to the squeaking of mice.

To get the prize of Rome, applicants had to submit to a rigorous examination process inconceivable to the BritArt pack of today, with two shortlists and the making of an exam-

ROMA · MCMXXIV

ROBIN SARGENT AUSTIN RA (1885-1973)

Ss Carlo & Giacomo.

Rome Scholar in Engraving 1922-25. Graduate of RCA. He married Ada Harrison, Gilchrist Student 1922-23, who worked on the Academies of Rome. Member & Hon Secretary of Faculty of Engraving 1926-51; Fellow of the Royal Society of Painters, Etchers & Engravers; he was lecturer then Professor of Engraving at RCA.

DAVID EVANS (1874-1959)

(above) David Evans' studio.

(right) David Evans (1923).

Rome Scholar in Sculpture 1923-26. After his first year at the British School Ashby wrote of him: '...Mr. D. Evans has produced a good deal of small work and numerous drawings, and his results, considering the short time he has been here, promise well for the future'. He produced portrait busts of Thomas Ashby, Eugénie Strong, Dorothy Ashmole and Winifred Knights, but his studio reveals him working successfully on bas-reliefs. Evans continued producing portraiture after his time in Rome. His commissions included such people as Sir Hugh Walpole, Sir Arthur Evans and John Galsworthy. On his death in 1959, his widow recalled: 'Our memories of our years in Rome are very sweet and pleasant'.

ination piece. In order to continue each year, they had to submit to more examinations, pass the scrutiny of the distinguished board of artists and obtain the crucial character reference from the Director; behaviour was thus wonderfully controlled. Even Winifred Knights with whom everyone was in love, administrators included, was reprimanded for leaving Rome and visiting the Abruzzi without permission which had to be obtained from London. Some scholarships were not renewed, some not appointed, some left rather quickly, some managed to charm Evelyn Shaw to permit them to visit Spain instead. The debate, which still continues down to the present day was always the same: should the artists be supervised, taught even. But other than the infrequent provision of short visits from faculty artists, no teaching or even an encouraging appointment was ever made. To date, in a hundred years no Director or Assistant Director has ever been an artist. Eugénie Strong did provide lectures on art history, but her advocacy of the Baroque would not have gone down well. After 1925 there was nothing. The artists, provided they behaved themselves, were left to their own devices. Nevertheless some artists, like other scholars, were inspired for the rest of their lives by both Ashby and Strong. For example, Alan Sorrell, Painting Scholar in 1928, who became a leading exponent of archaeological reconstructions, originally commenced in 1936

JOHN SKEAPING RA (1901-1980)

(above) Portrait of Barbara Hepworth.

(right) Self portrait.

Gold Medallist of the Royal Academy Schools (1919-21), he held the Rome Scholarship in Sculpture 1924-27, returning six months early because of ill health. Single when appointed to his scholarship, he met Barbara Hepworth in Rome (having missed the Rome Scholarship, she held a travelling scholarship from the West Riding), and they married in Florence in the summer of 1925, moving into the School thanks to Ashmole's liberal policy. Later he became Professor of Sculpture at the RCA (1953-9).

for the *Illustrated London News*. His dramatic reconstruction, *Caerwent, Gwent. A bird's eye view of a Roman Town* (1937) can almost be seen as a homage to Ashby's earliest excavations. Today Sorrell is regarded as an influential Neo-Romantic painter.

There was a social purpose to the intention of sending artists to Rome, which explained the interest of the 1851 Commission, that of the 'Monumental Art,' of mural decoration, which would enhance buildings back home. It was propagated in particular at the RA by John Singer Sargent and Edwin Austin Abbey who worked together on the murals for the Boston Library. Abbey's legacy, after his death in 1911, was to become a key source of support for painting in later years. Thomas Monnington, scholar in 1922 (later President of the RA), became their finest exponent, but the notion did not really succeed because the world changed in the meantime. The primary subjects were Architecture, Sculpture and *Decorative* Painting, the latter two being mere enhancements for the mother of all arts, the space that contains, that is, Architecture (for which there was a scholarship from 1907 onwards). Henry Tonks of the Slade believed that painting directly onto walls was the only real way for a painter to perform - but unfortunately the mural paintings on the corridor walls were always covered over for the next lot. The assumption was that the tradition would prevail; that you had to learn your craft, be able to draw using Renaissance formulas and techniques, that teaching was derived from a history rooted in the classics and training in the copying and imitation of art works. All students were monitored as if they were children in care and all problems solved, other than the inadequacy of the heating and too little to eat. Artists have always been a liberal lot, their values strange when set against the average, and in this environment, with its emphasis on academics (whom the artists regarded as parasites feeding on the bones of practitioners), with its rules and regulations, the artists had to bend, no wonder some snapped.

It is wrong for any selection process to pretend to itself that it can recognise the 'best': a selection panel can only ever select others like itself. The rigorous selection by the panels reflected the politics of the art school establishment: of 61 offers of scholarships, 53%

EDWARD IRVINE HALLIDAY (1902-84)

Gulliver's Travels (self portrait).

Rome Scholar in Painting 1925-28. George Clausen judged him 'evidently a man of exceptional ability; he knows what he wants and is making the best use of his time'. After his time in Rome Halliday returned to Britain and painted three mural panels on the subject of the Greek goddess Athena for the Athenaeum Club Library in Liverpool. He became a notable society portrait painter, particularly of the Royal family (Princess Elizabeth in 1948; Prince Philip in 1949; many paintings of Queen Elizabeth, he also painted the Queen Mother and Prince of Wales). He was appointed C.B.E. in 1973.

went to the Royal College of Art, 15% to the Slade, 13% to the Royal Academy School and a mere 11% to the entire rest of the nation, where no doubt departments did not bother to advise their students to apply. The composition of the Faculties was profoundly connected to the RCA and, to a lesser extent, to the Slade; to others hardly at all. Highly influential in front and behind the scenes was William Rothenstein, principal of the RCA. The 'best' meant, in effect, *their* best students. The original memorandum, 'free from sectional control' was conveniently ignored.

Sculpture seems to have fared worse than the enthusiasm for 'decorative painting' for its faculty was heavy with what, alas, was to become the war memorial variety, Derwent Wood, George

ALAN SORRELL (1904-74)

Self-portrait.

Rome Scholar in Painting 1928-30, Sorrell earned the approval of A.H. Smith. 'He has, I think, made much progress during his two years in Rome, and his conduct as a member of the School has been excellent' (Smith, 26.6.1930). 'I think he is undoubtedly interested in Italy, and profiting by his Scholarship' (Smith, 14.6.1929).

Sorrell's own views of Smith were very much less warm (Alan Sorrell, *Barbarians in Rome* (unpublished typescript), quoted in Wiseman, *Short History*, p.16). He became a distinguished exponent of perspectivist archaeological reconstructions.

Frampton, and later the greatest exponent, Charles Jagger, who never made his scholarship to Rome. While the tradition of clay modelling of the figure held supreme, the scholars are best remembered now for the impact of John Skeaping (1901-80) in taking up marble carving after he had been taught by Giovanni Ardini, and for his influence on his young wife, Barbara Hepworth. Hepworth herself, who lost the scholarship but married the holder, was able to stay in the School courtesy of Ashmole. While Italy was to remain a profound influence on Hepworth, Skeaping was to become well known for his horses and other animals. Yet monumental *gravitas* was recognised by no less than five sculpture scholars making it to RA (Hardiman, Jagger, Ledward, Skeaping, Woodford), while the other two disciplines scored only two each (Lawrence and Monnington in Painting, Freeth and Austin in Engraving).

The new Engraving (later Printmaking) Faculty, established in 1920 by the generosity of Stephen Courtauld, was the most consistently successful of the three subjects. During this period prints were like internet shares, with editions being bought and sold *before* issue and ending up in bank vaults. This attractive commercial proposition was therefore in line with memorial sculpture and mural decoration. The prints of D.Y. Cameron (Council member) were among the most bankable. The Print Revival lasted until the

Wall Street Crash. While the printmakers who came were also picked as traditionalists, they did produce a steady stream of excellent exponents, now coming into their own once more: Job Nixon, Robin Sargent Austin, William E.C. Morgan, Edward Bouverie Hoyton, Evelyn Gibbs, James T.A. Osborne, William Fairclough, Andrew Freeth - difficult to leave anybody out. Their success was probably due to the hijacking of the whole enterprise by the inspirational teacher Frank Short, Chairman of the Faculty from its inception and his fellow exponents, D.Y. Cameron, Muirhead Bone, Campbell Dodgson of the BM, Charles Shannon, all with some connections to Short's department at the RCA or his presidency of the Royal Society of Painter Etchers. Of the 22 scholars, a staggering 80% came from his department, only 14% from the rest of the entire country, with a mere one scholar from the Slade. The composition of the Faculties obviously played a crucial role in who got what. This cosy world of power and patronage set amongst the myth of mad unpolitical artists was greatly assisted by having faculty members who stayed on and on until they dropped dead, to be replaced by handpicked former scholars.

Rome the city, as opposed to Italy and its countryside, was in some ways the wrong place for British temperament – for artists and archaeologists alike. For artists, the overwhelming characteristic was the rejection of Rome and the adoption of 'Tuscan' values.

WILLIAM GRAHAM HOLFORD, RA (1907-75) (LORD HOLFORD)

View of Piazza del Popolo

Rome Scholar in Architecture 1930-33, Holford was born in Johannesburg, and studied at Liverpool. While in Rome he worked with

Richmond on the town plan of Verona, published in PBSR XIII (1935). He became Professor of Civic Design at Liverpool in 1937, Professor of Town Planning at UCL 1948-70, President of RIBA 1960-62, RA 1968, knighted 1953, life peer 1965. He was eloquent about the impact of his Roman experience:

'Visual impressions of the Rome of to-day are curiously strong; as if they were fired on to the mind by the sun, and thus made permanent. The architect in particular is impressed, since he is sensitive to the appearance of solid forms in light. I can recall with peculiar distinctness any one of a hundred Roman pictures, each complete in its atmosphere and detail. I can see the exact and luminous shadow cast by the obelisk in the Piazza del Popolo...' (*Journal of* RIBA 1937, 537).

+ PIAZZA + DEL + POPOLO +

This whole period is set in an Imperial Rome, amidst the growth of fascism and the dictatorship of Mussolini. In true Grand Tour fashion the artists continued to ignore the people and their concerns; their world consisted of an abstraction. The 'primitive' simple life of the farmer and the organic syncopated domestic architecture of a hill town set in the sunshine was to be the paradise, Claude Lorrain updated. The scholars fled Mussolini's playground and settled instead for Anticoli Corrado, 60 kilometres west of Rome in the Sabine Hills beyond Tivoli. As Miss Knights wrote in 1921: 'I have never imagined a more beautiful place, it hardly seems real.' It was an idealised world: 'the town is a pigsty, you meet herds of swine running quite loose in every street.' Virtually all of the prints produced and many of the paintings show this idealised Italy. Colin Gill, first scholar, found it that first summer; it was to be the nearest they could all get to Tuscany. He commenced the tradition, handed down to the next arrivals, of spending the hot summer months sketching there and working them up later as paintings in the studio. J.M. Benson, the next painting scholar after Gill, actually married a girl from Anticoli. Today artists still make the same pilgrimage just to see if it is still there.

The British artists were lovers of Giotto and Masaccio, and they virtually reinvented the long forgotten Piero della Francesca (the first monograph on the artist, Robert Lunghi's, did not appear until 1927). The pilgrimage was not to the Vatican to see Raphael's 'decorative painting' but to Sansepolcro to talk with an angel. It was the Quattro/Cinquecento artists that influenced them, and the assessors back home, such as Charles Ricketts, felt likewise; it had very little to do with Rome, which was vulgar in comparison. Their work was in the wake of Cézanne, of Roger Fry and his advocacy of Post-Impressionism - Impressionism was definitely out. Art had to have 'significant form', solidity, order, structure, intellect, and the mysteries of the Golden Section. It was Puvis de Chavannes country, Blake's all bounding line, a renewal of classicism with much the same solutions as the generation of German Romantics had found in their 'Rome' a century earlier. The mannered, hard edged, stylistic devices were not derived from Fascist Futurism but were of the English Vorticist variety.

Left to fend for themselves, the artists found their own world in their imagination, a remarkably consistent one for over twenty years. Looking back it is as if Mussolini's dictatorship with its huge modern building programme outside their door had never existed. The early period was plagued by politics, with mass destruction and two world wars but you would never guess any of it from looking at the art produced. It is as if they all lived a private life outside the scrutiny of their chaperons in Rome or beyond the dictates of their paymasters. In effect they behaved as artists generally do.

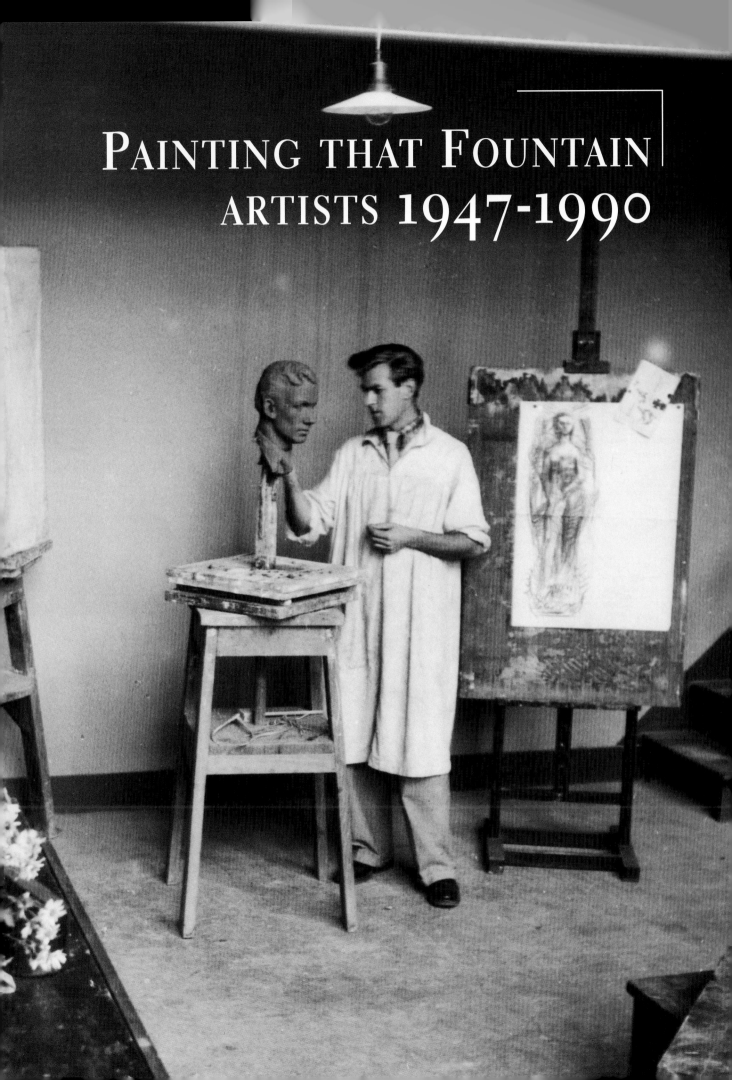

PAINTING THAT FOUNTAIN
ARTISTS 1947-1990

Painting that Fountain: Artists (1947-1990)

by Stephen Farthing

Not very early one Sunday morning during the spring of 1976 I remember seeing a man driving a Fiat 500 slowly around Rome's big ring road: he had the curb side window rolled down and what looked like a large leather strap flapping around both inside and outside the car, on the end of that strap on the hard shoulder was a trotting beige Great Dane. At this point I realized there were no strange events in Fellini's *Roma* and that what I had seen in his film was a fairly accurate collage of the eternal city.

To share fully my perspective of post-war Italy at the BSR it is important to keep that jogging dog in mind. Artists tend to make a habit of picking up on the moment. They may be drawn to the façade of a palazzo and begin to study its proportions but when a shadow falls across it or the pigeons go up, that's often when the work begins. Their job is to mesh the past with today through acts of constructive distraction.

'The Rome Scholars in the Fine Arts, whose awards were intermitted on the outbreak of war, have been advised to postpone resuming them until the autumn of 1947.'

Scene two opens in the faded September colours of 1947 when Rome Scholar, Douglas Wain-Hobson, dressed either in a cream linen jacket and gray flannels, or a rather too warm for the time of year tweed, arrives at via Gramsci 61, pushes open its impressive oak door and walks into the traces (so it seems to him) of a decommissioned Nazi Hospital. He stands there surveying what is to be his home for at least the next two years.

Bryan Neil, RA (b. 1930, Sculptor, Rome Scholar in Mural Painting 1949, brother of Nigel Neil, the man at the BBC who wrote *Quatermass*), provides a friendly voice-over:

'The place' he says 'closely resembled an installation by Joseph Beuys, awash with hundreds of chamber pots and pairs of wooden skis, we used the chamber pots to mix plaster and paint in'.

Although clearly a mess, it must have been the kind of mess that someone who

(above and previous)
Douglas Wain-Hobson
(RS Sculpture 1947)
At work in his studio.

had just gone through the war in Britain would be accustomed to, so he stands reflecting on the warmth, sunshine and personal success that has allowed him to escape a post war and monochrome Britain and offered him the opportunity to spend time in Italy, the artists' Galapagos.

If you talk to artists who were at the school at this time the lingering impression is of an experience that falls mid-way between two rather splendid mid twentieth century black and white films, *An American in Paris* and *Roman Holiday*. Both stories are devoid of irony, packed with limpid honesty and linger on falling in love with a place and a person. In these films earnest young men smoke cigarettes in dark studios then go out to meet pretty young girls in headscarves and sunshine to sight-see on the backs of Lambrettas. That was the middle of the last century.

In the next scene we cut to a terracotta building at the top end of Exhibition Road, London, just after the museums and just before the entrance to the park. In a wood-panelled boardroom is a large wooden table surrounded mainly by men, most of whom, between lungfuls of smoke, are drinking tea and eating Rich Tea biscuits. Each knows the other, they are the London-based high-achievers in their field, some ex-Rome scholars, some independently successful professionals, the rest teachers from the leading postgraduate courses. There is an

MICHAEL ANDREWS (RS Painting 1953)
Portrait of Lorenza Mazzetti at the Spanish Steps.
Mazzetti later cast Andrews in one of the leading
roles in her Free Cinema film *Together*.

161

JOE TILSON (RS Painting 1955)
John Ward-Perkins and Joe Tilson in
1955, at a joint exhibition with
the American Academy.

(above) Anticoli Corrado.

(left) Oranges.

atmosphere of healthy competition. They are the Faculties and Selection Panels, the people who choose the scholars and as such provide the cast and to some extent the script for the story which unfolds in Rome. If you talk to scholars who were sent in the early fifties they talk about the stranglehold Camberwell had on the scholarships, and later, in the seventies, they will tell you that the Royal College and the Slade appeared to have had the patch divided up between them.

But in the end I think we must work with the assumption that what the selection panels were looking for were aspirant artists and architects who would go on to become winners, wherever they came from and whoever they knew.

To give a feel of the kind of people we had in the casting department (not all of them, the list would be massive) I will run a few names. This is a list that readers other than cognoscenti should probably skip.

In 1945 the Architects were Professor Cordingley, Professor Holford and Mr Jellicoe; the Painters, Thomas Monnington and Gilbert Spencer; the Sculptors, Frank Dobson, James Woodford; and the Engravers, Stanley Anderson and Andrew Freeth. At this time each Faculty appears to have been something of a rule unto itself but membership did change.

By 1955 the picture included some women and looked like this: the Architects elected Mr Ansell to the Chair, Monnington became the Painting Chairman and Vanessa Bell and Duncan Grant also joined. Sculpture elected Woodford to the Chair and Charoux,

GERALDINE KNIGHTS (RS Sculpture 1956)
View of Knights' studio.

Skeaping and Wain-Hobson became members, while Engraving elected Mr Henry Rushbury to preside over Miss Gertrude Hermes, Andrew Freeth and John Nash.

By 1965 Sheppard Fidler had taken over the Chair of Architecture, Monnington remained in the Painting Chair with new blood emerging in the form of R.B. Kitaj and Ceri Richards.

The 1975 Faculty of Architecture was chaired by Mr Mills. Painting, by today's standards, was dominated by the two big postgraduate schools, the Royal College of Art and the Slade, led on one side by Professor Peter de Francia, and on the other Professor Sir William Coldstream.

What this highly edited list of names tells us is that over a forty year period many of the key players in the London art and architecture world gave time and thought to shaping the fine arts at the British School. Coldstream, De Francia, Kitaj, Blake, Weight, Fullard, Moynhan, Monnington and Jellico are names that for me stand out in bold.

STEPHEN FARTHING (Abbey Scholar 1976) *Cloud Burst of Material Possessions.*

What becomes clear if you scan the list of elected scholars and begin to put the big names into bold, is that amongst them are just as many impressive careers as there were on the selection committees; there are just a few more spaces between. This I think is to be expected, because just like betting on horses, selecting artists is not an exact science and experience tells us that early promise does not always translate into lasting reputations. Before I give a taste of this list there is one important detail that we need to build into the equation. The Edwin Austin Abbey Memorial Awards are best introduced by this extract from the 1986 Report of the Faculty of Painting:

'The Abbey Scholarships Council established the Abbey Major Scholarship in Mural Painting in its existing form in 1937, as a second award in the Rome Painting competition, and made the first appointment in 1938. The stipend and allowances which the Abbey Council provide are the same as those of the Rome Scholarship, and the ordinary tenure is for one year, although on a number of occasions the Abbey Council has been able to fund a second year renewal when

CAROLE ROBB (RS Painting 1979) *Landscape of a Fountain.*

the School has been able to accommodate the Scholar. The Council also generously pay an annual grant towards the overhead expenses involved in housing the Scholar. Only on two occasions since the war has the Abbey award not been made.'

To this I should add an important footnote, which is that not all Abbey Awardees actually went to Italy and Rome: some took off on their motorcycles in other directions.

Two Abbey Awardees stand out in the list because of the quality of their work and their international reputations, they are: Euan Uglow (1953), a brilliant, measured and scholarly painter who died this year in London, and John Walker (1961), also a painter whose career has placed him at the top of his profession in Britain, Australia and now the USA, where he also lives. Of the Rome Scholars Michael Andrews and Joe Tilson, both Awardees during the early 50s, have to my mind achieved a similar status and level of achievement.

An interesting group of Rome and Abbey Scholars, which in some respects is very British, are those that went on to not just make their names as artists but to work at the top end in education as well. Graham Nickson (RS Painting 1972), now Director of the New York Studio School, Stuart Brisley (Abbey Awardee 1959), who became head of department and Professor at the Slade School, Glynn Williams (Gulbenkian Scholar 1961), long Professor of Sculpture at the Royal College of Art, and I suppose myself (Abbey Scholar 1976) as the Ruskin Master of Drawing at the University of Oxford during the 90s and now Executive Director of the New York Academy of Art.

If you look at the work of these artists you will find that for some the influence of Rome has conspicuously remained, but for others there never was an obvious visual connection between their studies in Rome and their mature output as artists. But this said, just about every artist who ever went to the School describes the time as a powerful and formative time in their life, mostly because of the city, the art and the opportunity to travel but also because of the contact it enabled with scholars in other fields. It is important to remember that at this time there were few university courses in art and that independent art schools were by today's standards intellectually isolated places, so for many artists it was their first taste of a bigger intellectual world.

Michael Andrews (RS Painting 1953) went on to become one of Britain's most highly respected post-war painters. He turned topographical painting back into a fashionable subject, and in doing so neatly linked his student studies to his mature output and the past to the contemporary art of his day. Michael Andrews went out to Rome at the age of 25, having just completed two years National Service and three years at the Slade School. His time at the school was a mixed one and after only six months he returned to England. Andrews' assessment of the situation at the time was that 'I have made up my mind to stay in England, because of a preoccupation with the environment, not because I didn't like Italy, in some ways I loved it.' While at the school he did however complete at least one

RICHARD TALBOT (RS Sculpture 1980) and ANDREW STAHL (Abbey Scholar 1979) present their work to the Duke of Edinburgh.

ARTISTS AT WORK (1983)

MARK WINGRAVE
(Abbey Scholar 1982)

DENISE DE CORDOVA
(RS Sculpture 1983)

DENZIL FORRESTER
(RS Painting 1983)

HELEN WILDE
(RS Printmaking/Engraving 1983)

ROGER PARTRIDGE
(RS Sculpture 1983)

STEPHEN CHAMBERS
(Abbey Scholar 1983)

PAUL HAWDON (RS Printmaking/Engraving 1988).

significant painting, of which Lawrence Gowing said this:

'Michael Andrews went to Italy with the Rome Scholarship and there devised an image, with the Spanish Steps for background, of a Slade friend Lorenza Mazzetti... By this time he had formulated, and probably written down, his thoughts on the issue of vagueness and definition, which separated him from the systematic positiveness of figurative painting at the Slade; he now thought it wrong to attempt to look into a region where no certainty was possible. He was beginning to admire Velasquez. In the context of his own approach, it was the absence of strain that astonished him in the even gaze. But the influence behind the steady embodiment of the woman and the example that meant most to him was Piero della Francesca...'

Joe Tilson (RS Painting 1955) went out to Rome at the age of 27 having just completed his studies at the Royal College of Art. The director at the time, Ward-Perkins, wrote this of him on the subject of his renewal for a second year:

'Tilson presents no problems, and I need not waste the Faculty's time with a lengthy report. A cheerful, hard-working scholar, he has got through a lot of travel and a lot of painting. He certainly seems to make excellent use of his time. He has acquired fluent Italian and has many friends outside, both among Italian artists and in the Villa Medici. As an individual, he is obviously the sort to make the best possible use of a Rome Scholarship; he fully deserves, and will make full use of, a second year.'

Joe Tilson (who both owned a Lambretta and married a beautiful young woman in a head scarf, in Venice) was at the school from the autumn of 1955 to the summer of 1957. He drew and painted from life to produce dark, passionate landscapes and still lives which are a long way from the work I know him for, as one of the fathers of Pop Art and one of the most influential British modernist painters. He talks about his time in Rome as a time to study, not a career break.

Ronald Brooks Kitaj (Abbey Awardee 1961) was born in Cleveland, Ohio and took up

CORNELIA PARKER

(Rome Fine Arts Awardee 1989 and

Henry Moore Sculpture Fellowship 2000)

Chalk drawing on tennis court wall.

his award at the age of 29. In 1957 he completed his National Service for the American Military, went to the Ruskin School in Oxford and then the Royal College of Art for a total of four years. Professor Carel Weight said of him at the time:

'He is perhaps the most intellectual of all students in the Painting School this year, and also a painter of great originality. He has a charming manner, he is a very popular figure at the College, he is a leader in discussions, and in every way a very mature man indeed.'

Glynn Williams (Gulbenkian Scholar 1961), now Professor of Sculpture at the Royal College of Art, went out to Rome from Wolverhampton at the age of 22 and studied Etruscan art, which at the time must have been a fairly off-beat pursuit, but with hindsight seems a perfectly natural thing to do. In his second year he built the fountain that still stands in the gardens.

The artists and architects sent by the Faculties to Rome, up until a transitionary period which I will place as existing between 1975 and 1985, saw themselves as students not members of a profession, and as such went there with a single project which was to learn through wide-open eyes not tightly defined projects.

I will let Carole Robb, the 1979 Rome Scholar in Painting, construct the images and be the voiceover in the closing sequence:

'Each person finds their own Rome and you have to leave to discover it. My Rome was an airship flashing the message over the British School, "Roma è bella per la notte." My Rome was Bernini's Apollo & Daphne and the neglected Canova fountain with a dead cat floating in its pools. When I left for America, Apollo & Daphne became the central theme of my work for 8 years. Now I'm back in Rome, painting that fountain.'

INTO THE MILLENNIUM
1995-2001

INTO THE MILLENNIUM
(1995-2001)

TO TELL THE STORY OF THE SCHOOL in its present regime would be premature. Even so, the reader will want to know how the present team is facing up to the challenges which, as the foregoing chapters have shown, may partly remain constant over time, and yet change with the circumstances of a changing world. The School is a small fragment of European history: Europe's great wars, the competitiveness of its nation states, the fluctuating international relations embodied in its exchange rates, all determine the context within which British scholars and artists have pursued their interests in Rome. The Rome of the turning millennium has a renewed role to play in European cultural relations, as Britain continues to hesitate, as it has for centuries, over just how European it wants to become. Rome is one of the most fruitful places where we can try to find an answer to that question: artists and scholars are also engaged in a constant experiment of how continental they wish their work to be, and the extraordinary cluster of academies of Rome still make it a place to relate not only to Italy, but to the whole range of European cultures, with local traditions of scholarly and artistic practice that after centuries of mutual influence remain resolutely diverse.

In the following pages, members of the team responsible for the School's range of activities comment on how their own departments are facing up to the challenges of the new millennium. The first point to underline is the importance of the fact that this team exists. So much of the School's history is about a poorly-resourced institution with very broad ambitions finding itself unable to do everything expected of it without appropriate staff. For decades Directors have had to double up as Administrators and Academic Project Leaders (not to say Editors in Chief), Assistant Directors as Librarians, and there was long nobody on the core staff to look after the artists except occasional visitors sent out from Britain by the Faculty. If the School is able to sustain more coherent activity now than at some periods in the past, it is because a decision has been made to focus the scarce funds at its disposal on the essential team to keep the pulse of activity beating. The title

(above and previous)
Libby Fellingham (Geoffrey Jellicoe Scholar 1996),
The Tiber.

of Assistant Director is now shared by three people, one of whom runs the Academic programmes, one the Archaeology, and one the Fine Arts. The Gallery Curator and the
Publications Manager play new but no less important roles; and the Library and Archive
is now run not by academics on short-term contracts, but by a professional Librarian able
to safeguard the collective memory of the institution. Nor could the scheme for expansion of the building have been attempted at its present ambitious level without a dedicated Project Manager.

These will speak with their own voices in the following pages, but we should pay tribute too to the staff who do not generate activities but provide the essential support for all
we do. The complex demands of running a residential community with a substantial staff,
maintaining building and equipment, and keeping the books are met by a professional
Administrator (Alvise Di Giulio), backed by a Hostel Manager (Geraldine Wellington)
and a Domestic Bursar (Renato Parente). Running the Committees, even in their
slimmed down version, and especially the scholarship competitions, is a large administrative burden: with the closing of the London office in 1991 this function was transferred
to Rome, where Cassy Payne as Registrar set a model of elegant efficiency. On her resignation in 1998, Gill Clark took back this function to London, in our splendid new quarters hosted by the British Academy in Carlton House Terrace, while Katherine Wallis
took over the functions of Director's Assistant. Maria Pia Malvezzi as School Secretary
leaves generations of scholars in her debt, above all for securing access to closed sites and
museums (already Thomas Ashby was dealing with a flood of such requests). The
School's Italian staff lie behind every activity, from the daily life of the residential community to the flurry of preparation that lies behind every lecture or art show; and they
remain entwined in the most affectionate memories of the scholars.

Activity in Rome is dependent on two things: the right sort of support at home in
Britain, and a sufficient flow of funding. In both, things have changed greatly for the better in the last decade. Relations with London have been transformed since the days of
Evelyn Shaw, and in retrospect it is awesome to look back at the cumbersome creation of
the new constitution negotiated in 1912, with its array of Council, Executive Committee
and five Faculties, involving the supervision of Rome's activity by as many as one hundred committee members back in Britain, and the formidable bureaucracy of control in
1 Lowther Gardens. The Supplemental Charter finally laid before Privy Council in 1995,
which came into effect on 1 January 1996, dramatically cut back this thicket of
Committees, and following the guidelines of the Charity Commission gave full responsibility to a board of 15 Trustees (Council), supported by such subcommittees as necessary
and two Faculties to provide advice and validation in the disciplines of the Humanities
and the Fine Arts.

The experience that Roddy Cavaliero brought from a career in the British Council, and
the efficacy of his negotiations with the many parties concerned, allow him to rank as the
School's most important reformer since Evelyn Shaw. He grasped the balancing act that
was necessary: between giving the staff in Rome the authority and initiative to pursue activities, and the need to plug into the academic and artistic worlds back at home for support
and guidance. Those who have made real contributions to the School's success by unpaid
work on these committees are too numerous to thank or even to list, but it will always be

remembered that an institution flourishes not just on the performance of its officers, but by the shared commitment of many to a cause that matters to them. To name the Chairmen of Council who have done so much to help refashion the School, Sir Alan Campbell, Professor Fergus Millar, and Professor Geoffrey Rickman, is to recall by association the many who have served with them.

The second prerequisite of success is funding. We have suggested above that in parting company with the 1851 Commission, the School rather than being damaged came of age. The relationship, at least up to the Second World War, had tended to be paternalistic, with Lord Esher threatening to resign if there was any public appeal. Yet the School had been founded on the basis of the subscriptions and contributions of individuals and institutions that shared its aims. Even if the income so raised was inadequate, it was the strength and breadth of public support that persuaded the Government to provide the first grant of £500 in 1905 – twenty printed sides of signatories to the petition to Prime Minister Balfour were eloquent expression of the broad base of interest. Government support has grown today to over £800,000, and is only part of the funding that the Department for Education gives to the British Academy for its constellation of Foreign Schools, Institutes and Societies (BASIS), under the watchful but understanding eye of Mortimer Wheeler's successor, Peter Brown. Yet it is no complaint to say that additional funding from a broad range of non-governmental bodies and individuals is as critical as ever to success. The partnership of private and public is essential: without core funding from the state, it is unlikely the School could survive, but with this solid basis, the School is in a strong position to attract funding from a wide range of supporters, in the Arts, academia, industry and charitable foundations.

The substantial support received from these private sources has enabled the School both to quicken the pace of its activities and to extend its building to a significant extent. Caroline Egerton relates below the success of the Development Appeal which has secured funding for capital projects worth three million pounds over six years. Much else has been made possible by private funding – the conservation of rare books and prints in the Library, exhibitions, publications (including the present one), archaeological projects, and above all the funding of scholarships. The breadth of the School's activity is the breadth of its appeal, but the especial power of the institution lies in the synergy it creates between different but converging interests. One donor may like conservation of old books, another cutting-edge contemporary art, one may like excavations, another new buildings: put them together and they all benefit each other and create an excitement which a more focused and limited 'School of Archaeology' could never have had.

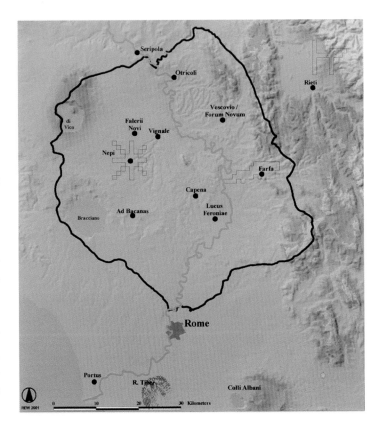

THE ARCHAEOLOGY PROGRAMME
by Helen Patterson, Assistant Director for Archaeology

The distinctive advantage of operating an archaeological project from a permanent base in Rome, rather than a university in Britain, is that it is possible to develop ambitious large-scale projects over time. Ashby could never have developed his study of all the roads and aqueducts that radiate from Rome on the basis of modern university research funding, nor could Ward-Perkins have surveyed 850 square kilometres of South Etruria over two decades. It was a new policy, following the recommendations of a report by Gill Andrews in 1995, that the School should again concentrate its resources on a major project directed by an archaeologist recruited for the purpose, moving away from the small funding of multiple projects typical of the seventies and eighties.

The choice of the Tiber Valley, or rather the stretch of the valley of the middle Tiber that flows north of Rome up to Otricoli on the border of Umbria, suggested itself for many reasons: the longstanding commitment of the School to the study of landscape, the logistical advantages of proximity, but above all the untapped resource offered by the still unpublished South Etruria Project. The re-evaluation of this survey material is a central element of the Tiber Valley Project. Never fully catalogued or published, the material has remained stored at the School - over 300 crates containing over 80,000 fragments of pottery, glass, marble, and building materials representing more than 2000 years of human activity from the Bronze Age to the Medieval period. With the passage of time and the

(opposite) Tiber Valley Project research area and related projects.

(right) The River Tiber with Monte Soratte in the background.

(above) Excavation at Forum Novum - Vescovio. From left: Mary Harlow, Will Clarke, Helga di Giuseppe, Rob Witcher, Helen Patterson.

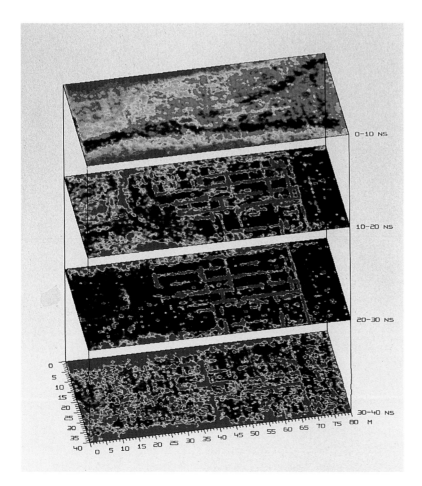

(left) Georadar time slices of the site at Forum Novum - Vescovio.

(opposite) Distribution of sites along the via Cassia (south of Lake di Vico), on a computer-modelled landscape.

continued destruction of the archaeological record, the value of this remarkable dataset has become increasingly apparent. Armed with a far more detailed understanding of pottery dating, a team of British and Italian specialists has been able to revise the old analysis completely.

Thanks to generous funding from the Leverhulme Foundation, we were able to appoint two research fellows for three years to work on the project, Helga di Giuseppe to sift through the archaeological bibliography and Rob Witcher to develop a database and Geographical Information System (GIS). With the support of two research assistants, they have brought together the data relating to settlement, economy and communication history. It has been possible to identify more than 5000 sites, ranging from scatters of a few sherds to entire cities, such as Rome's greatest rival, Veii.

At the same time, we did not wish merely to revisit old terrain. New data was needed to set alongside the old. And rather than study exactly the same patch of land, it seemed more interesting to redefine the boundaries, and to put the river Tiber at the centre instead of the edge. The Tiber divides two areas contrasting both in geography and in human history: the Etruscan west bank with its volcanic tuffs, and its history of densely clustered settlements, and the limestone hills of the Sabine east bank, with a historical reputation for sparser, more rural settlement. These contrasting terrains could be used to tell a common story: of the development of Rome to an imperial power, transforming the economy and social relations of its hinterland, and then the transformation of those relationships with the decline of Rome's imperial power, and the rise of the papacy as the dominant local force.

The team depends on the collaboration of colleagues from a dozen different UK institutions who are pursuing a range of projects closely linked with the core dataset. Annual workshops have enabled colleagues to bring different projects into relation with one another: specific aspects of the landscape such as roads, water management, building materials and sanctuaries.

New fieldwork projects feed into the broader initiative. The most notable gap in the older survey material, especially given the intensity of archaeological work on rural settlement, is the study of urban centres; this is the focus of the new fieldwork initiatives. The majority of these once lively, bustling centres have been abandoned for centuries and are now buried under fields. Temples,

HM The Queen with Helen Patterson.

streets and houses are being brought back to life through the use of remote sensing techniques which produce x-ray images of the buried structures.

The results are spectacular. As part of a study of urbanism in the Tiber Valley directed by Simon Keay and Martin Millett, survey at the Roman town of Falerii Novi has revealed a complete plan - street grid, public buildings including the forum, the theatres and its portico and even individual houses and rooms. At the Roman town and bishopric of Forum Novum (Vescovio) in the Sabine hills, a triple alliance of the School (Helen Patterson), the British Museum (Paul Roberts) and the University of Birmingham (Vince Gaffney) is combining remote sensing techniques with excavation to examine the layout and changing character of the centre through time. The town centre lies in part under modern structures, but georadar survey has proved invaluable revealing the clear plan of a villa and an amphitheatre, whose existence was previously unknown, and the podium of a large temple which now lies under a car park. The excavations are allowing us to trace the history of the centre, in particular during that elusive period which saw the decline of the Roman town and its emergence as a bishop's seat in late antiquity.

The Tiber Valley Project draws on and takes a step further the School's long tradition of innovative landscape archaeology. Already the project has stimulated several new research initiatives. It is especially pleasing to note that a number of younger British and Italian scholars, some of whom came to the School as research assistants, are now developing their own research as part of the School's Tiber Valley Project. This is something that Tim Potter, who played a key role as Chairman of the Faculty in developing the project, and as Chairman of the Project Committee in launching it, would have greatly appreciated.

If the Tiber Valley Project represents the main thrust, it by no means excludes other projects. The Director's own project at Pompeii deserves mention. In collaboration with Michael Fulford and a team from the University of Reading, his group has since 1994 studied a block of houses (*insula*) of Pompeii excavated in the 1950s, but left unpublished. Financed by a major grant of £60,000 from the European Union, matched by equal funding from Enterprise Oil, and with similar funds for excavation

Michael Fulford (left) in
the House of Amarantus
(I.9.11), Pompeii, 1997.

Section and
reconstruction by
Nicholas Wood of the
House of Ceres (I.9.13),
Pompeii.

from the British Academy, their close study of a group of houses is helping to rewrite
the history of the city as a whole, with the surprising revelation of a much larger
Etruscan settlement in the sixth century BC. Innovative use of computer technology
has enabled the virtual reconstruction of the block in a 3D model and a vivid documentation of the buildings and finds of a neighbourhood that ranged from ostenta-
tious good living to little workshops of craftsmen. This project sits alongside the work
on Falerii Novi and Forum Novum, together with Amanda Claridge's ongoing study
of the Vicus Augustanus at Castelporziano, and Janet DeLaine's study of an *insula* at
Ostia, as part of a larger rethinking of the many-faceted urbanism of the Roman
world.

The Academic Programmes
by Andrew Hopkins, Assistant Director

If archaeology is the most visible academic activity of the School, its broader disciplinary range has always determined the School's character. That range is present in the scholars who reside and work here, and share their experiences over dinner. The aim of our academic programme, as developed in recent years, has been to exploit and encourage that range by offering a regular programme of lectures and conferences.

The History of Art from antiquity to the modern is an area of central interest to users of the School, academics and artists alike. A renaissance of Art History occurred under the direction of Clare Hornsby who between 1996 and 1998 arranged a programme of regular lectures and conferences. Her conference on the Grand Tour, a theme which brings together art and architectural historians, museum curators and archaeologists, led to the first of a new series of publications in History of Art *(The Impact of Italy: the Grand Tour and Beyond)*, reviving a tradition that goes back to Ellis Waterhouse.

The recent programme has aimed to develop areas of disciplinary overlap. A joint series of seminars with the American Academy on 'Responding to the Antique' brought together classical art historians with students of the classical tradition; that on 'Santa Maria Antiqua', co-sponsored by the Norwegian Institute and the Soprintendenza of Rome, brought together those responsible for restorations with archaeologists and art historians. 'Roman Bodies', run in association with the American Academy, the Dutch Institute, and the Palazzo delle Esposizioni, brought together papers ranged in subject from headhunters in the Roman army, to the representation of disabled bodies in late antiquity and the middle ages, to papal funeral practices in Baroque Rome.

Architecture for the School is a cross-over discipline par excellence, with its mix of academic and artistic skills. As the focus of architecture radically shifted in the post-war period from measured drawings of ancient monuments to the celebration of modernity, Rome lost some of its draw for young architects. But Rome has recovered its interest as a place where the modern encounters the old. With the creation of a series of Sargant Lectures in Architecture, we have been able to invite architects such as Daniel Libeskind, Rick Mather and Sir Jeremy Dixon. Our own architect, Lutyens, is a special focus of interest. The conference jointly organised with Gavin Stamp, 'Lutyens Abroad', assembled entire cast of Lutyens experts in one of his most conspicuous buildings to discuss the architect's work outside Britain.

Since 1980 we have offered an undergraduate Ancient Rome Summer School: it has played a significant role in encouraging the scholars of the future. As an extension of this, five years ago the School launched its City of Rome Postgraduate Course. This annual eight-week course, directed by a tutor financed by the legacy of Max Cary as Cary Fellow, combines site visits with seminars and special lectures, including many distinguished Italian academics and Directors of the other academies in Rome. A growing number of UK universities now participate in this scheme. An important Australian link is the Renaissance and Baroque taught course from the University of Melbourne run by David Marshall, which has now been integrated into the School's own programme. We aim to develop increasing participation in this course from post-graduates registered at UK universities, and although these initiatives require development over many years, the results of the City of Rome course indicate how worthwhile these collaborative institutional undertakings can be.

The key to the success of the academic programme and the life of the School is the award of the scholarships by the Faculty of Archaeology, History and Letters. The two annual scholarships traditionally awarded (one before, one after AD 1000) gave little chance to cover the disciplines of archaeology, history, art history and literary studies from prehistory to the present. However, the funds previously distributed in research grants were used to create a third scholarship and four shorter awards; a fourth scholarship was added when the former Director Ralegh Radford, on his death in 1998 at the age of 98, left the School a legacy of nearly a quarter of a million pounds. A senior fellowship has been generously sponsored by the Paul Mellon Centre in London, the first dedicated specifically to the History of Art. In addition, the cultural range of School activities is extended by the welcome sponsorship by Jaguar Italia of an award

Daniel Wrightson (RS Fine Arts 1999), *Pantheon.*

for a musician from the Royal College of Music. The School has no higher priority for the future than to consolidate and add to its scholarships, and already it has proved possible to maintain a broad programme of activity reflecting this diversity.

After a century of academic activity, with lectures held principally in the dining room, we will finally in 2002 move into a purpose-built space for lectures, conferences, seminars and workshops, the Sainsbury Lecture Theatre. It will provide the ideal space required for our increasingly active academic programme; it will also allow us to combine various activities, including lectures linked to art gallery events, thus enhancing its cross-over appeal to artists and academics.

THE FINE ARTS PROGRAMME
by Jacopo Benci, Assistant Director for Fine Arts

Why Rome for artists? A widespread art-world prejudice sees Rome as nothing more than a tourist resort or a theme park, a place with an immense history behind it but incapable of producing anything worth looking at in terms of contemporary culture. Is this the truth? If one makes a list of things that happened in Rome over the last fifty years, one will have to include several major aspects in contemporary (high- and low-) culture, such as: neo-realist cinema, and world-acclaimed film 'auteurs' such as Fellini, Pasolini, Antonioni; cutting-edge fashion designers; post-avantgarde theatre from the 1960s onwards; the Rome chapter of the Arte Povera movement, and the Transavantgarde; 'Roman American' artists such as Cy Twombly, Sol LeWitt, and Joseph Kosuth. Rome has been cradle to all these things and many more because, as the ancient saying has it, 'all roads lead to Rome': sooner or later anyone and everyone who makes sense in the creative fields will pass through Rome, bring something to it, and take something else from it.

These are just some of the reasons why the foreign cultural institutes in Rome, over three centuries after the creation of the French Academy and two centuries after the height of the Grand Tour, still make a lot of sense. At some periods artists have felt nervous that in going to Rome they would be cut off from the lively scene in London and Britain. During the 1990s the idea of a residency in Rome regained its relevance to the live issues of contemporary practice. The range of their artistic practice of the scholars selected broadened to encompass painting (both figurative and non-figurative), sculpture, photography, installation, site-related projects, film & video, and multi-media. This development brought a new appeal to the Rome scholarships. The School has always had its fair share of up-and-coming and respected artists among its scholars

Fred Crayk (Abbey Scholar 1996), *Ecco Roma.*

Libby Fellingham (Geoffrey Jellicoe Scholar 1996), *The Tiber.*

(recent examples were Cornelia Parker in 1989-90, Kathy Prendergast and Daphne Wright in 1992-93), but from the mid-1990s onwards Fine Arts award holders included each year several artists already well known in the UK and abroad (a partial list should include Rose Finn-Kelcey, Julie Roberts, Edward Allington, Gillian Ayres, Anya Gallaccio, Alison Wilding, Adam Chodzko, Jaki Irvine, Tania Kovacs, Shauna McMullan, Mark Wallinger, Chantal Joffe, Bethan Huws, Lucy Gunning and Tim Stoner).

The shift has proved intellectually challenging and artistically stimulating to all Fine Arts award holders. The Gallery programme also played an important role in arousing local Italian interest in British artistic and cultural debate, and in creating new links for the resident artists with critics and galleries in Rome. These changes have been recognised both in Rome (as shown by the many exhibitions and events BSR artists and architects were invited to take part in) and in Britain. Unchanged has remained the artists' and architects' involvement in the city of Rome with its myriad historical, artistic and cultural layers, and their engagement in fruitful discussion and shared enterprises with the other BSR scholars – archaeologists, historians, and researchers. The illustrated talks by artists and architects give everyone at the School an opportunity to tune into the practices and the ideas being carried forward, and conversely the talks and lectures by Humanities scholars pave the way for mutual understanding, discussion, and collaboration. And one should not overlook the privileges artists and architects at the BSR share with their colleagues, such as gaining access to monuments and sites normally rarely or not at all accessible to the general public, or being taken to visit countless sites of archaeological, artistic and environmental interest throughout Rome and Italy.

One factor that significantly added to the attractiveness of our art scholarships was the

Adam Chodzko (RS Fine Arts 1997), *Salò Reunion.*

Marion Coutts (RS Fine Arts 1998), *Souvenir.*

John Riddy (Sargant Fellow 1998), *Rome (Argentina),* 1999.

Euan Heng (Australia Council Resident 1999), *Messenger*.

Catherine George (RS Fine Arts 1999), *Aegis*.

restructuring of the studios. The old wooden mezzanines, despite their bohemian charm, were unacceptable on health and safety grounds. The new glass and concrete living quarters installed in the second half of 1996, complete with ensuite bathrooms, transformed the studios into up-to-date facilities, while preserving the sense of space and light. That, together with the more vibrant tempo of the fine arts programme, helped to attract funding for a sequence of new scholarships that took the place of the old 1851 Commission funding. A senior fellowship in sculpture funded by the Henry Moore Foundation, together with a fellowship in memory of Helen Chadwick funded by the Arts Council of England in combination with the Ruskin School of Drawing and Fine Art in Oxford, took their place alongside the established Sargant Fellowship as opportunities for established artists. The Australia Council for the Arts established a new residency, together with the revived South African Architecture Scholarship, a welcome acknowledgement of our longstanding tradition of links with the Commonwealth. The Wingate Trust provided support for a new scholarship from 2000. And most recently, the Linbury Trust of Lord and Lady Sainsbury of Preston Candover in generously funding two scholarships for young painters and sculptors has revived the tradition of scholarships lasting for two years which characterised the early years of the School.

The Gallery Programme
by Cristiana Perrella, Gallery Curator

Since the age of the Grand Tour, young British artists have come to Rome in search of a Mediterranean experience to take back home with them. Essential to the experience was the meeting with a different quality of light and with the Antique. But Rome, at the end of the second Millennium, is much more than ruins, Baroque and blue skies: a contemporary metropolis, vivid and contradictory, a major European capital with an intense and up-to-date cultural life. After ninety years of existence, a new target was set for the School, to engage actively with Rome's contemporary cultural life, offering resident artists a good opportunity to encounter their peers in Rome. Setting up a Contemporary Arts Programme was an essential means of making this change.

A series of solo shows and lectures by major contemporary British artists started in 1991, thanks to the combined efforts of the former Director, Richard Hodges, and of Marina Engel, the Arts Adviser, who set up and curated this programme until the beginning of 1996. Striking works were conceived specifically for the difficult but fascinating space of the gallery: a former living room with fireplace, wooden floor and big panel windows

Mona Hatoum, *Untitled*, 1995.

False Impressions exhibition, 1997.

(Mona Hatoum's glass bead carpet plays on this domesticity). The School's gallery was soon viewed as a lively space for contemporary art, with a major role to play in representing the UK to the Italian artistic community. The gallery programme was also a fundamental stimulus for the resident artists who had an opportunity to exchange ideas with the artist showing in the gallery and because it regularly attracted Italian art critics and gallerists, making the events in the gallery a vital moment of exchange and a chance for new encounters.

When in 1997, Alison Jacques took over as curator, she continued to provide a showcase for British art in Rome and at the same time, allowed the programme a more confrontational attitude. She brought together eight artists, challenging the traditional reading of the portrait genre in the group show *False Impressions*. Subsequently she put on two dialogue-shows between a British and an Italian artist: Martin Creed/Massimo Bartolini and Tania Kovats/Carlo Guaita; and she curated Fiona Rae's first solo show in Italy.

Since taking over the curatorship in 1998, my intention has been to strengthen the links between the Contemporary Arts Programme and the Italian art scene, in order to create a stimulating atmosphere of debate in which to work, fundamental also for the artists in residence at the School. A series of three shows titled *London Calling* was dedicated to British art in Italian private collections (including seminal works by David Hockney, Gilbert and George, Alan Charlton, Anish Kapoor, Damien Hirst, Jake and Dinos Chapman, etc.). A programme of artists' commissions dedicated to Rome has been set up, which includes works by Cerith Wyn Evans (1998), Mark Wallinger (2000), Scanner (2001) and Yinka Shonibare (2001). At the same time, Italian artists Vedovamazzei (1998), Francesco Vezzoli (1999) and Paolo Canevari (1999), have been invited to show works with a close reference to British culture. Video programmes such as *Sweetie – Female Identity in British Video* (1999), or *VideoVibe – Art, Music and Video in the UK* (2000) after being presented successfully at the School, have toured in other Italian and European institutions.

The artists exhibited in the School's gallery in these first years reflect the whole ferment that began in the UK with the famous *Freeze* exhibition of 1988 and exploded at the beginning of the nineties. They demonstrate the vitality of British art and not only the more manifest phenomenon of visual sensationalism. If on one hand major works have been produced, strong in impact, ambitious in aim, scandalous and scandalising in their break with the past, on the other British art in the nineties has been anxious to maintain the difficult but constant balance between innovative force and contact with tradition. The School sees its function not as being to privilege any one brand of art, but to stimulate debate, and, above all, a dialogue between tradition and the contemporary.

Cerith Wyn Evans,
Untitled, 1998.

Mark Wallinger,
Threshold to the Kingdom, 2000.

PUBLICATIONS
by Gill Clark, Publications Manager

'PBSR' is a familiar sight in the notes and bibliographies of so many works on things Italian, and its traditional gold-lettered green spines take their place on many library shelves. Although it appeared sporadically in the School's earlier years, it has been annual since 1948, and in our centenary year we see the appearance of volume 69. We are particularly happy to note the success of the present Editor, Bryan Ward-Perkins, in ensuring that the *Papers* have come out regularly in November for the past five years.

Disciplinary range is one of the most persistent and striking features of the *Papers*. From its inception, the subject-matter of the *Papers* has been varied. However, over the last decade, under two successive Editors, John Lloyd (1991–5) and Bryan Ward-Perkins (1996–2002), we have seen a consistently broad range, with a significant increase in the number of pages. To take just one example, volume 67 (1999) started with a survey of hunting and farming in prehistoric Italy, from the Palaeolithic (some three quarters of a million years ago), and concluded with a study of a nineteenth-century photographer — a journey through time and down the length of Italy.

1991 marked a watershed in the School's publications programme. From 1923, supplementary volumes on a range of historical, art historical and archaeological subjects had been published, the first four being published on behalf of the School by commercial publishers. By the end of the 1980s, these amounted to some 18 volumes. A series of Archaeological Monographs was launched in 1991, under the impetus of John Lloyd as Chairman of the Publications Committee, with four volumes appearing in that first year. That same year also saw the appointment of the Publications Manager, a clear commitment on behalf of the School to its publications programme. Some 20 volumes have come out under the School's imprint in the last ten years.

The publications programme has moved since 1995 beyond archaeology, to art history, interdisciplinary conferences, and fine art studies and catalogues. Guided by Chris Wickham (Chairman of the Publications Committee 1996–2000), we have published *The Impact of Italy: the Grand Tour and Beyond* (edited by Clare Hornsby), exploring the cultural, social and artistic phonemenon known as the 'Grand Tour', *Remote Sensing: Drawings from the British School at Rome* by Kate Whiteford, drawings that arose from Kate's discovery during her time at the School as Sargant Fellow of RAF aerial photographs of Italy taken during the Second World War, as well as *Visions of Rome: Thomas Ashby, Archaeologist* (by Richard Hodges), chronicling the life and achievements of the School's first Scholar and third Director.

Collaboration in various forms has been a fundamental element, from the School's publications of *In Vino Veritas* (published by the School in association with the American Academy at Rome, the Swedish Institute at Rome, the Istituto Universitario Orientale di Napoli and the Università di Salerno) and *'Roman Ostia' Revisited* (published by the School in collaboration with the Soprintendenza Archeologica di Ostia) to the publications by others on behalf of the School of photographic material from the School's Archives.

As the School's activities increase, so does the potential for publishing, and for giving the activities a solid and long-lasting testimony. Much thought has been given over the last six years to the best ways forward. With the signing of an agreement with Cambridge University Press, we have a prestigious, effective and fitting means of publishing the School's research in art history. This, together with other collaborations and our own independent ventures, will combine to manifest in published form the multifarious work to be undertaken by the School as it enters its second century.

SUBSCRIBERS
by Jo Wallace-Hadrill, Subscriptions Secretary

Support from subscribers has always been vital to the British School at Rome, though over the past hundred years the nature of this support has changed somewhat. When the School was first launched in 1901, it was on the basis of a public appeal for subscriptions. For its first five years, the subscriptions and donations of up to 500 individuals and institutions constituted, incredibly from a modern perspective, the sole source of funding for the School. For the following five years, after the arrival of the Government grant of £500 per annum, the income from subscriptions was still sufficient to match this sum. Today we still have 500 or so subscribing individuals and institutions, but a rough calculation shows that if they were to manage to match state funding, they would currently need each to contribute an average of £1,600 per annum. In actual fact their contribution, though still most welcome, makes up only a fraction of the grant.

But although the subscribers no longer bear such crucial responsibility for the financial survival of the school, in latter years their role has developed in other, no less important, ways. These days, the body of subscribers forms a kind of supporters' club, an unique repository of memories and living history of the School in its various epochs and incarnations, bonded by the vast fund of goodwill which the School inspires in so many. Many are moved to keep in touch, and in recent years, attempts have been made to foster these good feelings. Regular lectures and social events have been organised, both in Italy, and more importantly, in London where subscribers can learn of recent events at the School and meet up with old friends. In recent years the newsletter *Notes from Rome* has been revived in order to keep subscribers informed about current activities and scholarships at the School. The centenary calendar, with its juxtaposition of archive and modern photographs, charting both the School's year and moments in its evolution, embodied the link between distant memories and current realities. We trust that this fund of warmth and enthusiasm, which has given the School so much support and encouragement over the past century, will continue to bear fruit for many years to come.

THE ARCHIVE
by Valerie Scott, Librarian and Archivist

It is easy to forget that what we do today, whether writing a letter, making a decision, taking a photograph or scribbling a note, quickly becomes tomorrow's history and how much more acute has that become in the recent past with the advent of e-mail, digital images, CDs and the ever-changing technology that is so radically affecting the way we work and the way in which history is recorded.

Leafing through over 600 box-files that make up the Administrative Archive one wonders at the scrupulousness of its first administrators: copies of every single typed letter, however mundane, on tissue-thin paper held together with rusting pins, although it would not be overly cynical to suggest that the motivation for this was probably political and had little to do with the more noble activity of writing history. However, it survives and since it has been moved to Rome from the office in London to join the photographic and archaeological Archives, its importance has at last been understood and appreciated. It has already been the main resource, not only for this publication, but also for the biography of Richard Hodges, *Visions of Rome: Thomas Ashby, Archaeologist.*

A prominent figure in our history, Thomas Ashby's name occurs many times throughout this volume in many contexts, as Director, archaeologist, topographer and biblio-

James Graham (1806-69) Paestum, Temple of Ceres from the SW, 1860.

Miss Bulwer (Agnes?), Huts at Osa.

phile. His wide-ranging interests also included photography from an early age and, just as his remarkable collection of rare books forms the nucleus of the Library, so his own photographs, more than 8,500 taken between 1890-1930, form the core of the photographic Archive. The 18 albums of prints ordered chronologically can be read as a visual autobiography of his life and interests. Choosing an album at random, we find Ashby travelling around Sardinia photographing nuraghe and local costumes, then back to the Campagna Romana on the via Latina, at Tivoli, Ferentino and along the via Appia, followed by Rome and Giacomo Boni's excavations in the Forum; on to acqueducts in the Roman countryside followed by a trip to England and 'rough sea' at St. Margaret's Bay, then to Malta, Carthage, Dougga ending up with another trip to Sardinia – all also recorded in the School's very detailed Annual Report for 1907-8. An indefatigable scribbler of notes, usually in pencil and often on the backs of envelopes, Ashby's annotations covering all areas of his wide-ranging interests run to thousands of pages. It is a miracle that these were not destroyed. The School, thanks to the generosity of its Treasurer, W. Russell, was able to purchase Ashby's library and photographs, but reading through the correspondence it becomes clear that no-one in the School was interested in the notes. Ashby's wife, May, however, understood their value and wrote in a letter of 19 February 1933 to the Director, Colin Hardie, 'before my husband died he often said these notes and mss were the most valuable of all he had and if he went first I was to see that they didn't share the fate of Lanciani's which were loose in the Vatican and scattered and soiled and it used to grieve T. to see them and so his own mss are to me a sacred trust'.

It is remarkable how many of the collections of late nineteenth and early twentieth century photographs belonging to the BSR, most of which are still unknown and unpublished, can be linked to Ashby's name. He was a member of the British and American Archaeological Society of Rome founded by John Henry Parker, himself a photographer who also employed others to carry out a photographic campaign documenting classical and medieval architecture and topography in Italy, and particularly Rome, in the nineteenth century; the Society's copy of the Parker collection of nearly 2,400 prints found its way to the School. One of the main activities of the Society was to organise trips into the Roman Campagna to visit archaeological sites and photography must have played an important part of those visits for not only were Parker and Ashby keen photographers but so were other members, for example, the Bulwer sisters, Agnes and Dora, and the Dominican monk Rev. P.P. Mackey. They were technically more skilled than Ashby, whose main interest was the significance of the object in question, whether a Roman road or a Sardinian traditional costume, not composition or lighting or just producing a beautiful image; both these collections were donated to the School via Ashby.

We must not forget the indomitable Eugénie Strong, scholar of Greek and Roman sculpture and Assistant Director during Ashby's Directorship. She was a great collector of commercial photographs of works of art, particularly sculpture, and has left a remarkable collection of over 12,000 prints, many taken by important photographers, Alinari, Anderson, Faraglia, Moscioni and Tuminello, to name just a few, as well as a

Father Peter Paul Mackey (1851-1935), Roman Arch at Priverno, near Latina.

collection of nearly 5,000 postcards. The importance of early photographs as a record of the past does not need emphasising but what is interesting and sadly ironic, is that the photographs taken by J. B. Ward-Perkins, Director 1945-74, during the South Etruria Survey in the 1950s and 60s are just as important as those much earlier images, thanks to the rate of urbanization to the north of Rome which has been greater over the past 50 years than probably the past 500, to the point that much of the historical landscape is simply unrecognizable today. His archaeological as well as military training meant that not only did he have an 'extraordinary understanding of terrain' during campaigns in North Africa but also recognised the future importance for archaeologists of the hundreds of thousands of air-photographs taken of Italy during the war by the RAF for military purposes. Not only did he manage to secure a copy of these for the School (subsequently deposited with the Italian National Aerofototeca in Rome in 1975) but also a collection of nearly 1200 photographs of Italian monuments damaged by bombing. Ward-Perkins, in fact, led the Sub-Commission of the Allied Government for Monuments and Fine Arts, which travelled the length and breadth of Italy at the end of the war to document the damage.

A rich and varied Archive then, containing over 100,000 items, neglected for many years and underestimated as an important resource for research, it is now receiving the attention it deserves. The Centenary Building Project, which will provide not only a new wing for the Library and a new home for the Photographic and Administrative Archives but also a Lecture Theatre and a new exhibition space offering much-needed facilities for events and activities, has stimulated a comprehensive project of reorganising, cleaning, conserving, digitizing and cataloguing that has already been valuable for the preparation of this volume and has also resulted in a number of new discoveries. Glass negatives are a conservation nightmare and as our collections include over 5,000 items, many still in their original boxes and all needing cleaning and conserving, this was where we began. The quality of the images, which became evident during scanning is remarkable and can be seen in many of the illustrations in this volume, in particular the photographs of work by our Fine Art Scholars from 1912 up to the 1950s which was recorded every year by a professional photographer. Sadly, this practice was dropped and was not resumed until the 1990s, resulting in large gaps in the collection.

It can safely be said that this Centenary Volume could never have been written or illustrated without our archives; but during its preparation the inconsistency of the contents became very noticeable. The answer to practically every enquiry regarding the early years of the School's history can, with patience, be found somewhere in those box-files; during the latter years, however, documentation, both visual and written, becomes more patchy. We have a responsibility not only to preserve and conserve the existing material but also to facilitate research and publication as well as ensuring that future generations have the means to understand and recreate the history of the BSR and its development throughout the twenty-first century.

DEVELOPMENT
by Caroline Egerton, Chair of the Development Group

The last years of the School's first century have involved continuous renewal and rebuilding. The major phase of the School's Development kicked off after the decision was taken in 1993 to renovate the North Wing of the School. This wing, containing the study-bedrooms and artists' studios needed complete refurbishment, and in addition it emerged that the entire School needed re-wiring. We started campaigning for the funds against the background of being comparatively unknown to the wider public and with the considerable handicap, as far as many grant-giving bodies were concerned, of being 'overseas'. The Baring Foundation, the Linbury Trust, the Headley Trust, the Monument Trust, Glaxo, the Rhodes Trust and so many others including the J.P. Getty Charitable Trust, the Manifold Trust and Mr Christopher Loyd gave substantially. An auction at Christies, for which our former Artist Scholars and friends contributed works, and private views of exhibitions organized at the Fine Arts Society by Paul Liss and Peyton Skipwith of our early scholars, Winifred Knights and Thomas Monnington, drew further attention to the cause. Without this extraordinary degree of support, we would never have succeeded in raising the £300,000 needed.

While crucial decisions were being taken about where the capital development programme should go next, at the end of 1996 we embarked on a fundraising programme for the Library, concentrating in particular on the conservation and rehousing of the rare books and prints, and the provision of extra shelving. There was also the necessity to catalogue and conserve the School's extraordinary Archive. Our old friends supported us, but we also got notable support from the Drue Heinz Trust, the Rayne Foundation, the Aurelius Trust, the British Library, Livery Companies and the many academic institutions who had links with the School. About £140,000 were raised. The new Rare Books Room was a triumph of the skill of Giuseppe Fioranelli, the School Carpenter.

During the years 1998/99 it became clear where our next efforts should be concentrated, namely to raise funds to extend the Library. On the urging of Lord Sainsbury of Preston Candover, we determined to build the urgently needed lecture theatre at the same time, though the target of over £ two million seemed daunting. With the vital encouragement offered by the Department for Education in providing one third of the sum needed,

Proposal for the library extension by Hugh Petter.

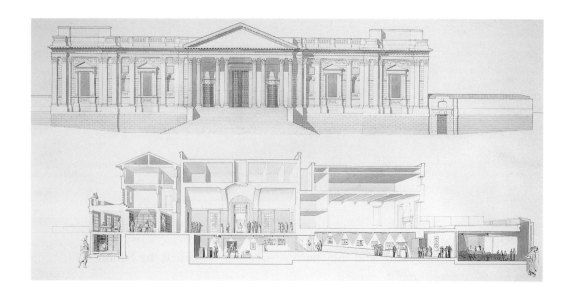

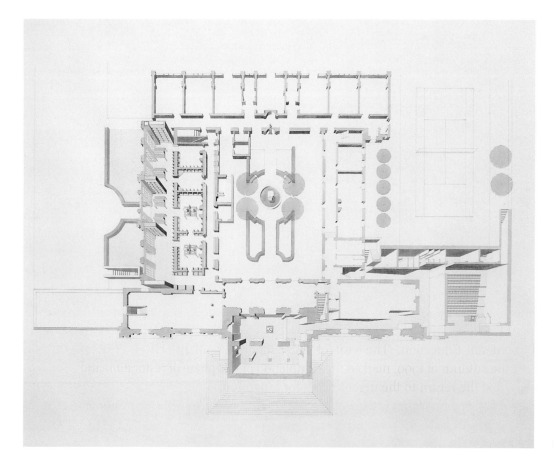

Plan of the School
by Nicholas Wood.

Lord and Lady Sainsbury's Linbury Trust and David Woodley Packard's Packard Humanities Institute emerged as the major sponsors, but valued contributions were received from many others, including the Weston Foundation, Lord Rothschild, the Commissioners for the 1851 Exhibition (as a parting gift) and old friends such as the Manifold Trust, the Rhodes Trust and the D'Oyly Carte Charitable Trust. We made new friends like the Michael Marks Charitable Trust and many others whose generosity enabled us to reach our target in two years.

The story would not be complete without an acknowledgement of the generosity of Richard and Janet Cooper who through their Charitable Trust enabled the School to celebrate its Centenary in style with a Private View at the Royal Academy of Arts in March 2000 of the *Genius of Rome* Exhibition. The money raised has enabled the publication of this volume.

The School owes a debt to all who have helped us along the way and the results are there for all to see. I also owe a personal debt to Christopher Mann and Rita Chapple who have been part of the team since 1993. I knew nothing at all about fund-raising when I started. They taught me all I know and they have advised and sustained the School's campaigns throughout the last eight years.

The Centenary Building Projects
by Jane Thompson, Project Manager

The first priority for any building is to ensure that what you have is in good working order. Robert Adam (Architecture Scholar 1973) was called in to advise on future plans for expansion in 1991. His masterplan, updated and developed by Francesco Garofalo and Sharon Yoshie Miura in 1995, addressed the three most urgent needs of the School: room for the Library to expand, a proper lecture space, and more private accommodation for the staff. His proposal to create two new houses in the garden for Director and Assistant Director fell foul of the planning authorities; but it was also overtaken by the gradual realization that the building fell short on virtually all health and safety standards, and that a major overhaul was needed before any new building could be contemplated.

Renovations, already started with the façade (1994), continued with the studio wing (1996): the elegant designs of Francesco Garofalo and Sharon Yoshie Miura gave a new life to these spaces. The unglamorous mission of rewiring, replumbing, and inserting fire doors in the rest of the building was made possible by a generous grant of £250,000 from the Department for Education. The visit of the School's President, HRH Princess Alexandra, in the autumn of 1999, marked the completion of this phase of restoration and improvement, and the return to the urgent needs for expansion.

The Adam masterplan was revisited in 1998 by Hugh Petter (Architecture Scholar 1990). Alternative solutions were offered for both the Library and the Lecture Room designed to respect the sensitivity of the planning authorities to any increase of the built surface in a 'green belt' area of gardens and cultural institutes. For the Library, the original Lutyens design which had foreseen a veranda along the west wing outside the Library offered an ingenious solution: we would be finishing off a Lutyens plan long since approved by the Roman authorities. For the Lecture Room, rather than the inconvenience of converting and relocating the kitchen, we could construct a new space at the level of the kitchen, which being subterranean as far as the ground plan of the School was concerned, would not add to our ratio of built to unbuilt space. Happily, the same 'subterranean' area would open directly on the street, allowing the public direct access for lectures.

These proposals were received positively by the Comune, thanks above all to the vigorous support of Professor Eugenio La Rocca; and they at once found an enthusiastic supporter, as Lady Egerton explains, in Lord Sainsbury. His early promise of support set a good example for a host of other donors, and ensured that the two million estimated costs were swiftly raised. When the School appointed a Project Manager in spring 2000, the scheme design, again by Francesco Garofalo and Sharon Yoshie Miura, was well advanced, and the funding was nearly in place; yet much was still to do. The role of a Project Manager, as main interface between the client body and the design team and builders, is to ensure that the client gets what is wanted, to the standard required, on budget and on time. But the client can be a many-headed beast, not always quite knowing what it wants, and the plans were to undergo significant development over the coming months. What had started out as two projects for new buildings on each flank of the original building grew over the following months into a more wide-ranging reappraisal and transformation of the School's physical resources. The willingness of the School to review the scope and impact of the projects, and dedicate more funds and fundraising skills accordingly, has undoubtedly reaped its own rewards and will make the centenary year one of historic change.

The major shortfall of the Library extension plans as initially proposed and costed was that they would only provide a relatively limited future growth. The outstanding generosity of the Packard Humanities Institute in late Spring 2000 enabled us to add a full basement under the extension, making the whole expansion of the Library a substantial affair and the disruption the more worthwhile. The opportunity to bring most of the School's Archive together in one location with space for growth which could offer the appropriate fire and environmental systems to protect its longevity brought obvious benefits for this unique asset of the School and triggered a whole series of benefits elsewhere in the existing building.

Just as the Library extension has benefited from David Packard's personal interest in ensuring the best outcome for the School, so the Lecture Theatre has benefited from Lord Sainsbury's insistence on high standards. The idea of three moving platforms, borrowed from Dulwich Art Gallery, ensure that the space will be flexible in use, as a raked lecture theatre, or a level space for exhibitions and other events. The latest audio-visual technology will open it up not only to slide projection, but video and computer projection, while the terrace above, accessible either from the theatre or the dining hall, will offer a superb space for entertainment linked to events.

A series of separate factors encouraged the School to rethink the relationship of the new facilities to the existing fabric at a late stage in the project development. The pressing need to address disabled access, the difficulty of maintaining beneath the front steps a carpenter's workshop that respected health and safety rules, the need to rationalise the old heating systems and the ludicrous detours of its pipe-work, the opportunity offered by the move of the archive from its previous home in the 'ping-pong room', but above all the need to rationalise the division of public and private activities within the building, led to a radical revision of the scheme.

Some modest juggling of the circulation and relocation of service access to the back of the building was instigated, giving the School the opportunity to manage its rich pro-

The new link corridor between
the gallery and Lecture theatre.

gramme of activities with a new clarity and ease. The conversion of the old service stair behind reception into a grand public route to the new lecture theatre has established an elegant connection between street level and the new lecture theatre and the existing main public areas of the building. The insertion of a lift beside the new stair not only gives the disabled access to all four floors of the building, but greatly helps the staff moving heavy materials. In conjunction with the lecture theatre, the School will have at its disposition an entire arts complex with direct street access and lift connections up to dining and fine terraces overlooking the Borghese gardens. The lower ground floor of street frontage will become the public face of the School where lectures, conferences, exhibitions, dances and concerts can take place without a negative impact on the residents. The upper ground floor will remain the public face of the School with the Lutyens entrance hall, the fine courtyard and the dining hall still welcoming guests and the Library and Archive still welcoming outside readers. The floors above and beyond, circling the court-

yard, will become the safe haven of residents and scholarly activity unhindered by visitors and the excesses of the events programme.

The new Gallery has become the third major initiative of the Centenary Building Project. The surprisingly large space liberated beneath the front steps lends itself to an exhibition area with a contemporary feel, so releasing the former Gallery in the heart of the residential area for its former use as a common room. The benefit of a flexible exhibition space that can take on a variety of uses is evident. Exhibitions of the Contemporary Arts Programme and the resident artists, but also from the Archive with its collections of photographs and drawings, or archaeology projects can run alongside a rich events programme of related or unrelated lectures, conferences, film shows and even parallel wall-mounted exhibitions in the Lecture Theatre.

The sum benefit of all the interventions described is far greater than anything we could have hoped for. The legacy the Centenary Building Projects will leave the British School is not only that of a top class new lecture room and library wing and gallery, but a series of improvements, the benefits of which are already being felt by the resident community.

(1995–2001)

INTO THE MILLENNIUM

AFTERWORD

by Geoffrey Rickman,   Chairman of Council

In 1958 I went to the School as the Henry Francis Pelham Student from Oxford. After a 36-hour journey by boat and train, as a near-penniless postgraduate, I caught a bus from the railway station to via Gramsci. On the bus a lively debate developed as to exactly where and what the British School was, and where best I should get off. I remained silent. Only now, after many more visits, and reading this volume, might I speak in such a debate with real confidence.

That first visit marked me for life, as it has many others before and after me. It aroused a passion for Italy, and a long, slow-burning, love for the School. It was profoundly educational precisely because the School was not a purely academic institution, set in the marvellous cultural location of Rome, but included, as part of its very essence, practising artists as well. A different, non-verbal, world of effort and achievement was opened up.

However intense the experience, I like others, still knew little of the origin, development, and continuity of the School. Now, after reading these pages, I understand much better. As the past comes back, names long forgotten start to whisper insistently in my

Visit of HM The Queen,
October 2000.

203

head, as different ones will in all who know the School. Some are mentioned in the text, some are not. The story of the School is full of unsung heroines and heroes, who deserve acknowledgement. They include the School's Italian staff, who have always done so much to make the School a home for its residents. Significant among them must be the Director's wife. In my time it was Margaret Ward-Perkins, universal mother, aunt, nanny, nurse, and graceful hostess to passing generations; recently Jo Wallace-Hadrill, in addition, has taken on the special care of the Subscribers, the living heart of the School's support.

But I should perhaps conclude by thanking especially all those, including my distinguished predecessors as Chairman, who have served on the School's Council and other committees, selflessly and for no reward. From different backgrounds and walks of life, they represent that wider constituency, vital to the School and its future, who I hope will be particularly interested and intrigued by this centennial history.

With its magnificent building refurbished and enlarged, with the original, comprehensive and inspiring vision of the founders brilliantly implemented by the present Director, Andrew Wallace-Hadrill and his team, the School can look forward to its next century with confidence and a sense of exhilaration.

HRH Princess Alexandra with Tilly Cooper and Sophie Wallace-Hadrill at the Royal Academy *Genius of Rome* private view, sponsored by the Richard Cooper Charitable Trust.

The British in Rome
(to 1900)

1. See *Executive Committee minutes* 4 Dec 1912.
2. I am indebted to Anthony Majanlahti for the following account of the English in medieval Rome.
3. See Andrew Wilton and Ilaria Bignamini, *Grand Tour: the Lure of Italy in the Eighteenth Century* (exhibition catalogue, Tate, London 1996); also Clare Hornsby (ed.), *The Impact of Italy: The Grand Tour and Beyond* (BSR 2000).
4. Clare Hornsby, 'Carlo Labruzzi: an album of thirteen aquatints dedicated to Sir Richard Colt Hoare', *Apollo* 2000, 3-8.
5. Frank Salmon, 'The impact of the archaeology of Rome on British architects and their work c.1750-1840' in *The Impact of Italy: The Grand Tour and Beyond*, ed. Clare Hornsby (BSR 2000), 219-43.

The Early Years
(1900-1910)

1. Reported by the Times, 23 Nov 1904.
2. See R. Hodges, *Visions of Rome*, 21ff.
3. See T.P. Wiseman, 'Con Boni nel Foro: I diari romani di W. St. Clair Baddeley', *Rivista dell'istituto nazionale di archeologia e storia dell'arte* 8-9 (1985-86), 119-49; T.P. Wiseman, *Short History of the British School at Rome* (1990), 3.
4. See T.P. Wiseman, 'The first Director of the British School', *PBSR* 49, 1981, 144-63.
5. Ashby PBSR VIII (1916), 81f.
6. J.E. Sandys, 'James Peddie Steele', PBSR IX (1920), 1-15.
7. Ashby, *PBSR* I (1902), p. 137.
8. *Notes from Rome by Rodolfo Lanciani* edited by Anthony Cubberley (BSR 1988).
9. A.H. Smith, 'Thomas Ashby, 1874-1931', *Proceedings of the British Academy* 17 (1931), 515-41
10. Ashby, *PBSR* I (1902), p.136.
11. J.L. Myres, 'Sir Henry Stuart Jones 1867-1939', *Proceedings of the British Academy* 26 (1940), 467-78.
12. See Wiseman, 'The first Director of the British School', 159-60.
13. See Mary Beard, *The Invention of Jane Harrison* (Cambridge, Mass. 2000) p.23.
14. *PBSR* V (1908), plate 38.
15. A.J. Toynbee, *Hannibal's Legacy: The Hannibalic War's Effect on Roman Life* (Oxford 1965), preface p.v refers to the visit.
16. S.J.A. Churchill, 'The goldsmiths of Rome under the Papal authority', *PBSR* IV (1907), 161-226.
17. Executive Committee minutes, 5 March 1907.
18. D. MacKenzie, 'The dolmens, tombs of the Giants, and nuraghi of Sardinia', *PBSR* V (1910), 87-137.
19. T.E. Peet, 'The early iron age in South Italy', *PBSR* IV (1907), 283-96.
20. T.E. Peet, 'Contributions to the study of the prehistoric period in Malta', *PBSR* V (1910), 139-63.

The New Building
(1911-1925)

1. John W. Simpson, *British School of Architecture at Rome. Second Memorandum* (November 1909), p.2.
2. Lutyens, letter to Exec Ctee, 26 April 1911.
3. The following account of the history of the building is based on material prepared by Andrew Hopkins; for a detailed account, see his contribution to the forthcoming volume, *Lutyens Abroad*.
4. Quoted from H. Petter, *Lutyens in Italy*, (1992), 14.
5. Quoted from Petter, *Lutyens in Italy*, p.11-18.
6. The four drawings were wrongfully removed from the London office and sold at auction in 1988.
7. Mary Taylor and H.C. Bradshaw, 'Architectural terra-cottas from two temples at Falerii Veteres', *PBSR VIII* (1916), 1-34.
8. H.C. Bradshaw, 'Praeneste: a study for its restoration', *PBSR IX* (1919), 233-62.
9. See Hodges, *Visions of Rome* 15; Emily Rothschild in *Winifred Knights (1899-1947)* (Fine Art Society and Paul Liss with BSR, 1995), 19-22.
10. The story is told in Hodges, *Visions of Rome* 69-82 .
11. Emily Vansittart, a friend of the Misses Bulwer, as Alistair Crawford pointed out to me. William Squire was Lutyens' project manager.
12. See Hodges, *Visions of Rome* 74; the above account slightly corrects the dates of the Committee meetings.
13. Mary Beard, *The Invention of Jane Harrison* (Cambridge, Mass. 2000) 14-29. The forthcoming biography by Stephen Dyson testifies to the continued impact of Strong.
14. Ashby to Shaw 24.6.25.

After Ashby
(1925-1939)

1. The entire list: Armando Bonora, Butler; Regina Bonora, sewing & laundry woman; Tina Bondi, dining-hall maid; Albertina Scartazzini, housemaid; Bruno Bonelli, hall-boy; Giovanni Vistoni, cook; Vittorio Di Giammarco, kitchen-boy; Felice Saletta, kitchen-boy; Pietro Corriere, house man (temporary); Camillo Tabacchiera, gardener; Antonio Oddo, night guard; Mr Pavey, stoker; and an unnamed kitchen porter.
2. Ashby to Shaw, 10.3.22, Box 87.
3. An allegation needless to say without foundation, as Mrs Stong protested to the Ambassador.
4. Smith to Shaw, 16.12.32.
5. Strong to Quick, 9.9.24, Box 87.
6. Esher to Shaw, 7.10.24, Box 87.
7. Shaw to Esher, 9.4.24, Box 117.
8. B. Ashmole, *An Autobiography* (1994), 30f.
9. B. Ashmole, *An Autobiography* (1994), 32ff.
10. Shaw to Ashmole, 11.1.26.
11. Ashmole to Shaw, 27.2.28.
12. Minutes of FAHL, 3.8.1927 for the decision.
13. Letter to T.P. Wiseman, 28.12.86.
14. Ashmole to Shaw, 27.2.28.
15. Shaw to Smith, 25.10.28.
16. Exec Ctee minutes 28.2.29.
17. Smith to Shaw, 1.3.30.
18. Ian A. Richmond, *The city wall of imperial Rome, an account of its architectural development from Aurelian to Narses* (Oxford 1930).
19. I.A. Richmond, 'The relation of the Praetorian Camp to Aurelian's wall of Rome', *PBSR X* (1927) 12-22.
20. R.A. Cordingley and I.A. Richmond, 'The Mausoleum of Augustus', *PBSR X* (1927) 23-35.
21. Published in *PBSR XII* (1932) plate V.
22. *The Classical Tradition in British Architecture: Rome Scholars in Architecture 1912-1982* (BSR 1982), 9-11.
23. Published in *PBSR X* (1927) plate XI.
24. Letter to T.P. Wiseman, 28.12.1986.
25. A. Minoprio, 'A restoration of the Basilica of Constantine, Rome', *PBSR XII* (1932) 1-25.
26. I.A. Richmond and W.G. Holford, 'Roman Verona: the archaeology of its town-plan', *PBSR XIII* (1935) 69-76.
27. Richmond to Shaw, 16.10.30.
28. Richmond to Shaw, 29.10.30.
29. Richmond to Shaw, 18.3.31.
30. Richmond to Shaw, 20.11.30 (collaboration); 28.11.30 (lunch).

31. Richmond to Shaw, 19.5.31.
32. Richmond to Shaw, 4.6.31.
33. Annual Report to Subscribers 1931-32.
34. FAHL minutes, 13.11.31.
35. Richmond to Shaw, 14.12.31.
36. Richmond to Shaw, 15.6.31.
37. Richmond to Shaw, 10.10.31; 21.10.31;
    24.10.31; 3.11.31; 3.12.31; 2.1.32; 31.1.32.
38. Richmond to Shaw, 13.4.32.
39. Richmond to Shaw, 8.6.32.
40. Richmond to Shaw, 3.8.32.
41. Smith to Shaw, 22.11.32. A guarded
    report on an interview with the School
    lawyer, Sir John Serrao, says Serrao
    'would feel bound to put an end to a
    scandalous situation' (Smith to Shaw
    21.12.32), the only whiff of scandal in the
    archive.
42. Richmond to Shaw, 14.10.32.
43. Smith to Shaw, 24.10.32.
44. Shaw to Hardie, 10.6.36.
45. Hardie to Shaw, 19.2.33.
46. Hardie to Shaw, 15.3.33.
47. Hardie to Shaw, 15.3.33.
48. Hardie to Shaw, 26.3.33.
49. Hardie to Shaw, 26.3.33.
50. Hardie to Shaw, 26.3.33.
51. Hardie to Shaw, 12.6.33.
52. W. Holford Journal of RIBA 1937, 538
    (cited in full above, Preface).
53. Hardie to Shaw, 29.4.33.
54. Hardie to Shaw, 19.11.35.
55. Hardie to Shaw, 24.11.35.
56. Shaw to Hardie, 25.5.36.
57. Hardie to Shaw, 22.1.36.
58. Hardie to Shaw, 16.4.35.
59. Hardie to Shaw, 14.6.36.
60. Wiseman, PBSR 49 (1981), 152.
61. Hardie to Shaw, 12.11.34.
62. Radford to Shaw, 11.10.37.
63. Shaw to Radford, 16.3.38.
64. Radford to Shaw, 24.9.37.
65. Mrs Barbara Craig, letter 16.4.98.
66. Letter to T.P. Wiseman, 28.12.86.
67. Radford to Shaw, 23.12.38, and 9.3.39.
68. The Classical Tradition in British
    Architecture: Rome Scholars in
    Architecture 1912-1982 (BSR 1982), 13.
    Hirst thought the visit was in 1937, but
    the coincidence of visitors is unlikely.
69. Radford to Shaw, 24.3.39.
70. Radford to Shaw, 13.10.44.
71. Minutes of FAHL, 28.1.37.
72. Shaw to Radford, 18.1.37.
73. Shaw reference in Radford file),
    20.10.41.

Il Dopoguerra (1945-1974)

1. Radford to Shaw, 25.3.40.
2. Radford to Shaw, 11.5.41; Shaw to
   Radford, 23.5.41.
3. Radford to Shaw, 17.9.39.
4. Firsthand accounts in Wiseman, Short
   History, p. 19.
5. Massimo Pallottino in PBSR XLVIII
   (1980), xvii.
6. Shaw to Radford, 25.3.45.
7. Radford to Shaw, 17.8.38 for Wheeler,
   18.6.45 for Ward-Perkins.
8. Cited in Petter, Lutyens in Italy, p.29.
9. See "Nobile Munus": Origini e primi
   sviluppi dell'Unione Internazionale degli
   Istituti di Archaeologia Storia e Storia
   dell'Arte in Roma (1946-1953), ed. E.
   Billig, C. Nylander and P. Vian (Rome
   1996).
10. Kate Whiteford, Remote Sensing:
    Drawings from the British School at
    Rome (BSR 1997).
11. 'The church of S. Salvatore at Spoleto:
    some structural notes', PBSR XVII
    (1949), 72-86.
12. A grant of £600 is reported in the Exec
    Ctee minutes of 14.9.56.
13. J.J. Wilkes, 'John Bryan Ward-Perkins
    1912-1981', Proceedings of the British
    Academy 69 (1983), 631-55 for a fuller
    account.
14. The inscriptions of Roman Tripolitania,
    edited by J. M. Reynolds and J. B. Ward-
    Perkins (BSR 1952).
15. The Shrine of St. Peter and the Vatican
    excavations, Jocelyn Toynbee and John
    Ward Perkins (London 1956).
16. J.B. Ward-Perkins and Jocelyn M.C.
    Toynbee, 'The Hunting Baths at Lepcis
    Magna', Archeologia 93 (1949).
17. See the account by T.W. Potter, first
    published in "Nobile Munus" (1996),
    187-96, reissued as part of the survey
    article: T.W. Potter and S.K.F. Stoddart,
    'A century of prehistory and landscape
    studies at the British School at Rome'
    PBSR 69 (2001), 3-34.
18. "Nobile Munus" p.194.
19. Exec. Ctee 24.9.70.
20. Exec. Ctee. 24.9.70.
21. Joyce Reynolds in PBSR XLVIII (1980),
    xvi.
22. Ward-Perkins, 18.6.1962, Box 228.
23. Eric Hebborn, Drawn to Trouble: The
    Forging of an Artist (Edinburgh 1991),
    190.
24. Mrs Hardiman to Shaw, 24.1.24.
25. Shaw to Ashmole, 16.3.26 – Sargant was
    a friend of Ashby and George Clausen;
    Ashmole to Shaw 7.4.26 is enthusiastic

about the property.
26. Shaw to Smith 13.11.28.
27. Smith Report to Exec Ctee, 5.11.30.
28. Exec. Ctee, 1.5.45.
29. Exec. Ctee. 1.3.55.
30. Exec. Ctee. 24.11.60.

New Challenges (1974-1995)

1. Minutes of the Finance and General
   Purposes Committee, 23.10.86: the
   pound fell from an average of 2450 lire
   during 1985/86 to 1960 lire on 23
   October 1986.
2. The following account is based on that
   of the Annual Report for 1983-84, which
   took the unusual step of bidding farewell
   to a Director with an account of his
   achievements.
3. Margaret Lyttleton and Frank Sear, 'A
   Roman villa near Anguillara Sabazia'
   PBSR XXXII (1977), 227-251.
4. Annual Report 78 (1983-84), 6.
5. The Archaeology of Mediterranean
   Landscapes edited by Graeme Barker
   and David Mattingly (1999-2001).
6. Excavations at Otranto. Volume I: The
   excavations. Volume II: The finds. (1992).
7. Neil Christie (ed.), Three South Etrurian
   Churches: Santa Cornelia, Santa Rufina
   and San Liberato (BSR 1991).
8. Minutes of Council, 12.12.86, 4.1.
9. Archeologia a Roma nelle fotografie di
   Thomas Ashby 1891-1930 (BSR/ICCD,
   Electa Napoli 1989).
10. Il Lazio di Thomas Ashby 1891-1930
    (Palombi, Roma 1994).
11. Published by the Istituto Poligrafico as
    The Twighlight of the Grand Tour. A
    Catalogue of the drawings of James
    Hakewill in the British School at Rome
    Library, Tony Cubberley and Luke
    Herrmann (1992).

APPENDIX

by Sarah Court, Sarah Hyslop and Katherine Wallis

PATRON

HM the Queen

PRESIDENTS OF COUNCIL

1912-21	H.R.H. Prince Arthur of Connaught
1921-36	H.R.H. The Prince of Wales (Edward VIII)
1936-42	H.R.H. The Duke of Kent (Prince George)
1945-65	H.R.H. The Princess Royal
1965-68	H.R.H. Princess Marina, Duchess of Kent
1970-	H.R.H. Princess Alexandra, the Hon. Mrs Angus Ogilvy
1945-74	WARD-PERKINS, John Bryan
1974-83	WHITEHOUSE, David B.
1984	BULLOUGH, Donald A.
1984-88	BARKER, Graeme W.
1988-95	HODGES, Richard
1995-	WALLACE-HADRILL, Andrew

CHAIRMEN

1899-1907	Prof. Henry F. PELHAM *Managing Committee*
1908-11	Prof. J.S. REID *Managing Committee*
1912-30	Viscount ESHER *Executive Committee*
1930-42	Lord RENNELL of RODD *Executive Committee*
1945-50	Sir Frederic KENYON *Executive Committee*
1950-61	Sir Alan BARLOW *Executive Committee*
1961-72	Dr T.S.R. BOASE *Executive Committee*
1972-87	Alwyn G. SHEPPARD FIDLER *Executive Committee*
1987-94	Sir Alan CAMPBELL *Council*
1991-94	Roderick CAVALIERO *Finance & General Purposes Committee*
1994-97	Prof. Fergus MILLAR *Council*
1997-	Prof. Geoffrey RICKMAN *Council*

Note:
The School was initially run by a Managing Committee. Under the new Charter of 1912, nominal control passed to Council, under a royal President, and effective control passed to an Executive Committee, while the old Managing Committee became the Faculty of Archaeology, History and Letters. In 1987, as a transitional measure the Executive Committee was abolished, and its functions transferred to a Finance and General Purposes Committee, while Council assumed real authority; under the Supplemental Charter of 1995, Council assumed full responsibility under the Charities Act.

DIRECTORS

1900-03	RUSHFORTH, Gordon McNeil
1903-05	STUART-JONES, Henry
1906-25	ASHBY, Thomas
1925-28	ASHMOLE, Bernard
1928-30	SMITH, Arthur Hamilton
1930-32	RICHMOND, Ian A.
1933-36	HARDIE, Colin G.
1936-39	RADFORD, C.A. Ralegh

ASSISTANT DIRECTORS AND LIBRARIANS

1903-05	ASHBY, Thomas *Assistant Director*
1906-07	DANIEL, Augustus M. *Assistant Director*
1907-09	YEAMES, A.H.S. *Assistant Director*
1909-25	STRONG, Mrs. Arthur (Eugénie) *Assistant Director*
1930-33	CROOKE, Richard L. *Librarian*
1933-36	WATERHOUSE, Ellis *Librarian*
1936-37	TRENDALL, Arthur Dale *Librarian*
1937-39	CRAIG, W. James *Librarian*
1946	MALCOLM, Donald *Librarian*
1946-48	CLEMENTI, Dione *Librarian*
1948-54	GOODCHILD, Richard G. *Librarian*
1954-57	CORBETT, G.U. Spencer *Librarian*
1957-62	BALLANCE, Michael H. *Assistant Director*
1962-67	MALLETT, Michael E. *Assistant Director*
1967-72	LUTTRELL, Anthony T. *Assistant Director*
1973-75	ROBERTSON, Ian G. *Assistant Director*
1973-89	VALENTINI, Luciana *Librarian*
1975-77	CORNELL, Timothy *Assistant Director*
1977-78	MICHAELIDES, Demetrios *Assistant to the Director*
1980-94	CLARIDGE, Amanda *Assistant Director*
1989-	SCOTT, Valerie *Librarian*
1996-98	HORNSBY, Clare *Assistant Director (Art History)*
1996-	PATTERSON, Helen *Assistant Director (Archaeology)*
1997-	HOPKINS, Andrew J. *Assistant Director*
1997-	BENCI, Jacopo *Assistant Director (Fine Arts)*

Note:
For most of its history, the School has had only one academic member of staff other than the Director. The Assistant Director also functioned as Librarian. Between 1925 and 1957, the title was changed to Librarian, and restored to Assistant Director in 1958. In 1973, the functions split, since when there has been a full-time Librarian, and, with intervals in 1978-80 and 1994-97, an academic Assistant Director. In 1997 parity of rank was given to those running the Archaeology, Art History and Fine Arts programmes.

STUDENTS (1901–1915)

1901 ASHBY, Thomas *Craven (Christ Church, Oxford)*
BLAKISTON, Cuthbert *Craven (Christ Church, Oxford)*
McINTYRE, Peter S. *St Andrews*
WEBB, Bernard H. *ARIBA*

1903 CUNNINGHAM, H.J. *Edinburgh*
DAVIES, W.J. *ARIBA*
JONES, E. Alfred -
WACE, Alan J.B. *Craven (Pembroke, Cambridge)*
WINSTEDT, E.O. *Craven (Magdalen, Oxford)*

1904 ALLEN, T.W. *Queen's, Oxford*
BURROUGHS, E.A. *Craven (Balliol, Oxford)*
KIRKWOOD, W.A. *University College, Toronto*
ORR, Frank G. *Glasgow*
RICHMOND, Oliffe L. *Craven (King's, Cambridge)*
YEAMES, A.H.S. *New College, Oxford; BM*

1905 DICKINS, Guy *Craven (St John's, Oxford)*
HAMILTON, M.B. *Carnegie (St Andrew's)*
JAMISON, Evelyn M. *LMH, Oxford*
MAINGUY, Alain *Exeter, Oxford*
TILLYARD, H.J.W. *Gonville and Caius, Cambridge*

1906 ERICHSEN, N. -
HENDERSON, A. Graham *RIBA*
HINDLE-HIGSON, J. *ARIBA*
MAINDS, Allan D. *Glasgow School of Art*
MAW, H. *Soane Medallist*

Louis de Soissons (Henry Jarvis Student 1913)
and Philip Hepworth (RS Architecture 1914).

MORLEY, Harry *RIBA*
RICHTER, G.M.A. *Girton, Cambridge; MMA, New York*
STUART, C.E. *Craven (Trinity, Cambridge)*
WELSH, Sylvia M. -
WHITELAW, James *Glasgow*
WILKINSON, Leslie *RA*

1907 BESSANT, J.A. *RCA*
CALDER, W.M. *Craven (Christ Church, Oxford)*
DROOP, J.P. *Trinity, Cambridge*
DRYSDALE, G. *ARIBA Soane Medallist*
GARRETT, H.F. *Pembroke, Cambridge*
HARTLEY, E. *Municipal School of Art, Manchester*
JACKSON, Arthur R.H. *RIBA*
JAMISON, E.A. *RIBA*
KIDD, A. *RCA*
LOYD, P. *King's, Cambridge*
NEWTON, F.G. -
PULLEY, R. *RCA*
SHEEPSHANKS, A.C. *Trinity, Cambridge*
WOOLWAY, G.R. *RCA*

1908 BEAZLEY, J.D. *Christ Church, Oxford*
COOPER, Harold *RIBA*
DAWSON, M. *RCA*
HARVEY, W. *British School at Athens*
PARR, H. *RCA*
PEET, T.E. *Craven (Oxford)*
RADCLYFFE, E.J.D. *Trinity, Cambridge*
ROBINSON, C.E. *Winchester College*
WRAY, E.W. *RCA*

1909 BEAUMONT, I. *Master House Painter's*
BUDDEN, Lionel *Liverpool School of Architecture*
DOD, H.A. *ARIBA*
DOUGLAS, E.M. -
DUCKWORTH, W.H.L. *British School at Athens*
HAMLYN, B. *Master House Painter's*
HARDY WILSON, W. *ARIBA*
JOHNSON, Lorna *Girton, Cambridge*
MILLER, W.O. *RCA*
NEAVE, S.A. *ARIBA*
PARKER, R.H. *RCA*
PEET, T.E. *Pelham*
PRESTON, L. *RCA*
ROBERTSON, D. *Glasgow School of Architecture*

1910 BARKER, A.R. *RIBA Soane Medallist*
BELLIS, A.W. *RCA*
CARUS-WILSON, C.D. *AA*
COWPER, S.A. *AA*
d'ORVILLE P. JACKSON, C *Edinburgh College of Art*
EDRIDGE, J. -

ENGLISH, E. -
FAREY, C.A. *AA*
GRIFFITHS, A. -
GROSE, S.W. *Gonville and Caius, Cambridge*
GUNN, R.W.M. *Glasgow Technical College*
HARDING, C. *Glasgow Technical College*
HARRISON, H.E. -
HETT, L. Keir *AA*
HOLLAND, P.E. *AA*
HOLME, K.D. *Edinburgh College of Art*
HORSNELL, A.G. *RIBA Soane Medallist*
JEWELL, H.H. *RA Gold Medallist*
JOWETT, P.H. *RCA*
KEITH, Christina *Edinburgh University*
LUBBOCK, H.T. *AA*
MacFARLANE, G.G. -
MASON, Arnold H. *RCA*
MOLYNEAUX, B.E. *Edinburgh College of Art*
MORGAN, E.E. *RIBA*
NEWBOLD, P. *Craven (Oriel, Oxford)*
PORTER, H.T. -
PRESTWICH, E. *Liverpool School of Architecture*
ROBERTSON, D.S. *Trinity, Cambridge*
ROBERTSON, D.S. (Mrs) -
ROBILLIARD, Miss *RA Gold Medallist*
SCOTT, A.T. *Glasgow Technical College*
SUND, Harold -
VYSE, C. *RCA*
WALGATE, C.P. *RCA*
WARK, F. *RCA*
WHATLEY, Norman *Hertford, Oxford*
WYNDHAM, Margaret -

1911 BARRY, F.R. *RIBA*
BEAUMONT, J.S. *Gilchrist (Manchester)*
BROOKE, Z.N. *Gonville and Caius, Cambridge*
LEAVER, N.H. *RCA*
LEITH, G. Gordon *Herbert Baker*
PAULIN, G.H. *Edinburgh College of Art*
SLATER, J.A. *AA*
TOYNBEE, A.J. *Balliol, Oxford*
WEBB, P.E. *RIBA*
WHITAKER, R. *Manchester School of Art*
WORTHINGTON, J.H. *Manchester University*

1912 ANGEL, J. *RA Gold Medallist*
ATKINSON, Donald *Pelham*
BELLOT, H.H. *Lincoln, Oxford*
BENNETT, J. *Glasgow School of Architecture*
BINNING, A. *ARIBA (RA)*
CONWAY, Agnes *Newnham, Cambridge*

de JONG, Piet *RIBA Soane Prizeman*
FOGGITT, G.H. *ARIBA (RA)*
GARDNER, R. *Emmanuel, Cambridge*
HORNER, Caroline *RCA*
LAWRENCE, Angel *Girton, Cambridge*
LIVOCK, S. *ARIBA*
LOCHHEAD, A.G. *Glasgow School of Art*
McMILLAN, W. *RCA*
MOERDYK, G. *RIBA*
MORLEY, C.S. *RIBA*
PEARSON, R.O. *RCA*
PRESCOTT, Constance *London University*
REVEL, J.D. *RCA*
RUDHALL, P.W. *AA; RCA*
SOLOMON, J.M. *Transvaal Association of Architects*
UTLEY, H.C. *Sheffield School of Art*
WILLIAMS, Margaret Lindsay *RA Gold Medallist*

1913 BAIRD, J.W. *Glasgow University*
FORGAN, Elizabeth *Aberdeen School of Art*
GARDNER, R. *Craven (Emmanuel, Cambridge)*
GHILCHIK, D.L. *Manchester School of Art*
HENDRIE, H. *RCA*
HERRICK, F.C. *RCA*
MURRAY, G. *Aberdeen School of Art*
PATERSON, Nora *Edinburgh College of Art*
POPE, J.K. *RCA*
ROBERTSON, M.W.U. *Gilchrist (Newnham, Cambridge)*

Portrait of R.P. Longden (Craven Fellow 1926)
by Edward Halliday (RS Painting 1925).

1913 SANDERSON, E. *Burnley School of Art*
    SLEEP, S.R. *Plymouth School of Art*
    SOUTER, J.B. *Aberdeen School of Art*
    TAYLOR, M.N.L. *Newnham, Cambridge*
    TAYLOR, M.V. *Somerville, Oxford*
    THOMPSON, W.H. *University of Liverpool*
    YOUNGMAN, H.J. *RCA*

1914 ARGENTI, P.P. *Christ Church, Oxford*
    BOXWELL, J. *University of Cape Colony*
    BOYD, J. *Glasgow University*
    BROWNSWORD, H. *RCA*
    CHISHOLM, D.J. *ARIBA; RA Gold Medallist*
    COLLIN, C.F. *RCA*
    CROIL, Gladys M. *Grey's School of Art, Aberdeen*
    FARRAR, J.H. *RCA*
    JONES, W.B. *Keble, Oxford*
    LLOYD, P. *RCA*
    RENWICK, W.L. *Glasgow University*
    SIMPSON, A.Y. *Master House Painter's*
    TAYLOR, G.G. *Master House Painter's*
    TAYLOR, M.N.L. *Gilchrist (Newnham, Cambridge)*
    WEBB, N.F. *RCA*
    WRIGHT, H.B. *RCA*

1915 DORELL, H. *Emmanuel, Cambridge*
    REES POOLE, V.S. *Transvaal Institute of Architects*
    THOMSON, J.W. *Gilchrist (Edinburgh) postponed*

Note:
In its early years, the School had no scholars, but 'students' admitted under strict rules by the Committee in London. Their names were listed in full in each Annual Report. The year given here is the first year of admission – several returned regularly. Their home institutions reveal their diversity: Royal Institute of British Architects (RIBA), Royal College of Art (RCA), the Royal Academy of the Arts (RA) and Architectural Association (AA) feature prominently. The Craven Fellowship and (from 1909) the Pelham Studentship, both awarded by Oxford University, were the closest equivalent to the later scholarships.

SCHOLARS IN FINE ARTS (1913-2001)

Year	Name	Award
1913	BRADSHAW, Harold Chalton	RS Architecture
	de SOISSONS, Louis	Henry Jarvis
	GILL, Colin	RS Painting
	LEDWARD, Gilbert	RS Sculpture
1914	BENSON, Jack M.B.	RS Painting
	CORMIER, Ernest	Henry Jarvis
	HEPWORTH, Philip Dalton	RS Architecture
	JAGGER, Charles Sergeant	RS Sculpture
1920	HARDIMAN, Alfred Frank	RS Sculpture
	KNIGHTS, Winifrid Margaret	RS Painting
	LAWRENCE, Frederick Orchard	RS Architecture
	NIXON, Job	RS Engraving
	St LEGER, Charles D.	Herbert Baker
1921	ARMSTRONG, Edward W.	Henry Jarvis
	McCONNELL, Leonard	Herbert Baker
	ROWLAND PIERCE, Stephen	RS Architecture
	WHITEHEAD, Lillian	RS Engraving
1922	AUSTIN, Robin Sargent	RS Engraving
	CHECKLEY, George	Henry Jarvis
	HOFF, George Rayner	RS Sculpture
	MONNINGTON, Walter Thomas	RS Painting
	WELSH, Stephen	RS Architecture
	WOODFORD, James Arthur	RS Sculpture
1923	CHAMBERS, Isabel M.	Bernard Webb
	CORDINGLEY, Reginald Annandale	RS Architecture
	EVANS, David	RS Sculpture
	LAWRENCE, Alfred Kingsley	RS Painting
	MURRAY, Charles	RS Engraving
	WILLIAMS, Edwin	Henry Jarvis
1924	LYON, Robert	RS Painting
	MORGAN, William Evan Charles	RS Engraving
	SISSON, Marshall Arnott	Henry Jarvis
	SKEAPING, John Rattenbury	RS Sculpture
1925	BAGENAL, Hope	Bernard Webb
	BUTLING, George Albert	RS Architecture
	HALLIDAY, Edward Irvine	RS Painting
	HOOGSTERP, J.A.	Herbert Baker
	JACOT, Emile	RS Sculpture
	MINOPRIO, Charles Anthony	Henry Jarvis
	WEDGWOOD, Geoffrey Heath	RS Engraving
1926	CONNELL, Amyas Douglas	RS Architecture
	HOYTON, Edward B.	RS Engraving
	JONES, Glyn Owen	RS Painting
	THEARLE, Herbert	Henry Jarvis
	WARD, Basil Robert	RS Architecture
1927	AUSTIN, Frederick George	RS Engraving
	BRILL, Reginald Charles	RS Painting

	CUMMINGS, Robert Percy	RS Architecture
	DYER, Harold Thornley	Henry Jarvis
	JARRETT, Eric B.	Bernard Webb
	PARKER, Harold Wilson	RS Sculpture
1928	BROWN, Cecil	RS Sculpture
	JONES, Eric Stephen	RS Engraving
	SORRELL, Alan Ernest	RS Painting
	WHITE, Leonard William Thornton	Henry Jarvis
1929	FINNY, Richard Jeffery	RS Painting
	GIBBS, Evelyn May	RS Engraving
	JELLICOE, Geoffrey Alan	Bernard Webb
	WRIDE, James Barrington	RS Architecture
1930	BROOKS, Marjorie	RS Painting
	EATON, Norman Musgrave	Herbert Baker
	HOLFORD, William Graham	RS Architecture
	KAVANAGH, John Francis	RS Sculpture
	OSBORNE, James Thomas Armour	RS Engraving
1931	AYRES, Arthur J.J.	RS Sculpture
	GIBSON, Charlotte Ellen	RS Sculpture
	HALL, Arthur Henderson	RS Engraving
	OAKES, Colin St.Clair Rycroft	RS Architecture
	ROBINSON, Madeleine Edith	RS Painting
	WHITE, Ian	RS Painting
1932	HUBBARD, Robert Pearce Steel	RS Architecture
	MEGGITT, Marjorie	RS Sculpture
	ROWE, Constance Dorothy Mary	RS Painting
	SPENCER, Charles Harold	RS Engraving
1933	BEACH, Adrian Gillespie	RS Engraving
	BRUCE, Frances Margaret	RS Sculpture
	BURNAND, Geoffrey Norman	RS Painting
	LEWIS, Owen Price	Bernard Webb
	SHEPPARD-FIDLER, Alwyn Gwilym	RS Architecture
1934	BISSET, Douglas Robertson	RS Sculpture
	BRUCE, Robert Alexander	Herbert Baker
	FAIRCLOUGH, Wilfred	RS Engraving
	MAUNDER, Fred Allard Charles	RS Architecture
	THOMAS, Brian Dick Lauder	RS Painting
1935	DEELEY, Geoffrey Hampton	RS Sculpture
	HOOPER, George Winstow	RS Painting
	LAVERS, Ralph	Bernard Webb
	TOD, Murray Macpherson	RS Engraving
1936	BENNETT, Hubert	RS Architecture
	FREETH, Hubert Andrew	RS Engraving
	HIRST, Philip Edwin Dean	RS Architecture
	NORRIS, Lawrence	RS Painting
	WILLIAMS, Garth Montgomery W.	RS Sculpture
1937	BEBBINGTON, Kenneth	RS Painting
	COWERN, Raymond Teague	RS Engraving
	McGILL, Marjorie	Abbey Major

	TOCHER, William Easson	RS Sculpture
	WALKER, William Thomas Christie	RS Architecture
1938	ARCHER, Frank Joseph	RS Engraving
	HAMMOND, Hermione Frances E.	RS Painting
	NEWLAND, Anne M.J.	Abbey Scholar
	POUNTNEY, Albert	RS Sculpture
	WYLIE, Alexander Buchan	RS Architecture
1939	COWAN, Ralph	RS Architecture
	LOWENADLER, Karin Margareta	RS Sculpture
1947	BARRY, Peter Henry	Abbey Scholar
	CARR, Alan Herbert	RS Engraving
	FRASER, Richard	RS Architecture
	WAIN-HOBSON, Douglas	RS Sculpture
	WRIGHT, Hilton	Bernard Webb
1948	HARPER, Jean Graham	RS Engraving
	PRANGNELL, John David	RS Sculpture
	PRICE, William	RS Painting
1949	BARNETT, Jack J.	Herbert Baker
	BELMONTE, Guido	RS Sculpture
	HARRIS, Ronald Walter	Rome Award
	HORSBRUGH, Patrick	Bernard Webb
	KNEALE, Robert Bryan Charles	RS Painting
	MELVILLE, Ian Scott	RS Architecture
	SEWARD, Prudence Eaton	RS Engraving
	SMITH, David Thomas	Abbey Scholar
	SPIRE, Sheila	Rome Award
1950	CARTER, Edward	RS Architecture

Portrait of Margery Deane (Bursar 1926-8)
by Glyn Owen Jones (RS Painting 1926).

EYTON, Anthony John Plowden	Abbey Scholar	
FRY, Anthony	RS Painting	
ROBINSON, Kenneth	Abbey Scholar	
SINDALL, Bernard Ralph	RS Sculpture	
YOUNG, James Kenneth	RS Engraving	

1951 BRADSHAW, Brian — RS Engraving
COOPER, Marion Menzies — RS Painting
LEE, Richard Dale — Abbey Scholar
RIZELLO, Michael Gaspard — RS Sculpture

1952 BLACK, Duncan Ian — RS Architecture
GIBSON, Sheila — Bernard Webb
GREAVES, Derrick Harry — Abbey Scholar
INLANDER, Henry Kurt — RS Painting
MIFFLIN, Bernard John — RS Engraving
WATT, Gilbert — RS Sculpture

1953 ANDREWS, Michael J. — RS Painting
FOZARD, Richard — RS Engraving
GRAHAM, John Anthony — RS Architecture
HERBERT, Albert Charles — Abbey Scholar
MacFADYEN, Neil — Bernard Webb
RICE, Brian Sean Liam — RS Sculpture

1954 CUMMING, Diana — RS Painting
FENN, Constance — Abbey Scholar
LACEY, Gerald Ian — RS Architecture
MONTFORD, Adrian Raphael — RS Sculpture
PERRIN, Brian Hubert — RS Engraving
STAUGHTON, Peter Samuel — RS Architecture

1955 BIDWELL, Timothy G. — Bernard Webb
FORD, Kenneth Charles — RS Sculpture
HASKELL, John Christopher — RS Architecture
TILSON, Joseph Charles — RS Painting

TUCKER, Walden Larimore — RS Engraving
WILD, David Paul — Abbey Scholar

1956 ALLEN, Clare Alison — Abbey Scholar
CAMPBELL, Kevin Patrick — RS Architecture
CLARKE, Geoffrey — RS Engraving
HERBERT, Gilbert — Herbert Baker
KNIGHT, Geraldine — RS Sculpture
NORRIS, Norman Thomas — RS Painting

1957 BURKE, Leslie Patrick — RS Engraving
ERITH, Raymond — Herbert Baker
JONES, Cordelia Margaret — Abbey Scholar
MILNER, Mary — RS Sculpture
RICHARDS, John D. — Bernard Webb
TURRAL, Gillian Mary — RS Painting
UYTENBOGAART, Roelof Sarel — RS Architecture

1958 CHALK, Robert Michael — Abbey Scholar
JONES, Leslie — RS Engraving
PLUMMER, Robin John — RS Painting
RIGBY, Alfred — RS Architecture
TAYLOR, Brian James — RS Sculpture

1959 GREAVES, Jack — Gulbenkian
HEBBORN, Eric George — RS Engraving
JEWETT, Jasper George — Abbey Scholar
MORRELL, Peter John — RS Painting
WHEWELL, John Alan — RS Architecture

1960 BALDWIN, Arthur Mervyn — RS Sculpture
CROZIER, Robin — Gulbenkian
FREETH, Peter Stewart — RS Engraving
NEWSOME, Victor George — RS Painting
WYLSON, Anthony John — Bernard Webb

1961 ATHERDEN, Ernest — RS Architecture
BEINART, J. — Herbert Baker
BOSEL, Charles Henry — RS Architecture
CHAMBERLAIN, Walter James — RS Engraving
HOUSDEN, Brian — Bernard Webb
LEE, Kenneth — Abbey Scholar
PEACOCK, Brian Arnold — RS Painting
PENNIE, Michael William — RS Sculpture
WILLIAMS, Glynn Anthony — Gulbenkian

1962 HAINSWORTH, George — Gulbenkian
MARTINEZ, Raymond Joseph — Abbey Scholar
MILLARD, Christopher John — RS Architecture
REYNOLDS, Michael Thomas James — RS Engraving
SANDERSON, Christopher Granville — RS Sculpture
SATINS, Mara — RS Architecture
THOMPSON, John Basil — RS Painting

1963 DUBSKY, Mario — Abbey Scholar
GREAVES, Terence Eugene — RS Engraving
IRWIN, Stephen Van Egmond — RS Architecture

Portrait of Richard Crooke (Librarian 1930-3)
by Majorie Brookes (RS Painting 1930).

212

	IVENS, Michael William	RS Sculpture	
	RHODES, Michael James	Gulbenkian	
	WELSFORD, Alan Robert	RS Painting	
1964	ELEY, Peter David Richard	Bernard Webb	
	FAIRCLOUGH, Christopher Michael	RS Engraving	
	JAMES, Richard Arthur	RS Painting	
	MacLAREN, Andrew Cunningham	Abbey Scholar	
	RHODES, Michael James	RS Sculpture	
	TILLOTSON, Edmund	Gulbenkian	
	WRIGHTSON, David Mainwaring	RS Architecture	
1965	ALLSOPP, Trevor Arthur	Abbey Scholar	
	JOYES, Jacqueline Patricia	Gulbenkian	
	MALENOIR, Mary	RS Engraving	
	PROUDFOOT, Peter Reginald	RS Architecture	
	SANSBURY, Geoffrey William	RS Painting	
	WESTON, Philip James	RS Sculpture	
1966	BRANSTON, Peter Martin Joseph	RS Architecture	
	COLLIER, Brian	RS Engraving	
	FURLONGER, Stephen Paul	Gulbenkian	
	STOCKHAM, Alfred Francis	Abbey Scholar	
	TERRY, Quinlan	Bernard Webb	
1967	PACKER, Linda Susan	RS Sculpture	
	ROONEY, Michael John	Abbey Scholar	
	TEASDALE, Geoffrey Grieves	RS Painting	
1968	ALLIX, Susan Jennifer	RS Engraving	
	DUNSTONE, Brian Albert	RS Sculpture	
	HOLTOM, Anna Elizabeth Josephine	Abbey Scholar	
	KITCHEN, Kenneth Harry	RS Painting	
	NICHOLS, Martin Henry	Gulbenkian	
	PEPPER, Simon Mark	Bernard Webb	
	REID, Richard Stuart	RS Architecture	
1969	BRUNELL, Geoffrey Reginald	RS Engraving	
	DIXON, Thomas Perry	RS Architecture	
	FAIRBANK, Andrew Lewis	RS Painting	
	SCOTT, June Carole	Abbey Scholar	
	TARRY, Susan	RS Sculpture	
1970	BORKOWSKI, Elizabeth Irena	RS Engraving	
	CRABTREE, Trevor	RS Sculpture	
	DEACON, Peter George	Abbey Scholar	
	FLEETWOOD, Roy Edric	RS Architecture	
	PEACE, Graham Rex Kenworthy	RS Architecture	
	TAYLOR, Donald	RS Painting	
	WESTLEY, Sheila Ann	Gulbenkian	
1971	ASTON, Frank Nicholas Paul	Abbey Scholar	
	BRANCH, Winston Nigel Patrick	RS Painting	
	GRAINGER, Ian Gavin Howard	RS Engraving	
	MORANT, Steven Alan	RS Architecture	
	PERREIRA, Karen Joan	RS Sculpture	
1972	ALSOP, Will	Bernard Webb	

	BATCHELOR, Anthony John	RS Engraving
	BENT, Trevor Edward	Gulbenkian
	GOULD, David Paul	Abbey Scholar
	MORTIMER, Graham	RS Architecture
	NICKSON, Graham Geoffrey	RS Painting
	PURSLOW, C.G.	RS Architecture
	WEST, Stephen Langley	RS Sculpture
1973	ADAM, Robert	ARCUK
	AIKEN, John Clifford	RS Sculpture
	DAVIES, Anthony John	RS Engraving
	EYTON, Anthony	Grocers' Fellow
	JONZEN, Martin Peter	RS Painting
	MARCHENT, Neil Philip	RS Architecture
	WATSON, Peter George	Abbey Scholar
1974	BASH, Elton	RS Painting
	CHADWICK, John Charlton	RS Architecture
	KIDD, Richard	Abbey Scholar
	KILN, Caroline Ann	RS Sculpture
	LEE, Sarah Frances Chepmell	Gulbenkian
	MARCHENT, Leonard	Grocers' Fellow
	MARTYR, Andrew	Bernard Webb
	MITCHELL, Errol Joseph	RS Engraving
	STRUTHERS, James Steele	RS Architecture
1975	FORSYTH, Michael Graham	RS Architecture
	LLOYD, Nicholas David	RS Sculpture
	ROGERS, William George	Abbey Scholar
	SILVER, Carole Anne	RS Painting
	WILSON, Terence Alison	RS Engraving

Peter Barry (Abbey Scholar 1947) in studio.

1976	DOUGLAS, Anne Elizabeth	RS Sculpture
	EVANS, Nicholas	Bernard Webb
	FARTHING, Stephen F.G.	Abbey Scholar
	HOLLAND, Michael John	RS Painting
	HYNES, Michael Edward	Gulbenkian
	KIMMERLING, Robert Michael	RS Architecture
	MASON, Michael	Grocers' Fellow
	POTTS, Martin Sydney	Abbey Scholar
1977	BLAKE, Jeremy Michael	RS Architecture
	BOWEN, Eleanor Mary	Abbey Scholar
	BRISLAND, John	RS Engraving
	GRIFFIN, Peter Lawrence	RS Painting
	JACKSON, Peter	RS Sculpture
	VOTICKY, Robert Leo	RS Architecture
1978	CHEO, Chai Hiang	RS Printmaking
	CHRISTOFIDES, Andrew	Abbey Scholar
	COWAN, Judith Anne	Gulbenkian
	GRIMSDALE, Sarah Ann	RS Sculpture
	McCALLION, Brian	Arts Council of N. Ireland
	McLAREN, Shelagh Morag	RS Architecture
	PLACE, Rodney S.	Bernard Webb
	WHITE, Jerry Nigel	RS Painting

Portrait of Shirley Bridges (RS Medieval 1948)
by Anthony Eyton (Abbey Scholar 1950).

1979	EGAN, Felim	Arts Council of N. Ireland
	GRIFFIN, David	RS Architecture
	NOBLETT, John Anthony	RS Printmaking
	ROBB, Carole	RS Painting
	STAHL, Andrew	Abbey Scholar
	TAVERNOR, Robert William	RS Architecture
	WOROPAY, Vincent Paul	RS Sculpture
1980	BLISSET, David Gordon	RS Architecture
	CAINES, Patrick David	RS Printmaking
	DIXON, Joseph	Abbey Scholar
	DRURY, Linda Louisa	RS Painting
	GINGLES, Graham Patrick	Arts Council of N. Ireland
	HENEGHAN, Thomas Anthony	Bernard Webb
	HOPEWELL, Barry Alva	Gulbenkian
	TALBOT, Richard Austin	RS Sculpture
1981	ALLIES, Edgar Robin	RS Architecture
	BODMAN, Virginia Mary	Abbey Scholar
	CARMICHAEL, Seamus James Gerard	Arts Council of N. Ireland
	GLEAVE, Lorraine Marie	RS Sculpture
	HODGSON, Carole	Grocers' Company Bursary
	KEIZER, Barbara	RS Printmaking
	MOONEY, James Jerard	RS Painting
	OLLEY, Peter J.	Grocers' Company Bursary
	SAUNDERS, Christopher	Bernard Webb
	SMITH, Stephen George	Abbey Scholar
1982	de THAME, Gerard Henry Charles	RS Sculpture
	DUBSKY, M.	Grocers' Company Bursary
	HEWITT, Vivien Alexandra	Arts Council of N. Ireland
	JONES, Lucy Katharine	RS Painting
	JONES, Robert Keith	RS Printmaking
	ROSSI, Mario Atilio	Gulbenkian
	WILSON-JONES, Mark Roland	RS Architecture
	WINGRAVE, Mark Cunliffe	Abbey Scholar
1983	CHAMBERS, Stephen Lyon	Abbey Scholar
	de CORDOVA, Denise	RS Sculpture
	FORRESTER, Denzil	RS Painting
	MAUDUIT, Caroline Elizabeth	RS Architecture
	O'CONNELL, Eilis	Arts Council of N. Ireland
	PARTRIDGE, Roger Howcroft	RS Sculpture
	WILDE, Helen Margaret	RS Printmaking
1984	CHILES, Prudence Irene Pamela	RS Architecture
	CRAIG, Shelley Margaret	Bernard Webb
	DOUGLAS, A.	Grocers' Company Bursary
	GILBERT, Richard Simon	Abbey Scholar
	HOYLAND, J.	Grocers' Company Bursary
	JAUSLIN, Catherine Erica	RS Painting
	LYSYCIA, Anthony John	RS Printmaking
	MacCANN, Brian	RS Sculpture
	MARA, T.	Grocers' Company Bursary

ROTHENSTEIN, M.	Grocers' Company Bursary	STAHL, Andrew	Rome Award
SHARPEY-SCHAFER, Sarah Jane	RS Architecture	THESIGER, Amanda Carolin	Abbey Scholar
TYE, Roderick John Scott	Gulbenkian	1990 BANAHAN, Christopher	Rome Award
1985 BRAIN, Nicola Joy	Abbey Scholar	BURNSIDE, Jane Denise	RS Architecture
BRILL, Patrick James	RS Painting	CARMICHAEL, Andrew	Rome Award
DALTRY, Hilary Jane	RS Printmaking	COCKER, Doug	Sargant Award
DONNELLY, Micky	Arts Council of N. Ireland	CRABTREE, Sam	Abbey Scholar
LARGEY, Kathryn	RS Printmaking	HALL, Sharon Janet	Rome Award
MacPHERSON, Iain Alexander	RS Sculpture	LEVERETT, David	Sargant Fellow
1986 CROCKER, Jeremy Richard	RS Printmaking	NURSE, Christopher	Rome Scholar
DESAI, Rajen	RS Architecture	OLIVER, Kenneth	Rome Award
ELSON, Stephen David	RS Sculpture	PETRIE, Nicola J.	Rome Scholar
KRUT, Ansel Jonathan	Abbey Scholar	PETTER, Hugh David Michael	RS Architecture
LANCASTER, John James Frank	RS Painting	RYDER, Charles	Sargant Award
POWELL, Felicity Jane	Gulbenkian	SNEDDON, Andrew Graeme	Rome Scholar
TEMPLE, Nicholas	RS Architecture	TAIT, Renny James	Rome Scholar
WATT, David Blair	RS Printmaking	TAYLOR, John	Rome Scholar
1987 BEER, Richard	Balsdon	WAKELY, Shelagh	Rome Award
BRUTTON, Hugo Philip Alexander	RS Printmaking	1991 BOWKER, Jonathan Mark	Abbey Scholar
LEE, Sarah	Abbey Scholar	BROUGH, Helen Elizabeth	Rome Scholar
MARTINA, Toni	RS Printmaking	BULLEN, Duncan	Rome Scholar
NAYLOR, Martin James	Balsdon	DEAN, Graham	Abbey Award
O'CONNELL, Deirdre	Arts Council of N. Ireland		
PEART, Margaret	Balsdon		
PERRY, Simon James	RS Sculpture		
WOLLAND, Peter Anthony	RS Painting		
WOOD, Robert Gary	RS Architecture		
1988 BONHAM-CARTER, Eliza	Abbey Scholar		
CHALKLEY, Brian	Rome Award		
CHEESEMAN, David Melvin	Gulbenkian		
DIXON, Jane Laura	RS Printmaking		
FRANKLIN, Jenny Ann	RS Painting		
HAWDON, Paul	RS Printmaking		
KIRKHAM, Edward T.	RS Sculpture		
McKEOWN, Harry Gregory	Rome Award		
MOSSMAN, Anna	Rome Award		
POTTER, Robert	RS Architecture		
WIGLEY, John	Rome Award		
1989 ALLEN, Kate	RS Sculpture		
DESMET, Anne Julie	RS Printmaking		
GANTER, Josephine	RS Printmaking		
GILL, Simon John	RS Architecture		
GILMOUR, Hugh Thomson	RS Painting		
HOUSDEN, Miranda Jane Elizabeth	Rome Award		
KERR, Bernadette	Rome Award		
KIVLAND, Sharon	Rome Award		
LATIMER, Elspeth Louise	RS Architecture		
PARKER, Cornelia	Rome Award		
REILLY, Simon	Arts Council of N. Ireland		

Portrait of Ernst Badian (RS Classics 1950) and Nathalie Badian by Richard Lee (Abbey Scholar 1951).

DERNIE, David	RS Architecture	O'DRISCOLL, Suzanne	Abbey Award
JOSEPH, Jane	Abbey Award	RUSSELL, Nicola	Arts Council of N. Ireland
McDONOUGH, Michael	Rome Scholar	SIKES, Brian Peter	Abbey Award
NAPIER, Philip Lindsay	Arts Council of N. Ireland	THOMSON, Roddy Alan	Rome Scholar
NEAGU, Paul	Sargant Fellow	WALKER, Denise	Rome Scholar
PICKSTONE, Sarah	Rome Scholar	WHITEFORD, Kate	Sargant Fellow
1992 ANSTEY, Timothy Ainsworth	RS Architecture	1994 CAPEL, Darren	RS Architecture
BANKS, Claire	Rome Scholar	CARTER, Tony	Sargant Fellow
DANT, Adam	Rome Scholar	CHEN, Gang	Abbey Award
DUNCAN, Stephen	Rome Award	CLARKE, Roger	Rome Scholar
GOALEN, Martin	Sargant Fellow	COOMBS, Daniel	Rome Scholar
HANSBRO, Brendan	Rome Award	DIGNAN, Paul	Rome Scholar
MOORE, Sally	Abbey Award	FREEMAN, Barbara	Abbey Award
PIERCY, Sioban	Rome Award	GOLDEN, Pamela	Abbey Award
PRENDERGAST, Kathy	Rome Award	HASELDEN, Ron	Sargant Fellow
RICHARDS, Jeanine	Abbey Scholar	JACKSON, Vanessa	Abbey Award
ROBERTSON, Carol	Abbey Award	McLEAN, Andrea	Abbey Scholar
SEAR, Helen	Rome Award	NEWMAN, Louise	Rome Scholar
WATSON, Christine	Abbey Award	OPIE, Julian	Sargant Fellow
WILSON, Susan	Abbey Award	ROONEY, Paul	Abbey Award
WRIGHT, Daphne	Rome Scholar	WILTSHIRE, Hermione	Rome Scholar
1993 BASS, David	RS Architecture	1995 BEDNARSKI, Cezary	RS Architecture
CHEVSKA, Maria	Abbey Award	CANNIFFE, Eamonn	RS Architecture
GALL, Neil	Abbey Scholar	CURRIE, Amanda	Rome Scholar
GUTHRIE, Karen	Rome Scholar	DESROCHERS, Brigitte	RS Architecture
KITE, Roger	Abbey Award	FERGUSON, Neil	Abbey Award
LANGLEY, Jane	Abbey Award	FINN-KELCEY, Rose	Sargant Fellow
LEWIS, David	South African Architect	FITZJOHN, David	Abbey Scholar
MacALISTER, Helen	Rome Scholar	GOUGH DANIELS, Liza	Abbey Award
MASON, Selina C.	RS Architecture	MALIES, Steven	Abbey Award
MAY, Nicholas	Abbey Award	MELVIN, John	Sargant Fellow

Ostia, 1958. From left: Patrick Burke (RS Engraving 1957), Anthony Blunt, Derek Hill (Artists' Adviser 1953-60), Martin Frederiksen (RS Classical Studies 1954), Geoffrey Rickman (Pelham Student 1958), Michael Ballance (RS Classical Studies 1948).

	NEWTON, Duncan	Abbey Award	McMULLAN, Shauna	Scottish Arts Council
	RAINEY, Michael	Arts Council of N. Ireland	PARKINSON, Stuart	Abbey Scholar
	ROBERTS, Julie	Scottish Arts Council	WEBSTER, Catrin	Abbey Award
	SMITH, Colin	Abbey Award	WILDING, Alison	Henry Moore
	STEEL, Carolyn	RS Architecture	1998 ALDRIDGE, James	Rome Scholar
	STRINDBERG, Madeleine	Abbey Award	BELL, Timothy	RS Architecture
	TALBOT, Emma	Rome Scholar	BOYD, Jane	Abbey Award
	TRANGMAR, Susan	Rome Scholar	COUTTS, Marion	Rome Scholar
	YOES, Amy	Abbey Award	DAVIS, Kate	Sargant Fellow
1996	ALLINGTON, Edward	Sargant Fellow	du TOIT, Suzanne	South African Architect
	AYRES, Gillian	Sargant Fellow	JOFFE, Chantal	Abbey Scholar
	BARAITSER, Alexandra	Abbey Scholar	KELLY, Paul	Scottish Arts Council
	CRAYK, Fred	Abbey Award	MALINOWSKI, Antoni	Abbey Award
	CREFFIELD, Dennis	Abbey Award	NALDI, Pat	Helen Chadwick
	FELLINGHAM, Libby	Geoffrey Jellicoe	RIDDY, John	Sargant Fellow
	FLANNIGAN, Moyna	Scottish Arts Council	ROGERS, Howard	Abbey Award
	FORTNUM, Rebecca	Abbey Award	ROLPH, Danny	Rome Scholar
	HARRIS, Anthony	Abbey Award	SMITH, Terry	Sargant Fellow
	JONES, Philip	Rome Scholar	STURGIS, Daniel	Rome Scholar
	KAUFMAN, Patricia	Abbey Award	SWAILES, Janet	Geoffrey Jellicoe
	LITHGOW, Katrina	Rome Scholar	WALLINGER, Mark	Henry Moore
	MASON, Charles	Rome Scholar	WRIGHT-SMITH, Andrew	Australia Council
	SNELL, Justin	South African Architect	1999 ALBERTS, Tom	Australia Council
1997	BARNES, Curt	Abbey Award	FAIRNINGTON, Mark	Sargant Fellow
	CARVALHO, Melanie	Rome Scholar	FRAIN, Rose	Scottish Arts Council
	CHAIMOWICZ, Marc Camille	Sargant Fellow	GAWRONSKI, Alex	Australia Council
	CHODZKO, Adam	Rome Scholar	GEORGE, Catherine	Rome Scholar
	CLARK, Samantha	Helen Chadwick	HARLAND, Beth	Abbey Award
	CUMMINS, Sean	Abbey Award	HENG, Euan	Australia Council
	GALLACCIO, Anya	Sargant Fellow	HUWS, Bethan	Henry Moore
	HODGSON, Clive	Abbey Award	JOFFE, Jasper Harry Nathaniel	Abbey Scholar
	IRVINE, Jaki	Rome Scholar	LLOWARCH, Andrew	RS Architecture
	KOVATS, Tania	Rome Scholar	LOWE, Brighid	Rome Scholar
	McGURRAN, Rosie	Arts Council of N. Ireland	MacLEAN, Mary	Abbey Award

Scholars outside east wing, 1983. From left: Virginia Bodman (Abbey Scholar), Sharon Fermor (RS Humanities), Barbara Keizer (RS Printmaking), Robert Jones (RS Printmaking), Jim Mooney (RS Painting), Stephen Smith (Abbey Scholar), Mario Rossi (Gulbenkian Scholar), Tony Trickey, Lucy Jones (RS Painting).

	NELSON, Stephen	Helen Chadwick	KEELING, David	Australia Council
	OLSEN, Geoffrey	Abbey Award	KIRWAN, Richard	Abbey Award
	O'MALLEY, Niamh	Arts Council of N. Ireland	LAMB, Tom	Sainsbury
	WALSH, Roxy	Abbey Award	MANGOS, Simone	Australia Council
	WEARY, Geoffrey	Australia Council	MURDOCH, Sadie	Abbey Award
	WISE, Kit James Edward	Wingate	PITTENDRIGH, Alexander	Australia Council
	WRIGHTSON, Daniel James	RS Architecture	RENSHAW, Tim	Abbey Award
2000	CATTRELL, Annie	Helen Chadwick	ROGERS, Henry	Abbey Award
	FISHER, James	Abbey Scholar	SILVER, Daniel	Rome Scholar
	FROST, Judith	Abbey Award	SMITH, Stephanie	Henry Moore
	GRAHAM, Christopher	Rome Scholar	STEWART, Edward	Henry Moore
	GUNNING, Lucy	Rome Scholar	WILLIAMS, Megan	RS Architecture
	HAWLEY, Cathy	RS Architecture	WILLIAMSON, Aaron	Helen Chadwick
	INMAN, Rachel	Rome Scholar		
	KANE, Paula	Abbey Award		
	KINDNESS, John	Sargant Fellow		
	MEREDITH-VULA, Lala	Sargant Fellow		
	STONER, Tim	Wingate		
	TAIT, Neal	Abbey Award		
	TRING, Valerie	Australia Council		
	ZUBRYN, Alexander	Australia Council		
2001	BILLINGHAM, Richard	Sargant Fellow		
	BOOYENS, Jaco	South African Architect		
	CRISP, Fiona	Wingate		
	GODBOLD, David	Rome Scholar		
	HOLDER, Kristin	Abbey Scholar		

Note:

Years listed are only the initial academic year of tenure.
The new constitution of 1912 provided for three Rome Scholarships (RS), each tenable for up to three years, in Decorative Painting, Sculpture and Architecture, awarded by the corresponding Faculties. In 1919 private endowment added a fourth scholarship in Engraving (renamed Printmaking in 1978). After the formation of multi-disciplinary award selection panels in 1994, Rome Scholarships were awarded in the Fine Arts (including Architecture), together with shorter Rome Awards. The RIBA funded the Henry Jarvis Scholarship in Architecture from 1913 to 1928. A legacy endowed the Bernard Webb Studentship in Architecture from 1923 to 1984. A fund established by Herbert Baker financed architectural students from South Africa from 1911 (see also under students) until 1961; this was revived in 1993 as the South African Rome Scholarship in Architecture. The Edwin Austin Abbey Foundation elected major scholarships from 1938, together with minor scholarships for travel, not necessarily involving visits to Rome; these were replaced by Rome Awards for senior artists in 1990. The Calouste Gulbenkian Foundation financed a second scholarship in Sculpture from 1959 to 1988. The Worshipful Company of Grocers offered fellowships, then bursaries, for senior artists between 1973 and 1981. The Arts Council of Northern Ireland has provided fellowships in Fine Arts since 1978, the Scottish Arts Council from 1995. The Sargant Fellowship was established, endowed by the legacy of FW Sargant, in 1990. The Landscape Foundation funded a scholarship in Landscape Architecture named after Geoffrey Jellicoe from 1996 to 1998. The Henry Moore Foundation funded a Fellowship in Sculpture from 1997, and in the same year a fellowship in memory of Helen Chadwick was set up in collaboration with the Ruskin School in Drawing and Fine Art, Oxford University, and sponsored by the Arts Council of England, the Foundation for Sport and the Arts and the Calouste Gulbenkian Foundation. The Australia Council for Arts established a residency for Australian artists from 1998. The Harold Hyam Wingate Foundation established a Rome scholarship in Fine Arts in 1999. The Linbury Trust of Lord and Lady Sainsbury of Preston Candover established two-year scholarships in Fine Arts inaugurated in 2001.

Artists of 1989 on the front steps. Back row from left: Simon Gill (RS Architecture), Josephine Ganter (RS Printmaking), Kate Allen (RS Sculpture), Elspeth Latimer (RS Architecture), Amanda Thesiger (Abbey Scholar), Anne Desmet (RS Printmaking). Front row from left: Miranda Housden (Rome Award Fine Arts), Andrew Stahl (Abbey Scholar), Jane Dixon (RS Printmaking), Simon Reilly (Arts Council of Northern Ireland Fellow), Hugh Gilmour (RS Painting).

Scholars in Archaeology, History and Letters (1919–2001)

Year	Name	Scholarship
1919	SANDYS, A.M.	Gilchrist
1920	FELL, R.A.L.	Craven (Cambridge)
	STRUCKMEYER, O.K.	Gilchrist
	THOMAS, E.E.	Mary Ewart
1921	ASHMOLE, Bernard	Craven (Oxford)
	BAILLIE-REYNOLDS, P.K.	Pelham
	FELL, R.A.L.	Gilchrist
	LAWRENCE, A.W.	Craven (Oxford)
1922	HARRISON, A.	Gilchrist
	JOLIFFE, N.C.	Gilchrist
1923	OMAN, Charles C.	Gilchrist
	WALKER, R.H.	Pelham
1924	RICHMOND, Ian A.	Gilchrist
	TOYNBEE, Jocelyn	Mary Ewart
1925	CHRIMES, Katherine M.T.	Gilchrist
	COX, Christopher W.M.	Craven (Oxford)
	HOLLEY, N.M.	Mary Ewart
	MEIGGS, Russell	Pelham
	RICHMOND, Ian A.	Craven (Oxford)
1926	LONGDEN, R.P.	Craven (Oxford)
	MOON, Noel	Gilchrist
1927	EDMINSON, Vera L.	Mary Ewart
	JACOBS, H.W.	Gilchrist
	SALMON, Edward Togo	Craven (Oxford)
	WALTON, C.S.	Pelham
1928	CARRINGTON, Roger Clifford	RS Archaeology
	SALMON, Edward Togo	Gilchrist
1929	LUCAS, Diana	Pelham
	MUNRO, Isobel	Craven (Oxford)
1930	GEDYE, Ione	Gilchrist
	WILSON, Frederick Henry	RS Archaeology
1931	BARRACLOUGH, Geoffrey	RS Medieval
	OSBORN, Margaret	Pelham
	STEVENS, C.E.	Craven (Oxford)
1932	BARGER, Evert	RS Medieval
	BINYON, Nicolette	RS Medieval
	WYNN THOMAS, Mary	Gilchrist
1933	ALLEN, Derek Fortrose	Pelham
1934	TRENDALL, Arthur Dale	RS Classical
1935	GRAY, Eric	Pelham
	JAMES, Arthur Walter	RS Medieval
	WARD-PERKINS, John B.	Craven (Oxford)
1936	BRETT, Gerard	Rivoira
	HAYNES, Denya Eyre Lankester	RS Classical
1937	DAVIES, William Hopkin	RS Medieval
1938	CHAPMAN, Barbara	Craven (Oxford)
	DAVIS, Godfrey R.C.	RS Classical
	FITZHARDINGE, Una G.	Pelham
	HARRIS, Ronald Walter	RS Medieval
	RENDALL, Francis John	Rivoira
1939	WILSON, Alan John Nibet	RS Classical
1946	BRUNT, Peter Astbury	Craven (Oxford)
	REYNOLDS, Joyce M.	RS Classical; Gilchrist
1947	BOORMAN, J.T.	RS Medieval
	MILLAR, Maureen	Mary Ewart
1948	BALLANCE, Michael J.	RS Classical
	BRIDGES, Shirley F.	RS Medieval

Scholars at the Villa d'Este, 1998. From left: Janet Swailes (Geoffrey Jellicoe Scholar), Vanessa Cloney, Evelyn Sperling, Paul Kelly (Scottish Arts Council Scholar), Marios Costambeys (RS Humanities), Roger Pitcher, Antoni Malinowski (Abbey Award), Kate Davis (Sargant Fellow), Graham Clarke (Trendall Fellow), Victoria James (Rome Award), Manon Janssens, Chantal Joffe (Abbey Scholar), James Aldridge (RS Fine Arts), Anna Bjerger, Suzanne du Toit (South African RS Architecture), Timothy Bell (RS Fine Arts).

1949	BARTLETT, John	Rivoira
	MacDOWALL, D.W.	Pelham
	MacFARLANE, Leslie John	RS Medieval
	OATES, E.E. David M.	RS Classical
1950	BADIAN, Ernst	RS Classical
	BULLOUGH, Donald A.	RS Medieval
	DIKIGOROPOULOS, A.I.	Rivoira
	SPIRE, Sheila	RS Medieval
1951	BULLOUGH, Donald A.	Rivoira
1952	CASELLS, John Seton	RS Classical
	PARKER, John S.F.	RS Medieval
	PARTNER, Peter	RS Medieval
	STRONG, Donald E.	RS Classical
1953	HAMILTON, Bernard Frank	RS Medieval
	HODGE, A. Trevor	RS Classical
1954	FREDERIKSEN, Martin William	RS Classical; Craven
	LARNER, John P.	RS Medieval
1955	TRUMP, D.H.	RS Classical
1956	DUNCAN, Guy Charles	RS Classical
	LUTTRELL, Anthony T.	RS Medieval
	RAWSON, Elizabeth D.	RS Classical
1957	JOCELYN, Henry D.	RS Classical
	MALLETT, Michael Edward	RS Medieval
1958	BROWN, Peter R.L.	Rivoira
	DRONKE, Ernest Peter Michael	RS Medieval

Augusto Valeri (Porter) guarding the front steps.

	RICKMAN, Geoffrey	Pelham
	WILKINS, John	RS Classical
1959	HARRISON, R.Martin	Rivoira
	JONES, G.D. Barri	RS Classical
	LEWIS, R.G.	Pelham
	ROBERTSON, Ian G.	RS Medieval
1960	COOPER, Paul Konrad	RS Classical
	GARDNER, Robert Donald Hugh	RS Medieval
	MARSHALL, A.J.	Pelham
	SMITH, Michael Quinton	Rivoira
1961	LLEWELLYN, Peter Awbry Burroughs	RS Medieval
	SMITH, Michael Quinton	RS Medieval
	WISEMAN, Timothy Peter	RS Classical
1962	CRAWFORD, Michael H.	RS Classical
	JAYAWARDENE, Sugathadasa A.	RS Medieval
	PHILLIPS, E. John	RS Classical
1963	SPRING, Peter W.H.	RS Classical
	WHITEHOUSE, David B.	RS Medieval
1964	ANTONOVICS, Atis Valdis	RS Medieval
	GARDNER, Julian	Rivoira
	SMALL, Alastair	RS Classical
1965	BARBER, Malcolm Charles	RS Medieval
	DUNBABIN, Katherine	Rivoira
	LING, Roger J.	RS Classical
	STEER, Lesley Ann	RS Medieval
1966	DUNBABIN, Katherine	RS Medieval
	HUSKINSON, John M.	Rivoira
	POTTER, Timothy W.	RS Classical
1967	DRUMMOND, Andrew	RS Classical
	PATERSON, Jeremy James	Craven (Oxford)
	WARD-JACKSON, Nicholas R.	RS Medieval
1968	LAW, John Easton	RS Medieval
	SEAR, Frank Bowman	RS Classical
	VOLK, Terence Rodney	RS Classical
1969	BARKER, Graeme William Walter	RS Classical
	CAMBER, Richard Monash	RS Medieval
	WRIGHT, Anthony Davis	RS Medieval
1970	HUCKLE, Alan Edden	RS Medieval
	MAXFIELD, Valerie A.	RS Classical
1971	KEPPIE, Lawrence J.F.	RS Classical
	WHITTON, David Raymond	RS Medieval
1972	ABULAFIA, David	RS Medieval
	ANDREWS, David Dormer	Rivoira
	WHITEHOUSE, Helen	RS Classical
1973	CLARIDGE, Amanda	RS Classical
	KNAPTON, Michael W.S.	RS Medieval
	PARKER, Robert	RS Classical
1974	ALDRIDGE, Dennis D.	RS Classical
	GORDON, Dillian Rosalind	RS Medieval

	WEISKITTEL, S. Ford	Pelham
1975	DAVIES, Glenys Mary	RS Classical
	RANKIN, Fenella Kathleen Clare	RS Medieval
1976	BURROUGHS, Charles	RS Medieval
	HOUSLEY, Norman James	RS Medieval
	LOWE, Claudia Joan	RS Classical
1977	DAVIDSON, Nicholas Sinclair	Rome Scholar
	DAVIS, Ian Charles	RS Medieval
	FORGACS, David A.	RS Classical
1978	CHATER, James	Rome Scholar
	GLUCKER, John	Hugh Last Fund
	OSBORNE, John L.	Rome Scholar
	PURCELL, Nicholas	Craven (Oxford)
	THOMAS, Hazel Claire	Rome Scholar
1979	BURKE, John	Rome Scholar
	CAMPBELL, Ian	Rome Scholar
	HALL, Belinda L.	Rome Scholar
	SMITH, Robert R.R.	Craven (Oxford)
	STERNFIELD, Frederick William	Balsdon
1980	CLARK, Gillian Lesley	Rome Scholar
	DEAN, Trevor	Rome Scholar
	DIXON, Joseph	Balsdon
	SPURR, M. Steven	Rome Scholar
	STODDART, Simon K.F.	Rome Scholar
	WHITE, Kenneth Douglas	Balsdon
1981	ARTHUR, Paul Raymond	Rome Scholar
	FRANKLIN, Jill Anne	Archival
	JENKINS, Rachel	Rome Scholar
	JONES, G.D. Barri	Balsdon
	MALONE, Caroline A.T.	Rome Scholar
	PATTERSON, John R.	Rome Scholar
1982	BLAGG, Tom	Hugh Last Fund
	BOLTON, Brenda Margaret	Balsdon
	BROWN, Rosalind	Rome Scholar
	FERMOR, Sharon Elizabeth	Rome Scholar
	HENRY, Elizabeth	Balsdon
	PATTERSON, John R.	Pelham
	SCOTT, Valerie	Archival
1983	BELLAMY, Richard	Rome Scholar
	MILLAR, Fergus Graham Burthulme	Balsdon
	SPIVEY, Nigel	Rome Scholar
	TAIT, Alan Andrew Hutton	Balsdon
	VERCNOCKE, Michael L.	Rome Scholar
1984	BROERS, M.	Rome Scholar
	HORSFALL, Nicholas Mark	Balsdon
	LOMAS, H. Kathryn	Rome Scholar
	PEARCE, M.	Rome Scholar
	WISEMAN, Timothy Peter	Balsdon
	ZERNIOTT, D.	Rome Scholar

1985	CHRISTIE, Neil	Rome Scholar
	GILL, David W.J.	Rome Scholar
	SHEFTON, Brian	Balsdon
1986	BEAVIS, Ian	Hugh Last Fund
	DELAINE, Janet	Rome Scholar
	KING, Helen	Rome Fellow
	MITCHELL, Shayne	Rome Scholar
	PERTILE, Lino	Balsdon
	TOMS, Judith	Rome Scholar
1987	CLARK, Gillian Lesley	Rome Fellow
	CLARKE, Georgia	Rome Scholar
	COLEMAN, Edward	Rome Scholar
	HILLS, Helen	Rome Scholar
	PATERSON, Jeremy James	Balsdon
1988	BOURDUA, Louise M.	Rome Scholar
	DITCHFIELD, Simon Richard	Rome Scholar
	LAW, John Easton	Balsdon
	SMITH, Christopher	Craven (Cambridge)
	SPARGO, Demelza Jane	Rome Scholar
1989	ALLISON, Penelope Mary	Rome Scholar
	BALZARETTI, Rossano	Rome Scholar
	COLYER, Christina Audrey	Balsdon
	GENTILCORE, David	Rome Scholar
	LAURENCE, Ray	Hugh Last Award
	LLOYD, John Alfred	Balsdon
	LOUD, Graham	Balsdon
	MURRAY, Oswyn	Balsdon
	ROBERTS, Paul Christopher	Rivoira
	SALMON, Frank Edwin	Rome Scholar

Pio Fiorini (Carpenter) and Giuseppe Fioranelli (Carpenter) with new work bench.

	WATSON, Alaric	Hugh Last Award
	WYKE, Maria	Hugh Last Award
1990	GRIFFIN, Alan Howard Foster	Balsdon
	LAURENCE, Ray	Rome Scholar
	O'CARRIGAIN, Eamonn Antoin Maire	Balsdon
	SKEATES, Robin	Rome Scholar
1991	BANAJI, Jairus	Rome Scholar
	DENCH, Emma	Rome Scholar
1992	ANDREWS, Frances Elizabeth	Rome Scholar
	GILLIVER, Katherine	Rome Scholar
	LUTTRELL, Anthony T.	Balsdon
	PLUCIENNIK, Mark Z.	Rome Scholar
1993	LINTOTT, Andrew William	Hugh Last Fellow
	THOMAS, Edmund Vivian	Rome Scholar
	WILTON-ELY, John	Balsdon
1994	BISPHAM, Edward	Rome Scholar
	COLLINS, Amanda	Rome Scholar
	LING, Roger J.	Balsdon
	SEAR, Frank Bowman	Hugh Last Fellow
1995	COATES-STEPHENS, Robert	Rome Scholar
	CRAWFORD, Alistair	Balsdon

Rino Ramazzotti (Waiter) with his portrait
by Kit Wise (Wingate Rome Scholar 1999).

	IZZET, Vedia	Rome Scholar
	KEPPIE, Lawrence J.F.	Hugh Last Fellow
	POBJOY, Mark	Rome Scholar
1996	BERRY, Joanne	Rome Scholar
	DAVIES, Alison	Rome Award
	de ANGELIS, Franco	Rome Scholar
	DENCH, Emma	Hugh Last Fellow
	GEE, Emma	Rome Award
	HAMILTON, Sarah	Rome Award
	HAYDEN, Christopher	Rome Scholar
	HUSKINSON, Janet	Hugh Last Award
	MANUZI, Martin	British-Italian Society
	MILLER, Honor	Rome Award
	PATERSON, Jeremy James	Cary
	TEPPERMAN, Hailey	Rome Award
	WYKE, Maria	Balsdon
1997	COOPER, Donal	Rome Scholar
	ELSNER, Jas	Hugh Last Fellow
	ISAYEV, Elena	Rome Scholar
	LAURENCE, Ray	Hugh Last Award
	MILLETT, Martin	Balsdon
	PILSWORTH, Clare	Rome Award
	RICHARDSON, Carol	Rome Award
	RIDLEY, Ronald	Trendall
	RUSSELL, Susan	Rome Award
	STACEY, Peter	Rome Scholar
	TOLFREE, Eleanor	Rome Award
	TOUCHETTE, Lori-Anne	Cary
	WRAGG, Simon	Rome Award
1998	CLARKE, Graeme	Trendall
	COSTAMBEYS, Marios	Rome Scholar
	CRAWFORD, Alistair	Archival
	DUNLOP, Anne	Rome Award
	FOX, Sarah	Jaguar
	GLINISTER, Fay	Hugh Last Award
	JAMES, Victoria	Rome Award
	RANKOV, Boris	Hugh Last Fellow
	RIVA, Corinna	Rome Award
	ROBSON, Janet	Rome Award
	SKINNER, Patricia	Rome Award
	SMALL, Alastair	Cary
	VELLA, Nicholas	Rome Scholar
	VOUT, Caroline	Rome Scholar
	WHITEHOUSE, Ruth	Balsdon
	WILKINS, John	Balsdon
1999	de WESSELOW, Thomas	Rome Scholar
	DELAINE, Janet	Hugh Last Fellow
	DOLAMORE, Hilary	Jaguar
	GIBBS, Robert	Balsdon

	GILLIVER, Katherine	Hugh Last Fellow	ASHTON, Sally-Ann	Rome Award
	HOLGATE, Ian	Rome Award	BEAVEN, Lisa	Rome Award
	LANGDON, Helen	Paul Mellon	COLBY, Richard	Rome Award
	MILBURN, Erika	Rome Scholar	CRAWLEY QUINN, Josephine	Rome Scholar
	MURPHY, Gillian	Rome Award	DAWSON, Helen	Rome Award
	NEWBY, Zahra	Rome Award	GRIG, Lucy	Rome Scholar
	RUSSELL, Camilla	Rome Award	MacKINNON, Michael	Rome Scholar
	SHEPHEARD, Mark	Pelham	McKITTERICK, Rosamond	Balsdon
	SKOIE, Mathilde	Rome Scholar	PILSWORTH, Clare	Rome Award
	SMALL, Alastair	Cary	PRICE, Jennifer	Hugh Last Fellow
	WILSON, Andrew	Rome Scholar	READ, Richard	Paul Mellon
2000	BIGNAMINI, Ilaria	Paul Mellon	WILSON, Roger J.A.	Balsdon
	BRIGSTOCKE, Hugh	Paul Mellon		
	BROADHEAD, William	Rome Award		
	CURTIS, Penelope	Balsdon		
	MANSOUR, Opher	Rome Scholar		
	MURPHY, Gillian	Rome Scholar		
	NEVETT, Lisa	Hugh Last Fellow		
	NOLD, Patrick	Rome Award		
	POLCI, Barbara	Rome Scholar		
	REVELL, Louise	Rome Award		
	SAUNDERS, Timothy	Rome Scholar		
	SMALL, Alastair	Cary		
2001	ALWIS, Anne	Rome Scholar		

Note:
The new funding of 1912 made no provision for scholarships in the Faculty of Archaeology, History and Letters (FAHL), though the Gilchrist Trust funded a studentship from 1919 to 1932, and until 1928 other awards were funded and selected by external bodies: Craven Fellows and Pelham Students selected by Oxford University, Mary Ewart Travelling Fellows and Craven Students selected by Cambridge University. In 1928 FAHL established its first Rome Scholarship (subsequently defined as Classical), and in 1931 a second in Medieval Studies. From 1978 the distinction of discipline between Classical and Medieval was dropped to reflect the extension of the scholarships to all Humanities disciplines. FAHL gave Grants in Aid of Research tenable at the BSR from 1962, regularised as Rome Awards in 1996. The Rivoira Studentship was funded from 1936 to 1972 by the legacy of the widow of Commendatore Rivoira. The Balsdon Fellowship for senior scholars was established in 1979 from the legacy of JPVD Balsdon, the Hugh Last Fellowships (and awards) in 1989, thanks to the legacy of Stefan Weinstock, the Cary Fellowships in 1996 thanks to a legacy from Max Cary, the Trendall Fellowships in 1997 thanks to a legacy from Arthur Dale Trendall. The Paul Mellon Centre for the study of British Art established a fellowship first held in 1999.

Fulvio Astolfi (Maintenance) and Renato Parente (Domestic Bursar) preparing for building work in 2000.

Image Credits

All images, unless otherwise stated, are drawn from the BSR Archive and are copyright of the BSR.

Photographs by Brian Donovan (for BSR)	Cover, p. 16, 23 (below), 36, 112, 116
Photograph by John Osborne	p. 25
Photographs by Claudio Abate (for BSR)	p. 28, 186 (above right), 187, 198
Courtesy of Trinity College, Oxford	p. 31 (above)
Courtesy of the National Portrait Gallery, London	p. 38, 113
Photographs by Andrew Wallace-Hadrill	p. 50 (above), 202
College Art Collections, University College, London	p. 56
English Heritage Photographic Library	p. 57
Private collection	p. 58
With permission of Paul Liss	p. 66, 72
Slade Archive, University College, London	p. 75
Produced by Rob Witcher	p. 106, 176, 179
Photographs by Helen Patterson	p. 108 (above left), 123 (above), 177
Photograph by Gill Clark	p. 123 (middle)
Photograph by Amanda Claridge	p. 126
Photograph by Graeme Barker	p. 132
Courtesy of Richard Hodges	p. 138
Photograph by Inge Lyse Hansen	p. 139
Photographs by Mimmo Capone (for BSR)	p. 142, 173/185, 188, 189, 203
Royal Academy of Arts Photographic Archive & Collection	p. 145
Courtesy of Paul Liss and Sacha Llewellyn	p. 147 (below)
Collection of the Museum of New Zealand Te Papa Tongarewa	p. 150 (below)
© Tate, London	p. 151 (above)
Private collection	p. 161
Courtesy of Stephen Farthing	p. 165, 166
Courtesy of Libby Fellingham	p. 173/185
Photographs by Helen Goodchild	p. 178 (above), 222
Produced by Dean Goodman, Yasushi Nishimura, Salvatore Piro	p. 178 (below)
Photograph by Ian Jones (for BSR)	p. 180
Courtesy of Marion Coutts	p. 186 (above right)
Courtesy of John Riddy	p. 186 (below)
Photograph by Albert Muciaccia (for BSR)	p. 201
Photograph by Photographic Records	p. 204
Photograph by Sarah Hyslop	p. 223

We are especially grateful to the following for their help in providing images:
Terry Danziger Miles, Silvia Ebert, Richard Hodges, Paul Liss, Federico Marazzi, Sandra Potter, the Royal Institute of British Architects, Alastair Small, Bryan Ward-Perkins and Margaret Ward-Perkins.